Shakespeare's Romantic Comedies

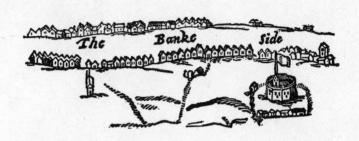

Shakespeare's Romantic Comedies

The Development of Their Form and Meaning

by

Peter G. Phialas

The University of North Carolina Press
Chapel Hill

For Ida, Mark and Katy

Acknowledgments

No one writing on Shakespeare today can be unmindful of his obligation to those who have preceded him in study of the dramatist. Accordingly, it is a pleasure to record here my great indebtedness to scholars and critics who have written on Shakespearean drama and especially the comedies. In particular I have found stimulation and aid in the work of H. B. Charlton, C. L. Barber, John Russell Brown, Bertrand Evans, and John Dover Wilson. As the notes indicate, I have profited also from other book-length studies as well as from scores of essays dealing with these plays.

Part of the work was drafted during a semester's leave-of-absence in the academic year 1963-64. For that leave and for other kindnesses done me I wish to thank the Department of English and especially the Chairman, Professor George Mills Harper. To my colleagues Professors Robert Boies Sharpe and Osborne Bennett Hardison, Jr., I owe a special debt for reading the manuscript and for making suggestions concerning content and organization.

Finally I wish to thank the University Research Council for financial aid in the publication of this book.

Peter G. Phialas

Chapel Hill, North Carolina
    November 1, 1965

[vii]

Contents

Introduction

This book is intended as an introductory aid in the study and interpretation of Shakespeare's romantic comedies. In particular, it attempts to define the nature and trace the development of some of the essential and distinctive features of these plays. The term "romantic" is here applied to those comedies in which the main action deals with a love story. The point needs stressing, for it distinguishes, at least in the present study, the romantic comedies from the farces, the so-called problem comedies, and the romances. In these plays the chief theme is something other than romantic love, although love and wooing form an important motif in them.

If it is true that the romantic comedies possess a distinctive form, a form evolved through experimentation, then their interpretation is inseparably connected with the process of Shakespeare's development of that form. Consequently, although each comedy is treated separately, an attempt is made in the present study to see these plays in their various relationships, noting especially their contribution to the general comic structure which is slowly emerging. For it is difficult, it is indeed impossible, to consider each play in isolation. The principle of experimentation and continuity is one of their most significant qualities, as it is of all Shakespearean drama. For that reason this study contains brief chapters on *The Comedy of Errors* and *The Taming of the Shrew*. Although belonging to another species, these two are included because they contribute significantly to the structure of romantic comedy which Shakespeare was gradually evolving. On the other hand, *The Merry Wives of Windsor* is excluded because it comes too late to have any bearing upon the development of that structure.

The aim of this study, then, has been to define in plain terms the distinctive qualities of the romantic comedies by an analysis of their proper action, by dealing with matters within the plays themselves. For that reason I have been concerned only incidentally with the literary genetics of various dramatic devices, type-characters, or other similar matters which may be relevant to the study of these comedies. Nor have I considered their structure and meaning in connection with Elizabethan theatrical conditions, or audiences or acting styles or any other historical influences. My chief concern has been with the action of each play, the nature and relationship of its parts, and the meaning or thought which that action dramatizes. On the other hand, I have tried to avoid the sort of approach which over-subtilizes the function or meaning of some aspect of structure or diction or imagery. In one or two cases I have dealt somewhat extensively with special matters of interpretation, for instance with the question of Shylock's role in *The Merchant of Venice* or of the unity of mood in *Much Ado About Nothing*.

Before proceeding to an analysis of a play's structure, each chapter touches briefly upon such questions as the play's date, its textual history, and its sources. The reason for this is that such matters have relevance to our interpretation of these as well as any other plays. Whether *As You Like It* was first written in 1593 or 1598-1600; whether its Folio text, the earliest we have, represents the original version (whether composed in 1593 or 1598-1600) or a substantial revision of it some time before 1623—these questions have much to do with our final estimate of the play's structure and characterization. Whether Shakespeare was able in 1593 to design the flawless structure of *As You Like It* and conceive its brilliant Rosalind is a question no study of the play and of Shakespeare's artistic development can overlook. And it is quite clear that a brief comparison of the play with its source, Thomas Lodge's *Rosalynde*, should indicate some of the special effects Shakespeare desired as well as the means of achieving them.

Of the components of drama, structure, theme, and character are the most important. Accordingly, the nature and mutual adjustment of these in each play form the chief subject of this study. What, in general terms, is the structure of Shakespearean romantic comedy? What sort of play is it and what is it about? In outline it follows the form of Menandrine comedy. It is non-satiric although, as we shall see, satire as a device is indispensable to it. But here satire, instead of being the chief end, is but a means or device in a larger conception of comic structure. That structure deals with a love story which, though for a time frustrated, is in the end brought to a happy conclusion. And it nearly always includes a secondary action of strife and conflict which impinges upon and obstructs the love story but which is likewise happily resolved before the end of the play. Although these two related actions are fundamental to all Shakespearean comedy, it must be stressed again that only in the romantic comedies is the love story at the center of the action. But the similarity in structure between the Menandrine form and Shakespearean romantic comedy is to be found only in this identity of broad outline. What gives Shakespeare's romantic comedies their uniqueness is the nature of the special conflict which for a time frustrates their love stories. For in addition to the external obstruction supplied by the secondary plot, and far surpassing it in significance, there is an interior conflict, a frustration or opposition coming from the lovers themselves. It proceeds from the attitudes and resulting actions of such characters as the King and his lords in *Love's Labour's Lost,* Benedick and Beatrice, Orlando and Phoebe, Orsino and Olivia, to name a few. As we shall see, the characteristic action of Shakespearean romantic comedy deals with the conflict and comic resolution of attitudes to love. One of these is the rejection of love by persons who later succumb to it; another is the sentimental idealizing of it; and a third is the realistic view of it, the concern with its physical aspect, a view generally serving to satirize and reduce the other two. Now the result of this diverting juxtaposition and comic reduction of these attitudes is two-fold: the achieving by the chief characters, whose attitudes are thus comically reduced, of a change or growth; and the emergence, stated or implied, of an ideal attitude, "ideal" here meaning the best that can be hoped for in the world we know. In the early plays that ideal view is merely suggested by the juxtaposition of opposed attitudes in different characters or in the same characters at different stages in the play's action. In the later plays, particularly *As You Like It* and *Twelfth Night,* that ideal attitude is represented throughout in the temperament of the heroine. Shakespeare's achievement of a Rosalind and a Viola seems to have been a deliberate aim in the years of experimentation. It is indeed true, as Professor Frye insists, that the theme of the comic "is the integration of society, which usually takes the form of incorporating a central character into it." But in Shakespearean romantic comedy a prior and indispensable step is the integration of the individual.

It is possible to trace, then, a steady progress in Shakespeare's ability to develop comic character and adjust it to the expression of his central comic theme in these plays. But there is also development in matters of dramatic structure: for instance in the nature and function of such features as the "enveloping action," the subplot, the play-within-the-play, and in the role of the clown as well as of song and music. Another striking development is in the means of commenting upon and reducing the extreme attitudes toward love. This is generally done through direct or ironic statement, or by means of rhetoric, or through the action of secondary characters. But in certain plays Shakespeare attempted to provide such comment by means of what we might call analogical structure, one of the most brilliant devices in Shakespearean drama. In *Love's Labour's Lost,* for instance, the satire of the extravagant attitudes toward language of both high and low characters is made to reflect upon their equally extreme attitudes toward love. Thus the comic reduction of attitudes toward love is enriched and sustained by a concurrent reduction of the use of extravagant language by the same characters. As we shall see, pastoralism is the theme presented in analogical relationship to love in *As You Like It,* while the theme of indulgence serves the same purpose in *Twelfth Night.* Indeed, Orsino's opening lines give us early notice of it by relating the two themes:

> If music be the food of love, play on!
> Give me excess of it, that, surfeiting,
> The appetite may sicken, and so die.

This analogical treatment of a secondary theme is not present in all of Shakespeare's romantic comedies but it is a feature of their final and perfected form represented by *As You Like It* and *Twelfth Night.*

Out of this development in structure and characterization there emerges a broad pattern of Shakespearean romantic comedy. It is not a rigid pattern but rather one admitting variation in both thematic emphasis and dramatic construction, a variation to be seen even in the last three plays, the so-called "joyous" comedies. Of these only *As You Like It* employs the sort of spatial symbolism found in *A Midsummer Night's Dream* and *The Merchant of Venice.* While *Much Ado* explores at length the theme of the disdainful lovers in the story of Benedick and Beatrice, *As You Like It* concentrates on the education of the romantic lover in the Orlando-

Rosalind affair, although of course both themes are dramatized in both plays. On the other hand, *Twelfth Night* gives the two themes equal emphasis but it excludes the secondary action of external conflict which for a time frustrates the love stories of the other two plays. Again, only *As You Like It* and *Twelfth Night* treat a subtheme in analogical relationship to the theme of love.

This pattern of Shakespearean romantic comedy, admitting variation as we have noted, is controlled and unified by the poet's overriding artistic purpose which is to expose to the searchings of the comic spirit the posturings of lovers and nonlovers and thereby point to an ideal view of love and of life's processes. Shakespeare's romantic comedies present a vision, then, which is given substance by their happy endings, their unions and reconciliations. Above all, that vision is made concrete momentarily by the wedding of the lovers who, having discovered the ideal hasten to pledge their allegiance to it. But a romantic lover's idealization of the beloved and of the experience of love itself—the very nature of the conceits he employs in his courtship—is but an expression of man's longing for a state of being that can be best described as spiritual. It is an expression of his longing for ideal forms, but that expression is here shown against human limitation; it is given a comic presentation. This is truly the heart of Shakespeare's romantic comedies: to present the lovers' ideal against the fact of man's physical being. And they generally present it enfolded within another larger ideal which underlies all Shakespearean drama: the ideal of a universal belief that love is the supreme value in life, that it gives measure and meaning to all enduring human relationships.

Shakespeare's Romantic Comedies

The Comedy of Errors

Chapter I

I

*T*he *Comedy of Errors*, though not belonging to the species of comedy with which we are concerned, nevertheless contains certain features of structure and theme, and even tone, which anticipate significant elements of Shakespeare's romantic comedies. As everyone knows, the play is an adaptation of Plautus' *Menaechmi*, but Shakespeare made changes and additions to the story which indicate clearly the way he was to follow in fashioning the special comic form which is the subject of this study. Perhaps the most significant over-all innovation is the presence of sentiment in Shakespeare's play, something utterly lacking in the Plautine source. Furthermore, *The Comedy of Errors* contains here and there a note of reflectiveness and serious purpose, a concern, however brief, with something deeper than accident and the surface show of things. And it happens that these things are especially prominent in the Shakespearean additions to the original. For although he retained and indeed expanded the farcical action of his source, Shakespeare gave the whole a slightly new coloring by complicating its structure and by adding two new themes to the extravagant realism of the *Menaechmi.* One of these is the framing story of Egeon and Emilia, the accidentally separated parents of the lost twin brothers, which makes possible the general family reunion at the conclusion of the play. Besides supplying this structural innovation, the story of the parents introduces the theme of loss, of strife and near-tragedy, which was to become an indispensable element in the later comedies. The other addition to the original story is the creation of Luciana and the episode of her wooing by Antipholus of Syracuse in III, ii, 1-70.[1] In view of Shakespeare's later comedies this is a far more significant addition since love and wooing became the chief concern of those plays. In introducing these two themes Shakespeare attempted for the first time what he was to do far more adroitly later in play after play, that is, to present in meaningful comic relationship elements of romance and realism. And as we shall see, this relationship will dominate the structure of his romantic comedies.

II

The Comedy of Errors has been placed at the beginning of Shakespeare's career, and most critics have seen it as the earliest of his comedies, although recently the rather late date of 1594 has been proposed.[2] Dating the play as late as December of that year places its composition after that of *The Two Gentlemen of Verona, The Taming of the Shrew,* and *Love's Labour's Lost.* This would not be a great matter since it has been impossible to fix the sequence in which these four plays were written. But it happens that the three plays above named deal more extensively and more deeply with love and wooing, the chief concern of Shakespearean romantic comedy. A priori, then, one would hesitate to accept so late a date for *The Comedy of Errors,* but such hesitation requires support, a matter we shall consider presently. Just now let it be said that the question of the play's date is of great relevance in the present study since we are here concerned in great part with Shakespeare's development as comic dramatist, especially as that development had to do with the invention and progressive refinement of ways to accommodate the theme of romantic love to a comic mode. If the play is indeed Shakespeare's initial attempt at comedy, what he did in it as regards romantic love, what aspect of it he chose to dramatize and how he did so—these matters take on special significance.

Though generally believed to be one of Shakespeare's early plays, *The Comedy of Errors* exhibits an astonishing command of his materials by the dramatist, a remarkable control of detail in adjusting the various themes to structure.[3] But it is doubtful that this was the feature which recommended the play to the members of Gray's Inn while they meticulously planned their grand entertainment of late December, 1594. Surely what they liked best must have been its multiple errors and mistakings and the sheer fun these generated, for the projected sports and revels were intended to surpass in hilariousness anything in that kind, the more so since such pastimes had been "intermitted by the space of three or four Years, by reason of Sickness and Discontinuances."[4] The account of the festivities printed in the *Gesta Grayorum* records that "upon Innocents-Day at Night" the members and their guests saw "a Comedy (like to *Plautus* his Menaechmus)." Since this was doubtless Shakespeare's play, December 28, 1594, is the time of its earliest recorded performance.

In the absence of other external evidence, we can assume no more than that the play is an early one, that it was written some time in or before 1594. But there are certain elements in it which may relate it in chronology to two other early comedies, *The Taming of the Shrew* and *The Two Gentlemen of Verona.* The extent and kind of treatment of certain motifs and especially love and wooing in these plays may help determine the sequence in which they were written. And that sequence is far more significant in the present study than the exact date of a particular play. *The Comedy of Errors* shares with *The Taming of the Shrew* a boisterous farcical action as well as the theme of the shrewish wife, a theme the latter play treats far more extensively. Furthermore, while *The Comedy of Errors* deals with love and wooing in a single episode, *The Taming of the Shrew* devotes its entire action to the wooing of the two sisters, Bianca and Katherina the shrew, although of course the wooing of the latter is of a special kind. In the third play, *The Two Gentlemen of Verona,* Shakespeare gives further prominence not only to wooing but also to romantic love which henceforth becomes the chief subject of his romantic comedy. This relative emphasis on wooing and romantic love in the three plays indicates strongly that *The Comedy of Errors* was almost certainly Shakespeare's earliest comedy, followed in turn by *The Taming of the Shrew* and *The Two Gentlemen of Verona*.[5]

III

The Comedy of Errors, it is clear, stands apart from the comedies which followed it, differing from them in many significant ways. It is, the Arden editor writes, "a special kind of play, not easily compared with the other exploratory works."[6] In particular, its plot, in part because of the story, lacks the complexity of the later plays. In his study of Shakespeare's comedies Bertrand Evans writes that "in his first comedy Shakespeare came nearer than ever afterward to placing his whole reliance upon an arrangement of discrepant awarenesses."[7] He finds the play unique in that it is built upon a single secret known only to the audience. Like the framing story of Egeon and Emilia, that secret remains static until the concluding episode: none of the characters deceive deliberately for none know the central fact before the recognition at the end of the play.

In thematic content, in structure, and in spirit, *The Comedy of Errors* is in the main a Roman, a Plautine comedy. And although there is another side of it created by the addition of two so-called romance themes, one of them may go back to a Roman original. Certainly the love-making of Antipholus of Syracuse is anything but Roman: it is in every detail a Shakespearean invention. But the other addition, the sentimental story of Egeon and Emilia which has been called romantic, may have been suggested by Plautus after all.

To the story of the twin Antipholuses which he took from the *Menaechmi* Shakespeare added the central episode of Plautus' *Amphitryon,* that is, Jupiter's taking the place of Amphitryon in Alcmena's bed and the attendant impersonation by Mercury of the servant Socia. On this is based the third act of *The Comedy of Errors,* some of the confusions of Adriana and the twin brothers, and especially her locking out of the house her own husband and entertaining instead his twin brother. For the story of the parents, their separation and reunion at Ephesus, Shakespeare may be indebted to the tale of Apollonius of Tyre, perhaps to John Gower's version in his *Confessio Amantis.*[8] In addition, analogues were available in other Greek romances as well as Italian comedies of the sixteenth century.[9] But it is also possible that the name Egeon and part of his story may have been suggested by yet another Plautine play, the *Captivi,* which in some important ways differs from Plautus' other comedies.[10] In the *Captivi* the father's name is Hegio, which Shakespeare could easily have turned to Egeon, although of course the exact form of the name may have come from the legends of Theseus and his father Aegeus, King of Athens.[11] Hegio, a wealthy Aetolian citizen, has lost two sons, one stolen while a child by a faithless servant, the other a war prisoner of the Eleans, with whom Aetolia is at present in conflict. In search of a way to recover the son held by the enemy, Hegio purchases a number of Eleans captured by his own country, hoping that among them he might find someone he can exchange for his own imprisoned son. Among the Elean prisoners is the aristocratic Philocrates attended by a devoted servant, who happens to be Tyndarus,

Hegio's stolen son. After a near-tragic complication the play ends happily through the revelation of Tyndarus' identity. But the action creates a mood which sets the play apart from Plautus' other comedies. Of this difference a point is made in the Prologue:

> Non pertractate facta est neque item ut ceterae,
> Neque spurcidici insunt versus, immemorabiles.
> Hic neque periurus leno est nec meretrix mala
> Neque miles gloriosus.[12]

The *Captivi* is indeed far removed from all this. It is a play of sentiment, of idealism, of powerful emotion. In order to enable his master Philocrates to escape slavery, Tyndarus exchanges identities with him, which in turn causes him to be put at hard labor in the stone quarries by his own father. In addition to sentiment generated by the devotion and friendship of the *captivi*, the play dramatizes extremes of passion, first in Hegio's violent indignation when he discovers that the two prisoners have duped him by exchanging identities, and second in the clash of emotions within Hegio when it is revealed that one of the prisoners is his own long-lost son. The passage describing Hegio's pain and joy at the moment of recognition is one that would have appealed strongly to Shakespeare. Upon the confession of Stalagmus, the servant who had stolen Tyndarus while a little boy, Philocrates calls out to Hegio now lost in wonder and perplexity:

> Quin est ipsust Tyndarus tuos filius. . . .[13]

To which Hegio replies:

> Et miser sum et fortunatus, si vos vera dicitis.[14]

Another feature of the *Captivi* which would have impressed a young dramatist is the play's structure, which Lessing called the best in existence. Aristotle, had he had such a play at hand, would have given high praise to the unfolding of the action which leads, step by step, to the recognition and dénouement.

In the *Captivi* Shakespeare would have found much to interest him, especially the accommodation of sentiment as well as conflict and powerful emotion in a comic structure. It is often argued that by bringing to life the father of the twins, who in *Menaechmi* dies before the play opens, Shakespeare rounds off the action with an unclassical picture of family reunion and reconciliation.[15] Although it is true that family reunion and reconciliation is very common in the prose romances and their derivatives, the theme is not altogether nonclassical. It is certainly a major element of the *Captivi*. And in the force of tearful happiness, of sheer emotion generated by such reunion, no comedy of Shakespeare's surpasses the closing scene of the *Captivi*. Very wisely Shakespeare approaches such intensity of emotion in only one or two of his comedies, perhaps most clearly in the Shylock scenes of *The Merchant of Venice*. The reason is that Shakespeare discovered that it was extremely difficult to adjust powerful emotion to the central theme of his comedy, be it romantic or farcical. For Plautus there was no such problem. In the *Captivi* he wrote what may best be described as a tragicomedy; in *Menaechmi* he composed a farce, a play completely innocent of feeling or sentiment. What Shakespeare tried to do in *The Comedy of Errors* and in later comedies was to combine the two, to frame the farcical and boisterous action dealing with mistaken identity with a poignant story of sentiment and compassion. What is of interest is that Plautus' influence may have operated even in this so-called romantic addition to the story of *Menaechmi*.

IV

Whether inspired by Plautus or not, the story of Egeon and and Emilia initiates Shakespeare's habit of opening his romantic comedies with a secondary story or subplot of strife and pain which ends happily at the conclusion of each play. The other and more significant link with the romantic comedies is the invention of Luciana and the episode of her wooing by Antipholus of Syracuse. Although the love theme is here given the briefest treatment, both its presence and the expression it receives are of the greatest consequence in Shakespeare's development as a comic dramatist. In this respect, *The Comedy of Errors* bears a distinct relationship to the comedies which followed and should not, therefore, be seen in unbridgeable isolation from them.

Although successful in creating a farce which surpassed the Plautine original so early in his career, Shakespeare showed but slight interest in this sort of play, and he returned to the species only twice, in *The Taming of the Shrew* and *The Merry Wives of Windsor*. But here his main concern is no longer with incident, as it is in *The Comedy of Errors*. What is comic in these plays, as well as the rest of the comedies, inheres in character, and its comicality is made to reveal itself through a special and individual response to circumstance. Furthermore, in the later plays Shakespeare would attempt, in Francis Fergusson's phrase, "the harmonizing of complementary perspectives." In *The Comedy of Errors,* it is clear, he made no sustained attempt at such harmonizing. But it is equally clear that he at least essayed to express, however briefly and obliquely —by placing side by side conflicting points of view—an idea concerning love and wedded happiness. The wooing of Luciana by Antipholus of Syracuse, and her own views about marriage, are juxtaposed with the contrasting attitudes of Adriana and Antipholus of Ephesus. And thus the protestations of love addressed to Luciana by Antipholus of Syracuse serve as a counterpoint to the mutual recriminations and to the strain and unhappiness of the married pair. Although the idea which the dramatist is trying to express never achieves explicitness, and although the relationship of Luciana and her Antipholus remains unresolved, what is of great significance is that here in a farce, in what may well have been his earliest comedy, Shakespeare introduces the chief structural principle of his romantic comedies: the juxtaposition of attitudes toward love and toward the ideal relationship of man and woman.

The contrast of attitudes is introduced early in the play, in II, i, where Adriana and her sister engage in semiformal disputation on the relations of husband and wife. Adriana, impatient and jealous, objects to her sister's "fool-begg'd patience," rejects the notion that the man should be master in the home, and wishes to curtail her husband's liberty. She blames him for everything, including her faded beauty, which she erroneously believes has driven him away:

> Hath homely age the alluring beauty took
> From my poor cheek? Then he hath wasted it. . . .
> What ruins are in me that can be found
> By him not ruin'd? Then is he the ground
> Of my defeatures.
>
> (II, i, 89-98)

Later on, believing that her husband had wooed her sister, she calls him

> deformed, crooked, old and sere,
> Ill-fac'd, worse bodied, shapeless everywhere:
> Vicious, ungentle, foolish, blunt, unkind,
> Stigmatical in making, worse in mind.
>
> (IV, ii, 19-22)

Here, then, is one of the causes of what Luciana calls Adriana's "troubles of the marriage bed." Adriana misconceives the proper basis of her union with her husband. In a startlingly romantic passage she recalls with pain his courtship of her which has now receded into the distant past:

> The time was once when thou unurg'd wouldst vow
> That never words were music to thine ear,
> That never object pleasing in thine eye,
> That never touch well welcome to thy hand,
> That never meat sweet-savour'd in thy taste,
> Unless I spake, or look'd, or touch'd, or carv'd to thee.[16]
>
> (II, ii, 115-20)

The attraction she is here said to have held for her husband appears gone, and this loss is precisely what she is lamenting. It should be noted, incidentally, that his courtship had been couched in the exaggerated phrasing of the romantic lover, the hyperbolic idealizing of the sonneteer! And now, she asks,

> How comes it now, my husband, O, how comes it,
> That thou art then estranged from thyself?
> Thyself I call it, being strange to me,
> That, undividable, incorporate,
> Am better than thy dear self's better part.

(II, ii, 121-25)

The conception of "undividable, incorporate" union of lovers seems beyond Adriana's capabilities, and in such passages we may perhaps detect a great deal more of the young dramatist himself than of his character. Nevertheless, what is significant is that Adriana, wooed in the romantic vein by her husband, and perhaps even possessed of the notion of an ideal union with him, misconceives the basis of such a union.

Adriana thinks of love in terms of possession, ownership, mastery. And this is not strange, seeing that the concrete basis of her marriage had been financial, in terms of gold in the form of dowry. And even as she may still control and even repossess that dowry, that is, take back what she has given, she insists also on possession of her husband's liberty, a possession she calls her "right." Adriana's concept of love is the right to possess, to receive and own and be master of, whereas both her sister and Antipholus of Syracuse oppose to that concept their view of love as giving.[17] It might be added here that the financial or commercial attitude towards human relationships is reinforced by the analogous misconception which underlies the Duke's judgment on Egeon:

> Therefore, merchant, I'll limit thee this day
> To seek thy [life] by beneficial help.
> Try all the friends thou hast in Ephesus;
> Beg thou, or borrow, to make up the sum,
> And live; if no, then thou art doom'd to die.

(I, i, 151-55)

The folly of possessiveness as contrasted with love's giving forms a very small part of the action. But its dramatization here anticipates the much more extensive and meaningful treatment of it in *The Taming of the Shrew* and especially *The Merchant of Venice*. In the latter play the contrast between the commercial and human relationships, between gold and love, is at the very center of the play's thought. One passage from it may illustrate the relationship between that later play and *The Comedy of Errors,* and thus demonstrate the unity and continuity of Shakespearean comedy. Before turning to that passage, let us note that in what may have been his earliest comedy, at least in the one treating of love most briefly, Shakespeare asks, however indirectly, the question: What is Love? And we should note also that that question, which is to be Shakespeare's continuing concern in the comedies, is most directly asked in *The Merchant of Venice*. "Tell me where is fancy bred," sings Nerissa while Bassanio, by some considered an ideal lover,[18] contemplates the caskets. Within the song the reply is indirect, offering tentatively what love is not, but a more pertinent answer is given by Portia and Bassanio a moment after he has made his choice. "Fair lady," says he, kissing her, "I come by note, to give and to receive." To which she returns the notes of the ideal:

> You see me, Lord Bassanio, where I stand,
> Such as I am. Though for myself alone
> I would not be ambitious in my wish
> To wish myself much better; yet, for you
> I would be trebled twenty times myself,
> A thousand times more fair, ten thousand times
> More rich . . . .

And she adds that she is happy that

> She is not bred so dull but she can learn;
> Happiest of all is that her gentle spirit
> Commits itself to yours to be directed,
> As from her lord, her governor, her king.

(III, ii, 150-67)

This surrender of the self to her husband, to her "lord, her governor, her king," is precisely what Adriana rejects in her colloquy with her sister, to which allusion was made above. Though she is aware of the uniting of lovers' identities, she invokes the principle in order to justify her rights of possessing her husband. In the concluding episode she refuses to let anyone minister to him. In this she comes into conflict with Emilia, and a tug-of-war follows the refusal of each to yield to the other the man who has sought sanctuary in the abbey, who happens to be Antipholus of Syracuse, not Adriana's husband. That her concept of love as possession leading to jealousy is unacceptable and indeed dangerous is enforced upon Adriana by the abbess:

> The venom clamours of a jealous woman
> Poisons more deadly than a mad dog's tooth. . . .
> The consequence is, then, thy jealous fits
> Hath scar'd thy husband from the use of wits.
> (V, i, 69-86)

There is no space in *The Comedy of Errors,* and perhaps neither inclination nor skill on Shakespeare's part, to pursue in detail the ideal basis for lovers' union and wedded happiness. This he was to do in the romantic comedies which followed. Nevertheless, he is able here to isolate, obliquely and in the briefest compass, one of the central conceptions of those later plays: that love does not possess, that it gives without needing to receive, for it gives to another self. "Call thyself sister, sweet, for I am thee," says Antipholus of Syracuse to Luciana.

Adriana's other misconception of the ideal union of lovers is the belief that such union is based on external beauty: that her husband has been driven away by her loss of physical attractiveness. That ideal love is not based on external beauty alone is much more directly and forcefully presented in the later comedies. And it is of especial interest to note that a much quoted passage in *The Merchant of Venice* which rejects the notion of love as possession—which opposes possession and love

—likewise rejects love's concern with external beauty. "All that glisters is not gold," the Prince of Morocco is told after choosing the golden casket. But the idea is given direct and unmistakable expression in Nerissa's song as well as in Bassanio's speech which follows it.

> Tell me where is fancy bred,
> Or in the heart or in the head?
> How begot, how nourished?
>   Reply, reply.
>
> It is engend'red in the eyes,
> With gazing fed; and fancy dies
> In the cradle where it lies.

(III, ii, 63-69)

And on his part Bassanio affirms that "The world is still deceiv'd with ornament," and that external beauty is but

> The seeming truth which cunning times put on
> T'entrap the wisest.

(III, ii, 100-1)

In *The Comedy of Errors* the idea is viewed from the other side: Adriana fears that she has lost her husband's love because her beauty is gone, and the bitterness of that loss turns into jealousy and vents itself in violent nagging. And that nagging, born of disappointment with the motion and change of things, sends our minds over a half dozen comedies to the tête-à-tête of Orlando and the disguised Rosalind in *As You Like It*. To his bookish protestations that he will love her "for ever and a day" she replies: "Say 'a day,' without the 'ever.' No, no, Orlando. Men are April when they woo, December when they wed; maids are May when they are maids, but the sky changes when they are wives. I will be more jealous of thee than a Barbary cock-pigeon over his hen, more clamorous than a parrot against rain, more newfangled than an ape, more giddy in my desires than a monkey." (IV, i, 146-53) The managing of the complex ironies here was quite beyond Shake-

speare's abilities when he wrote *The Comedy of Errors.*
Yet there is a palpable contact between the two plays and
another instance of the unity of Shakespearean comedy. What
puzzles Adriana, what in her own conduct remains beyond
her awareness, is for Rosalind the most obvious fact in the
nature of things. Both husbands and wives change, but their
happiness need not be touched by such changes since that
happiness should be based on something that remains constant:
not outward beauty, not physical attraction, but inner beauty
and worth.

The multiple attitudes toward love which are most skillfully
woven into the fabric of *As You Like It* have no place in *The
Comedy of Errors.* Here what we should note is the presence
of the master-principle which controls the structure of Shakespeare's romantic comedies, namely the juxtaposition of attitudes toward love represented by different characters. This is
a most significant aspect of *The Comedy of Errors,* a play
dealing in the main with matters quite alien to romantic love.
And it is certainly surprising to find that Shakespeare, in a
severely limited space, could put in such a play so much of
what was to be the chief matter of his romantic comedies. The
treatment of love and the related motifs which we have noted
above is elementary, lacking utterly the incisiveness as well
as the ironic dramatization which we find in the later plays.
But the fact remains that *The Comedy of Errors,* though in
the main concerned with the farcical mistakings of identity,
touches briefly a theme of far greater significance, the ideal
relationship of man and woman. And it is here, rather than
in the confusions of identity, that we find the element of reflectiveness and concern with something deeper than accident
and the surface show of things to which we alluded at the
beginning of this chapter. It is true that upon arriving at
Ephesus, Antipholus of Syracuse is driven by his strange reception there to question his own identity:

> So I, to find a mother and a brother,
> In quest of them, unhappy, lose myself.

> (I, ii, 39-40)

But it is likewise true that he discovers not only his identity but a new and larger self in his love of Luciana. In her, he tells her, he has found

> mine own self's better part,
> Mine eye's clear eye, my dear heart's dearer heart,
> My food, my fortune, and my sweet hope's aim,
> My sole earth's heaven, and my heaven's claim.
>
> (III, ii, 61-64)

In these matters, then, *The Comedy of Errors* prefigures some of the significant features of Shakespeare's romantic comedies. It shows his general predilection for combining multiple actions into mutually qualifying relationships. More particularly, it initiates his custom of enclosing a comic action within a serious or near-tragic framing story or subplot. And most important of all it introduces into a farcical story of classical origin the theme of romantic love and attempts, in elementary fashion, to comment upon that theme by representing contrasted attitudes to it. In so doing, the play employs for the first time in Shakespeare's career the central thematic and structural characteristics of his romantic comedies.

The Taming of the Shrew

Chapter II

I

The Taming of the Shrew records a most significant step in the development of Shakespearean romantic comedy. Its action has to do with the wooing of two sisters, although "taming" is the term employed to describe Petruchio's courtship of Katherina. But wooing is the main concern of the play, and in this as well as in other matters it anticipates a good deal which we shall find characteristic of the romantic comedies which followed it. The play has been thought by most scholars to follow *The Comedy of Errors* in composition, but an accurate dating of it will be accomplished only after the vexing problem of its relationship to *The Taming of a Shrew* has been solved. For it makes a great deal of difference in dating *The Shrew* whether the anonymous *A Shrew,* printed in 1594, is a version of Shakespeare's play or whether it inspired or derived from it.[1] With one or two exceptions, scholars have agreed upon 1593-94 as the probable date of Shakespeare's comedy, and the choice is apparently supported by the record that the Chamberlain's Company acted a play entitled *The Taming of a Shrew* in June, 1594. This has been identified as Shakespeare's play on the reasonable assumption that the titles *The Shrew* and *A Shrew* were interchangeable in Shakespeare's day.[2]

But it must be borne in mind that the dating of the play will be conjectural so long as its relationship to *A Shrew* continues in its present bewildering state.[3] No doubt the debate concerning that relationship will continue, but whatever emerges as the final and all-convincing conclusion, the fact will remain that *The Taming of the Shrew* as we have it represents for practical purposes the work of Shakespeare, a work done some time between 1592 and 1594. To be sure, the question of authorship has been raised, and scholars have posited one or even two collaborators. As with other Shakespearean works, there has been a tendency to attribute to some collaborator or reviser parts of the play which seem inferior to the rest. For instance, the Bianca story, either all or in part, has been assigned to one or two other poets.[4] But recent researches have succeeded in defending the Shakespearean authenticity of the whole play. Through a careful analysis of the style, diction, and imagery of the two plots, Ernest P. Kuhl, and more recently K. Wentersdorf, among others, have helped to bring about a wide acceptance of Shakespeare as the sole author of the play.[5]

Whether Shakespeare wrote unaided the subplot of *The Taming of the Shrew* is of the greatest relevance in the present study of his development, since all aspects of each work must be brought into the account we are giving of that development. And the Bianca episodes make their own special contribution. The character of Bianca herself, and of her suitors, the smooth articulation, both structural and thematic, of the two plots, the use of a master image—here that of taming, which runs through the entire play including the Induction —all these elements are precisely those with which Shakespeare experimented in these early plays. They are the materials he kept manipulating until, in the later years of the decade, he arrived at certain dramatic modes which seemed successful, modes he thenceforth employed again and again.

II

It is, then, well that we may begin our interpretation of *The Taming of the Shrew* with at least a measure of certainty in the matter of its Shakespearean authorship and probable date. Before proceeding further, let it be said that in the present study it is not an absolute necessity to establish an unalterable sequence in the composition of Shakespeare's comedies. It is quite probable that the dramatist did not follow step-by-step a forward and steady progress toward the comic modes he finally achieved. Indeed we know that he was not rushing from a comparatively unsuccessful treatment of a theme or motif in one play to a successful dramatization of it in the next work. A number of plays separate *Love's Labour's Lost* from *Much Ado About Nothing*. Shakespeare's need for variety in subject matter and for constant experimentation, whether early or late in his career, is manifest in every play. And yet reading his comedies in their chronological sequence, so far as this is possible, yields greater satisfaction and affords clearer insights into what he was about than viewing them in some haphazard way. Such a reading enables us to see clearly certain relationships among the plays which indicate a continuity and development in thematic treatment as well as dramatic construction.

The connections between *The Comedy of Errors* and *The Taming of the Shrew* are fairly extensive. Both are what have been called experimental plays, that is to say, both deal with certain themes or motifs and they employ schemes of structure in tentative fashion. *The Taming of the Shrew* takes up in earnest the popular theme of the shrewish woman, a theme treated more tentatively in *The Comedy of Errors,* but its approach in *The Shrew* is equally experimental, and its most subtle dramatization is achieved by Shakespeare in a much later play, *Much Ado About Nothing.* In addition, the scene in *The Taming of the Shrew* (V, i) in which Vincentio is barred entrance into his son's lodging, though probably derived from George Gascoigne's *Supposes,* looks back to a similar scene, borrowed from the *Amphitryon,* in *The Comedy of Errors* wherein Antipholus of Ephesus is shut out of his own house. Another motif common to the two plays is the expression of love in financial terms, and as with the theme of the shrewish wife, *The Taming of the Shrew* carries the treatment of this other theme a great deal further. But again, as with the theme of the shrew, the most successful dramatization of the love-gold relationship is achieved in a later play, in this case *The Merchant of Venice.* Again, like *The Comedy of Errors, The Taming of the Shrew* dwells in great part upon a world of appearances and situations, but with greater concern for the creation of psychologically penetrating and consistent characterization.[6]

In the matter of structure the two plays bear witness to a remarkable control of materials on the poet's part, and in *The Shrew* to a skill in interweaving two plots and an Induction into a structural coherence seldom surpassed in the later comedies. Dr. Johnson thought the construction of *The Taming of the Shrew* so successful, the two plots so masterfully united, that one could hardly speak of them as two plots without doing injury to the art which bound them together.[7] Like *The Comedy of Errors, The Taming of the Shrew* presents its main action—the play proper—within a framework, although Sly's story has far less to do directly with the main action than the story of Egeon and Emilia does in their own play. The connections between the Induction and the play proper are in terms not of story but rather of theme, metaphor, and tone.

In all these matters, then, the two plays show a close relationship, with the very clear indication that in certain important details *The Taming of the Shrew* exhibits an advance over *The Comedy of Errors*. Its structure is more complex but no less successful; its characterization, though again deriving in part from Latin comedy, shows progress in the sharper delineation of certain characters, particularly Sly, Petruchio, Katherina, and Tranio. Furthermore, *The Taming of the Shrew* introduces a feature somewhat unusual in the early comedies, namely a running image, a symbolic metaphor which appears throughout the play including the Induction, through which the poet expresses the chief idea of the comedy. This idea being the catching and taming of a shrewish woman, the dramatist chooses to represent it by means of the analogous action of taming a hawk for the purpose of falconry. Hence the images from falconry, bird hunting, and snaring which are distributed throughout the play.[8]

III

Earlier in this chapter mention was made of the desirability of reading Shakespeare's comedies as nearly as possible in the order of their composition. Such a reading might reveal something of what Shakespeare was trying to do and also some of the steps he followed in achieving a general comic mode he considered successful. This point of view has its dangers, particularly in the case of doubtfully dated plays, as is shown by certain critical assessments of *The Taming of the Shrew*. Professor Charlton, for instance, whose *Shakespearian Comedy* is a pioneering work of great importance, believes that "*The Taming of the Shrew* is literally Shakespeare's recoil from romance."[9] According to this notion, in a great deal of its action the play represents a violent turn from the dramatization of a romantic story to something not only different but its direct opposite. This of course assumes that *The Taming of the Shrew* followed in composition a play of romantic love with which the dramatist was utterly dissatisfied. "It may very well be," Professor Charlton writes, "that when Shakespeare finished *The Two Gentlemen,* oppressed by the devastating effect of its internecine war between the comic and the romantic, out of sheer physical disgust he turned for an antidote to an old play of shrew taming which had scarcely been contaminated at all by any romantic sentiment."[10] In composing *The Taming of the Shrew,* Shakespeare "was certainly enjoying a boisterous retaliation on the very sanctum of romance."[11]

Professor Charlton's view may be quite accurate, and it is of course impossible to refute it with incontrovertible evidence. But evidence is lacking also for his assumption that *The Two Gentlemen of Verona* preceded *The Taming of the Shrew* in date of composition. Indeed, the majority of scholars assign 1594-95 as the date of *The Two Gentlemen of Verona* and place it after *The Taming of the Shrew* and before *A Midsummer Night's Dream.* Furthermore, it might be argued a priori that *The Taming of the Shrew,* with its close thematic connections with *The Comedy of Errors,* follows in composition that play instead of the *Two Gentlemen of Verona.* But Professor Charlton's dating of *The Shrew* as following *The Two Gentlemen* must be met on its own ground, that is, on the ground of thematic choice by the dramatist, a choice dictated by a personal dissatisfaction with romance.

That Shakespeare recoiled from romance in the early days of his dramatic career is quite impossible of demonstration. But it is even much more difficult to accept the notion that he recoiled from romance not once but twice in those early days. And here I think Professor Charlton's interpretation suffers rather seriously. "It is scarcely likely," he writes, "that *The Taming of the Shrew* was Shakespeare's first recoil from romance, though it is certainly a rollickingly emphatic one."[12] Before recoiling from the romance of *The Two Gentlemen of Verona,* the argument goes, Shakespeare had already fled that theme as he had treated it in another play. His first "recoil from the insouciant romantic formlessness of *Love's Labour's Lost* seems to have been a feeling that plays without backbone are hopelessly crippled."[13] And so, dissatisfied with *Love's Labour's Lost,* Shakespeare turned to classical comedy, "putting himself to school to Plautus for his *Comedy of Errors.*"[14] It may be so. And yet it is not likely that Shakespeare began his

career with *Love's Labour's Lost,* according to Professor
Charlton his first play; recoiled from it by writing *The Comedy
of Errors*; turned to romantic comedy in *The Two Gentlemen
of Verona* and once more recoiled from that with the composition of *The Taming of the Shrew*; and then he recoiled from
that play by writing *A Midsummer Night's Dream,* which Professor Charlton calls "the very ecstasy of romanticism."[15]
Shakespeare need not have been such an incorrigible recoiler.
Instead, he may well have proceeded by writing the two early
farces which, besides their own close relationship, are heavily
indebted to Plautine theme and tone; and it is equally likely
that *The Two Gentlemen of Verona* initiates in earnest the
entrance of romance into Shakespearean comedy, henceforth
to become its chief theme for which the dramatist is to fashion
his own special structure.

But are *The Comedy of Errors* and *The Taming of the
Shrew* in truth a recoil from romance? *The Comedy of Errors*
cannot be seriously considered as a reaction to a romantic play
not merely because it may itself be Shakespeare's first comedy
but also because it most clearly combines classical with romantic themes. As we saw in the first chapter of this study,
the most significant addition to the Plautine original in *The
Comedy of Errors* is the romantic affair of Luciana and
Antipholus of Syracuse, as well as the story of Egeon and Emilia.
Why would Shakespeare add two romantic themes to the plot
of a play which was to be a recoil from romance?

Now to return to *The Taming of the Shrew.* May we say
of the play that it is altogether a recoil from romance? It is
true that anti-romantic elements abound in the play, but this
is true of Shakespeare's romantic comedies as well. Petruchio's
treatment of the shrew as suitor and husband must be generally
accounted anti-romantic. And yet if we look closer we may
discover that his conduct, and especially his wooing, combines
romantic with anti-romantic matter. And this is true of the
whole play since the Bianca subplot, though ostensibly romantic, is diluted with episodes that are unmistakably anti-
romantic. Far from being an exception or even evidence of the

dramatist's recoil from romance, the mixture of romantic and anti-romantic elements becomes a structural principle in Shakespeare's romantic comedies. Benedick and Beatrice are much more violently opposed to romance than Petruchio and his shrew, and yet we can scarcely call *Much Ado About Nothing* an anti-romantic play. The point to be made, then, is that in his early as well as later comedies, Shakespeare's chief concern is not in rushing from one extreme attitude toward love and romance to its opposite from one play to the next, but rather in juxtaposing within the same play such attitudes for the purpose of pointing to an ideal attitude, something very different from stressing either extreme. Opposed attitudes toward love appear in *The Comedy of Errors* as well as in *The Taming of the Shrew*, but their juxtaposition, quite uncertain, points rather vaguely to what might be called a compromise. As we shall see, the dramatic achievement of that ideal came to Shakespeare at the end of a long and slow progress.

IV

The comic disposition of romantic and anti-romantic elements is given increasing complexity in successive plays. For instance the relationship of the two is structurally much simpler in *The Comedy of Errors* where Adriana's attitude toward love and wedded happiness is simply contrasted with her sister's. And there is also a clear dichotomy in the attitudes of the two pairs: Adriana and Antipholus of Ephesus represent in the main a classical if not an outright anti-romantic conception of marriage; Luciana and Antipholus of Syracuse stand for the contrasting romantic point of view. And yet even here, in what may have been his first comedy, Shakespeare adds at least some complexity by recording Adriana's reminiscence of her pre-marital wooing by Antipholus of Ephesus. That wooing, though now described by her in melancholy retrospect, bore some sure marks of the romantic:

> The time was once when thou unurg'd wouldst vow
> That never words were music to thine ear . . .
> Unless I spake. . . .

And a few lines later she adds:

> Ah, do not tear away thyself from me!
> For know, my love, as easy mayst thou fall
> A drop of water in the breaking gulf
> And take unmingled thence that drop again,
> Without addition or diminishing,
> As take from me thyself and not me too.
>
> (II, ii, 115-31)

Such sentiments, closely allied to the wooing of Luciana by Antipholus of Syracuse, offer striking contrast to Adriana's insistence, elsewhere in the play, upon complete mastery of her husband. The lines anticipate incidents as well as passages in the later plays: in short the voicing of romantic and anti-romantic sentiments by the same character in different scenes and under different circumstances becomes a structural motif. In the joyous comedies, wherein Shakespeare is finally able to enshrine the ideal in the person of a heroine, this juxtaposition becomes her most significant attribute, that is, it becomes an aspect of her characterization. In *The Comedy of Errors* it is somewhat confusing; the dramatist instinctively feels the need for the simultaneous expression of opposed attitudes or perspectives, but he is yet unable to adjust that seeming conflict to the all-important creation of character. Indeed, Adriana's lines of romantic reminiscence jar against everything else she says and does in the play.

But what the dramatist here and elsewhere hopes to achieve through the juxtaposition of romantic and anti-romantic elements is of the greatest importance, namely, a reconciliation of the two conceptions. In looking at his romantic comedies we discover that without any exception this is indeed the heart of their story. In *The Taming of the Shrew*, a play allegedly recoiling from romance, one would expect no such thing as an attempt to reconcile opposed conceptions of love. The reason is far too obvious to need comment: the taming of a woman into a dutiful wife appears scarcely capable of reconciliation with any romantic approach to the ways of a man with a maid. Professor Charlton expresses the general assessment of the play when he says that in writing it Shakespeare's "mood was to exhibit the love of woman more in the spirit of the Roman market-place than in that of his own modern Europe."[16] This is of course the apparent impression made by the taming action as well as by a related aspect of the Bianca plot. But is there any doubt that the play exhibits two kinds of wooing? It is true that Petruchio's initial concern is with the shrew's abundant gold:

> I come to wive it wealthily in Padua;
> If wealthily, then happily in Padua.
>
> (I, ii, 75-76)

And in the romantic subplot the shrew's father, sharing Petruchio's apparently financial concept of marriage, offers the hand of his younger daughter Bianca to the highest bidder. To Gremio, the old pantaloon, and to the other amorous suitor, the disguised Tranio, Baptista declares:

> 'Tis deeds must win the prize; and he of both
> That can assure my daughter greatest dower
> Shall have my Bianca's love. . . .
>
> (II, i, 344-46)

Whereupon the race to outbid begins. The bidding is surely no less outrageous than Petruchio's wooing. Gremio takes a score of lines to list his plate and gold, his basins and ewers, his hangings of Tyrian tapestry; his ivory coffers stuffed with crowns, fine linen, Turkey cushions bossed with pearl, valance of Venice gold in needlework, his hundred milch-kine, six score fat oxen. But Tranio in his turn overgoes him so that Gremio returns with more. But that, too, and anything soever he might add later, Tranio can surpass. He says that he will offer

> . . . three great argosies, besides two galliases
> And twelve tight galleys. These I will assure her,
> And twice as much, whate'er thou off'rest next.

To this the exhausted Gremio can say only:

> Nay, I have off'red all, I have no more;
> And she can have no more than all I have.
>
> (II, i, 380-84)

For the contest must come to a close, but of course it has nothing
to do with Bianca except to occupy Gremio and Baptista so
that in the meantime Lucentio, Tranio's master, may woo her
in the proper romantic fashion. The bidding of Gremio and
the disguised Tranio is so overdone that its sole aim must surely
be to mock itself. And it may be said in passing that such self-
mockery, beginning here, will be a recurrent device in the
later comedies. In other times and places and contexts the
king of Navarre with his courtiers, Benedick and Beatrice,
Duke Orsino, Orlando, all these and more will, through the
same outrageous exaggeration, gently mock themselves and
their attitudes toward love. Here the blatant excess of the
bidders turns upon the very concept they intend, or pretend, to
promote. And at the same time romantic love as acted out by
the other two wooers, Hortensio and Lucentio, is having its
wonted way.

Lucentio is the more important wooer, for he after all wins
Bianca and it is he who is contrasted with Petruchio, both as
wooer and husband. Like all sensible romantic lovers he loses
his heart at first sight of his lady. In Bianca's silence he sees,
he says, a

> Maid's mild behaviour and sobriety. . . .

In his next speech he likens her to a goddess:

> Hark, Tranio! thou mayst hear Minerva speak.

And in his third and longer speech he is in love:

> O Tranio, till I found it to be true,
> I never thought it possible or likely.
> But see, while idly I stood looking on,
> I found the effect of love in idleness;

> And now in plainness do confess to thee. . . .
> Tranio, I burn, I pine, I perish, Tranio,
> If I achieve not this young modest girl. . . .
>
> (I, i, 153-61)

Again he further protests that he

> saw her coral lips to move
> And with her breath she did perfume the air.
> Sacred and sweet was all I saw in her.
>
> (I, i, 179-80)

This is the sentiment and language proper to the romantic context, and it is these which Lucentio addresses to Bianca when he is with her. Initially, his wooing her is severely circumscribed by the presence of Hortensio, who, disguised as Bianca's music teacher and justly suspicious of his rival, limits the disguised Lucentio's communications to pseudo-translation of Latin poetry. But in the second scene of Act IV, Lucentio and Bianca are shown together beneath a tree reading a book. Their dialogue is that of romantic lovers in Shakespeare or anywhere else:

> *Lucentio.* Now, mistress, profit you in what you read?
> *Bianca.*   What, master, read you? First resolve me that.
> *Lucentio.* I read that I profess, the Art of Love.
> *Bianca.*   And pray you prove, sir, master of your art!
> *Lucentio.* While you, sweet dear, prove mistress of my heart!
>
> (IV, ii, 6-10)

The scene of the lovers, their language and sentiment, and their subsequent romantic elopement—these are surely the most common materials of romantic love.[17] But could a play with such matter in it be justly called a recoil from romance? For Lucentio's wooing of Bianca is placed in no ironic context; on the contrary, it is itself intended as a mocking contrast to the unavailing concept of bidding for a wife. And although Baptista promises that he

> That can assure my daughter greatest dower
> Shall have my Bianca's love,

his daughter belies him in word and act. To the romantic
lovers, Hortensio and Lucentio, she protests:

> Why, gentlemen, you do me double wrong
> To strive for that which resteth in my choice.
>
> (III, i, 16-17)

Clearly, then, the subplot brings on the stage at least two
perspectives concerning the way to marriage, and the romantic
approach, represented by Lucentio and Bianca, is given as-
cendancy. The opposing commercial or financial approach to
love both mocks itself by its own outrageous exaggeration and
furthermore it is mocked by the opposing romantic action. The
main plot, Petruchio's wooing and taming of Katherina, though
apparently quite different, follows the same pattern.

v

Earlier in this chapter it was noted that the dominant impression made by the taming plot is anti-romantic, but it was
also suggested that Petruchio's wooing is compact of romantic
as well as anti-romantic elements. As the wooing and winning
of Bianca includes both the commercial as well as the romantic
conceptions of love, so does the wooing of Katherina, although
at first sight it seems quite unlikely. The overtly anti-romantic
conduct of Petruchio seems to preclude the presence in his
wooing of the sentiment and language of romantic lovers.
But this incongruity is precisely what we have discovered in the
story of Bianca. How horrifying even to contemplate that
Lucentio's "Minerva," she whose beauty is like the beauty
of Agenor's daughter, even she should be sold to the highest
bidder! That Petruchio's wooing might borrow from the
ecstatic blazon of romantic lovers should appear no more
strange or startling.

First it is well to bear in mind that the over-all anti-romantic
impression produced by the taming plot is precisely the kind
most appropriate for the diversion of the somnolent Sly, the
spectator for whose delectation the players are presenting
their play. The servants tell him that the actors are about to

"play a pleasant comedy" to frame his mind "to mirth and merriment." "Is not a comonty a Christmas gambold, or a tumbling-trick?" asks the befuddled Sly. The taming action is indeed very like these things, and Sly, whether sober or drunken, would find it to his taste. But when the story of Bianca and her lovers takes the stage, it is no surprise if Sly nods and minds not the play. Nor is it hard to see why at the end of the opening scene he wishes that " 'twere done!" This part of the "comonty" is not his cup of tea. After all, he has not seen or heard Petruchio, and though the shrew has made her appearance, the action of that initial scene is the mildest of the entire play. If Shakespeare had wanted his pedlar-turned-tinker to mark the play, he should have opened it with Petruchio, some of whose sentiments Sly would have found congenial. For to Sly wives are shrews, and he is utterly puzzled by the way his own "lady" addresses him in the Induction. When the page, disguised as his lady, calls him her noble Lord, Sly misunderstands.

Page. How fares my noble lord?
Sly. Marry, I fare well, for here is cheer enough.
    Where is my wife?
Page. Here, noble lord; what is thy will with her?
Sly. Are you my wife and will not call me husband?
    My men should call me "lord"; I am your goodman.
Page. My husband and my lord, my lord and husband,
    I am your wife in all obedience.

                          (Ind. ii, 101-9)

The multiple incongruity of it is overpowering.

        Am I a lord? And have I such a lady?
        Or do I dream? Or have I dream'd till now?
        I do not sleep; I see, I hear, I speak. . . .[18]

                          (Ind. ii, 70-2)

Things are not so in the world Sly has known, and the story of Petruchio's taming of a shrewish woman is much more consistent with that other world.

But although the story of a woman-tamer might satisfy Sly's taste for "gambolds" and "tumbling-tricks," the dramatist's choice and treatment of such a story was not, of course, dictated by the Induction. What is significant is that in fashioning an appropriate Induction to the play Shakespeare tried to relate the two by means of similarities in theme, tone, imagery. Of special interest to us is the juxtaposition in the Induction of the same two broad conceptions of love and life in general. Surely Sly must be accounted the very incarnation of anti-romance. When he first comes upon him, the Lord exclaims:

> O monstrous beast! how like a swine he lies!
>
> (Ind. i, 34)

But the same Lord resolves that Sly shall "dream" he is a lord!

> Wilt thou have music? Hark! Apollo plays,
> And twenty caged nightingales do sing.
> Or wilt thou sleep? We'll have thee to a couch,
> Softer and sweeter than the lustful bed
> On purpose trimmed up for Semiramis. . . .
> Dost thou love hawking? Thou hast hawks will soar
> Above the morning lark.
>
> (Ind. ii, 37-46)

To which the Second Servant adds:

> Dost thou love pictures? We will fetch thee straight
> Adonis painted by a running brook,
> And Cytherea all in sedges hid,
> Which seem to move and wanton with her breath
> Even as the waving sedges play with wind.
>
> (Ind. ii, 51-55)

And the Lord once more:

> Thou art a lord, and nothing but a lord.
> Thou hast a lady far more beautiful
> Than any woman in this waning age.
>
> (Ind. ii, 63-65)

Here again, then, we have not only the placing side by side of
two attitudes but the exaggerated expression of each, the same
principle followed in the Induction as in the plot of Bianca
and her wooers. What we should note here as in the Bianca
plot is the violence of the incongruity: Apollo shall play his
immortal music for the drunken tinker! For the dramatist the
incongruity becomes a structural device, an indispensable means
of pointing toward what is yet an imperfectly limned ideal.
Here even the juxtaposition itself is merely described; mere
"palabris" as Sly would say. But in a year or two, in the enchanted woods beyond Athens and with the incomparable
Bottom wooing the Queen of Fairies, this strange "kind of
history" shall come to pass before our very eyes.

VI

It would be surprising if the juxtaposition of contrasted
attitudes or perspectives which we have found in the Induction
and the Bianca plot should be absent from the wooing and
taming of Katherina. We note first that the story begins with
the shrew, not with Petruchio. Katherina, whose shrewishness
has discouraged suitors, is delaying Bianca's marriage-day; the
shrew must be married first. And for a husband the dramatist,
as the story teller before him, must provide an appropriate
suitor. But a suitor for a shrew must be himself a greater
shrew, and this is what Petruchio tells Baptista:

> I am as peremptory as she proud-minded;
> As where two raging fires meet together
> They do consume the thing that feeds their fury.
>
> (II, i, 132-34)

John Masefield complained that Kate "is humbled into the
state of submissive wifely falsehood by a boor who cares only
for his own will, her flesh and her money."[19] It is so and yet
not so. Katherina is humbled, but not into a "submissive
wifely falsehood" nor by a boor of Masefield's description. In
Act II, scene i, Katherina appears in a very damaging scene

indeed. She enters the stage, whip in hand, with her younger sister Bianca, her "bond-maid and her slave," whose hands she has tied behind her. And the reason for this is made perfectly clear. To Baptista the shrew complains:

> Nay, now I see
> She is your treasure, she must have a husband;
> I must dance bare-foot on her wedding-day
> And for your love to her lead apes in hell.
>
> (II, i, 31-34)

It is not merely her jealousy of Bianca for having suitors; what Katherina dreads is that if Bianca should marry before her, then she herself would surely remain a maid. "Leading apes in hell," the proverbial occupation of old-maidhood, is precisely what Beatrice, that other but much more sophisticated shrew, dreads, though in her own subtly self-deceiving way she pretends to aspire to it. Katherina is both unreasonable and forgetful, for her father has already declared that he will not bestow his younger daughter before he has a husband for the elder.

This, then, is the shrew whom Petruchio must woo, wed, and tame. How must he do it, and what sort of person must he be? For of course the dramatist must make certain that in general Petruchio's wooing and taming of Katherina be consistent with his character. Well, as he has already boasted, Petruchio is peremptory, he is a raging fire, but his carefully laid plan for wooing Katherina is, by his own admission, not quite so fearful as that. While waiting for her to join him on the stage, he reflects on his strategy:

> I will attend her here
> And woo her with some spirit when she comes.

But then it turns out that by "spirit" he means something less than the action we should anticipate in a tamer. He explains:

> Say that she rail, why then I'll tell her plain
> She sings as sweetly as a nightingale.

> Say that she frown, I'll say she looks as clear
> As morning roses newly washed with dew.
> Say she be mute and will not speak a word,
> Then I'll commend her volubility,
> And say she uttereth piercing eloquence.
>
> (II, i, 169-77)

It is an excellent plan and with but one or two exceptions, he follows it through. But the exceptions, though quite serious and even startling, are roughly in character. Immediately upon Katherina's appearance Petruchio momentarily forgets his plan and answers fire with fire:

> *Katherina.* Well have you heard, but something hard of
>   hearing.
>   They call me Katherine that do talk of me.
> *Petruchio.* You lie, in faith; for you are call'd plain Kate,
>   And bonny Kate, and sometimes Kate the curst. . . .

But he soon recovers, turns to his plan, and woos as he had promised:

> But Kate, the prettiest Kate in Christendom,
> Kate of Kate Hall, my super-dainty Kate,
> For dainties are all Kates, and therefore, Kate,
> Take this of me, Kate of my consolation;
> Hearing thy mildness praised in every town,
> Thy virtues spoke of, and thy beauty sounded,
> Yet not so deeply as to thee belongs,
> Myself am mov'd to woo thee for my wife.
>
> (II, i, 184-95)

Petruchio's other lapse is likewise brief and unavoidable: when, after a line of bawdry he protests he is a gentleman, she offers to test him.

> *Petruchio.* What, with my tongue in your tail?
>   Nay, come again,
>   Good Kate; I am a gentleman—

> *Katherina.*   That I'll try.
>   [*She strikes him.*]
>   *Petruchio.* I swear I'll cuff you, if you strike again.

After that, his wooing returns to the exaggerated protestations
and general hyperboles of romance:

> *Petruchio.* Nay, hear you, Kate. In sooth, you scape not so.
> *Katherina.* I chafe you, if I tarry. Let me go.
> *Petruchio.* No, not a whit; I find you passing gentle.
>   'Twas told me you were rough and coy and sullen.
>   And now I find report a liar;
>   For thou art pleasant, gamesome, passing courteous,
>   But slow in speech, yet sweet as springtime
>   flowers. . . .
>   Why does the world report that Kate doth limp?
>   O sland'rous world! Kate like the hazel-twig
>   Is straight and slender, and as brown in hue
>   As hazel nuts and sweeter than the kernels.
>   (II, i, 242-57)

And when Baptista and the rest have joined the pair, Petruchio
speaks of Katherina as another Lucrece, "a second Grissel."
And finally he asks:

>   Did ever Dian so become a grove
>   As Kate this chamber with her princely gait?
>   O, be thou Dian, and let her be Kate;
>   And then let Kate be chaste and Dian sportful!
>   (II, i, 260-63)

Was ever shrew thus wooed and won? Is this outrageous
mockery of her (how Mercutio would have thrilled to it!)
the way to win her? Mocking or not, the words find their
target, for she is, as Hotspur would say, "but yet a woman."
And Petruchio, now certain of his suit, replaces his mocking
hyperboles with something more authentic:

>   And therefore, setting all this chat aside,
>   Thus in plain terms: your father hath consented

> That you shall be my wife. . . .
> Now, Kate, I am a husband for your turn;
> For, by this light whereby I see your beauty,
> Thy beauty, that doth make me like thee well,
> Thou must be married to no man but me;
>
> (II, i, 270-77)

"Setting all this chat aside," Petruchio speaks to her in "plain terms" indeed, terms which anticipate, though in a far different context, the wooing of the fair Katherine by the victorious Henry V. In plain terms, then, Petruchio declares that he is attracted by her beauty, for the shrew is indeed beautiful, as Hortensio had already announced:

> I can, Petruchio, help thee to a wife
> With wealth enough and young and beauteous,
> Brought up as best becomes a gentlewoman.
>
> (I, ii, 85-87)

Petruchio is challenged by her curstness, he is content with her dowry, he is attracted by her beauty: she must be his.[20]

For a "peremptory" tamer, Petruchio's wooing lacks something of that "raging fire" he had threatened. He is indeed rough, and in his own words "woo[s] not like a babe," but that roughness peeps through his wooing only twice, as we have seen. The rest of it borrows the accents of romance, the language of Lucentio and the lover before him, Antipholus of Syracuse. And it is the same Petrarchan hyperbole that all Shakespeare's romantic lovers speak, from *The Comedy of Errors* to *The Tempest*. But there is something more in the extremes of Petruchio's wooing, an attempt to suggest a middle position, something Shakespeare's romantic lovers will not achieve for some time to come; and when they do, we shall discover that with one or two exceptions the golden mean will be made explicit by the romantic heroines. Petruchio's exaggerated mockery of romantic wooing recoils upon and defeats itself just as the outrageously overdone bidding for Bianca does in the subplot. And again the purpose is to present through character and in a fleeting moment or two that middle position, the compromise between the extremes of hyperbolic Petrarchism on the one hand and of realism, or outright materialism, on the other. In *The Taming of the Shrew,* it is quite clear that two antithetical conceptions of love are mutually exposed, mocked, and, to an admittedly somewhat vague degree, reduced. Petruchio's mocking exaggeration of the language of romantic wooing is matched by the outrageous overdoing of the financial or commercial approach to love by the competitive bidding of Gremio and Tranio for the hand of Bianca. The first is made part of the taming plot, the anti-romantic story of the shrew, while the second is part of the romantic story of Bianca and her wooers. And here we observe a principle of structure which is to become an indispensable component of Shakespearean dramatic construction. While the subplot in its general matter and tone is contrasted with the main plot, the two actions lend each other motifs for the purpose of further comment and mutual clarification. This is the sort of complexity in structure towards which Shakespeare is advancing. And this complexity in structure will go hand in hand with a complexity in characterization.

VII

In *The Taming of the Shrew* both that complexity of structure and the dramatic expression of an ultimate vision are tentative, experimental. And the same can be said of their relation to character. Neither Petruchio nor Katherina can be construed as representing, even remotely, an ideal attitude towards love, although both are made to say so at the conclusion of the play. Their protestations are a dramatic necessity, particularly as these are contrasted with the feeble mumblings of the other two couples. But it would be unwise to take the "conclusion" too seriously. Professor J. R. Brown attaches a bit too much gravity to the proceedings when he says that Shakespeare manipulates the incidents "to embody his living image for the acting and recognition of love's truth."[21] Nor is it more appropriate to conclude with Professor Bullough that the "moral is not only that wives should be subject to their husbands, but that romantic marriages are no more likely to be successful than marriages of convenience."²² Such a conclusion assumes that the union of Petruchio and Katherina is a marriage of convenience, that Shakespeare advocates such marriage, and that the way to become master and lord of one's wife is to treat her as Petruchio treats his shrew. But all this is far from certain. As the marriage of Petruchio and Katherina follows the longest and most persistent wooing in the play, and as only a single line in that wooing refers to Katherina's dowry, their marriage cannot be called a marriage of convenience. Furthermore, we have noted that that sort of marriage is outrageously mocked by the bidding of Gremio and Tranio for Bianca. Nor does Shakespeare fail elsewhere to castigate it. Two instances in two different plays of this period may suffice. They are Egeus' attempt to force his daughter Hermia to marry Demetrius in *A Midsummer Night's Dream,* and Capulet's determination to bestow Juliet on Paris. There is no doubt whatever that Shakespeare, so often oblique, is direct to the point of savage bluntness here. Egeus begs the Duke of Athens to let him have his way:

> As she is mine, I may dispose of her;
> Which shall be either to this gentleman
> Or to her death. . . .

                                        (I, i, 42-4)

In almost identical words Capulet turns upon Juliet:

> An you be mine, I'll give you to my friend;
> An you be not, hang, beg, starve, die in the streets. . . .²³

                                        (III, v, 193-4)

As to gaining mastery over a wife by Petruchio's means, this is precisely what offended John Masefield's sensibilities, and Shakespeare would scarcely disagree. The self-mockery of the overdone taming as well as the bidding episodes preclude our taking too seriously the play as an exposition of a particular moral.

But if Shakespeare was unwilling to weight the boisterous action of *The Taming of the Shrew* with grave morality, did he exclude any implication of serious import from the play? This Shakespeare was evidently incapable of doing even in such a play as *The Comedy of Errors,* perhaps of all his plays the one most concerned with the external show and surface of experience. In *The Taming of the Shrew,* where individuality of character becomes central to the action, the dramatist manipulates or informs event in such a way that it expresses through character a particular psychological truth. Doubtless the most significant aspect of the play in terms of character is the portrayal of the shrew, an advance over the often indistinct lines of characterization in *The Comedy of Errors* including that of Adriana. What are depicted in the Bianca scenes and later in the taming action are simple psychological universals which go into the creation of a particular temperament. One is the often bitter jealousy between sisters which occasionally may issue in some act of cruelty. The other, much more significant here, is the universality of positive female response to romantic wooing. The former theme, being inimical to comic treatment, is replaced by the steadfast affection of a long line of heroines presented in twos or threes or even fours in the comedies to come. The second motif becomes one of the bases of Shakespeare's comic construction.

The character of Petruchio, depending for its special quality on the conception of the shrew, is nevertheless of import because it initiates its own line of Shakespearean characters, in comedy or elsewhere, whose common claims upon us are self-praised bluntness and self-conscious honesty. Among these are Falconbridge and Hotspur, Mercutio and Benedick, all self-appointed scourges of sentiment, by their own claim men of few words yet of incessant speech, cryptoromantics foisting themselves upon us as anti-romantic realists. They are all subtly and delightfully comic.

Though Petruchio initiates that line he is himself not so subtly conceived as the rest, and his characterization is subordinate to the needs of the action, its general direction and tone. But his wooing of Katherina is of the greatest significance since it employs an ironic attitude toward the Petrarchan convention of love. In *A Shrew* Ferando woos Katherina in irrelevant pseudo-Marlovian diction, whereas in his own play Shakespeare gives Petruchio the much more relevant language of the sonneteer. The Marlovian style has very little to do with attitudes toward love and wooing; Petruchio's exaggerated and mocking Petrarchism has everything to do with it. A particular attitude towards love and wooing is gently mocked by being exaggerated, even though, as so often in Shakespeare, it is ironically enough the very thing Petruchio is mocking which wins Katherina's apparently stubborn heart. But such comic reversal, if we may call it that, is unaccompanied by any comic recognition, as for instance we find it in Benedick and Beatrice a few plays later. In any case, Petruchio is not opposed to love and wooing and marriage. On the contrary he enters the stage in search of a wife. Consequently he fails to experience anything comparable to Benedick and Beatrice's self-revelation. Petruchio's characterization, though it anticipates theirs in some ways, is on a different level. It appears, then, that in terms of comic theme and, in part, of characterization, the play shows Shakespeare moving in a clearly defined direction. His choice of constructing a comic plot in which attitudes toward love are the chief matter is fatal to Plautine themes and characters, some of which nevertheless survive in *The Taming of the Shrew*. Though no fewer than four old men have substantial parts in the play, and though they are duped by the young men, the chief conflict here is not between old men and their young sons. Furthermore, the slaves waiting upon the young men in Plautine comedy are given smaller parts in *The Shrew*. Here such slaves, now servants to the young men, do not control or direct the action as they do in Plautus. It is Hortensio, not his servant, who devises the plan of having Petruchio propose him as a music teacher for Bianca. And Lucentio, on his part, having devised his own plan to become Bianca's schoolmaster, receives no aid from his servant Tranio. Can it be done, Lucentio asks, to which Tranio answers:

Not possible; for who shall bear your part,
And be in Padua here Vincentio's son,
Keep house and ply his book, welcome his friends,
Visit his countrymen and banquet them?

(I, i, 199-202)

Surely Tranio is an unworthy descendant of his Plautine namesake.

There is another area in which Shakespeare's slowly emerging comic construction differs from Plautine comedy and even from *The Supposes*, which supplied the Bianca plot. As in *The Comedy of Errors*, here too Shakespeare replaces the Plautine interest in illicit love affairs with the wooing of maidens leading to marriage. Even in *The Supposes*, from which Shakespeare took much, the action begins long after the wooing of Polynesta (Bianca) by Erostrato (Lucentio) has taken place. Indeed, as the nurse Balia (prefiguring the inimitable Angelica of *Romeo and Juliet*) likes to repeat, the lovers "have passed so many pleasant nightes togither."[24] But though he replaces illicit love with wooing which leads to marriage, Shakespeare nevertheless employs the physical aspect of love as an important countertheme to the romantic and idealizing wooing of his maidens. He goes further by introducing often startling bawdry into the language of those same heroines. As a structural component, the physical side of love is represented by lovers who are concerned with that aspect of it, by ubiquitous bawdry in dialogue and song, often particularly effective in the speeches of jesters and clowns. In *The Taming of the Shrew* such bawdry is present in Petruchio's wooing of Katherina as well as in the scenes of Bianca's wooing by Hortensio and Lucentio. The effect of such bawdry is in great part atmospheric: its presence tends to keep in balance so far as possible, or at least to keep nearer the world of this earth, the often hypersentimental wooing of romantic lovers. And this, as we shall see, becomes another indispensable element of Shakespearean romantic comedy.

Finally *The Taming of the Shrew* introduces in most ten-

tative fashion what might be called a symbolic structure, an
aspect of Shakespearean comedy most readily apparent in such
plays as *A Midsummer Night's Dream* and *As You Like It*.
The action of such plays is presented now in a world like our
own, now in a distant and idealized world, the world of make-
believe. The two juxtaposed worlds provide contrasting points
of reference, but their respective actions derive meaning when
seen against each other. This is especially true in the later
and greater comedies. In *The Taming of the Shrew* this structural device is much simpler, though much more advanced than
anything of the kind in *The Comedy of Errors*. There the
only hint of a contrast between two *loci* is the strangeness of
Ephesus, which puzzles Antipholus of Syracuse and his Dromio.
In *The Taming of the Shrew* the Induction is laid on the level
of alleged reality, the world of the drunken Sly, with its pointed
geographical and other references to Warwickshire. The world
of the play proper is sharply separate: it is the world of "a
pleasant comedy," as Sly is told, that other land of enchanted
woods and islands, in the later plays the land of Belmont and
Arden and Illyria. In *The Taming of the Shrew* this other level
is generally contrasted with the world of Sly. But even in this
early attempt Shakespeare introduces a principle which he follows throughout his romantic comedy. Each of the two contrasted worlds has elements of the other. Just as the Sly episode
includes references to Apollo's music, to the song of "twenty
cag'd nightingales," to Daphne and Cytherea, so the fictional
playworld counterpoints with its own bawdry, its boisterous
gambols, broken heads, the beating of servants, the bidding
for a wife, the mud and mire of country lanes in Warwickshire.
By such exchange of details the dramatist achieves a measure of
unity, which is quite necessary since the stories of the Induction and the play proper are independent. Unlike later plays,
The Taming of the Shrew simply and explicitly separates the
two worlds, and although each contains elements of the other,
the two do not mix; they remain sharply and awkwardly apart,
and this may be one reason why Shakespeare may have chosen
to abandon one of them early in the play.[25]

The Two Gentlemen
of Verona

Chapter III

*T*he *Two Gentlemen of Verona* is Shakespeare's first essay
in romantic comedy, and though it is not a successful
play, its faults as well as its merits have been somewhat exaggerated.[1] Furthermore, its promise of things to come has been
inaccurately identified. The play is promising, the modern
argument goes, in that it employs motifs and bits of action which
appear in Shakespeare's later comedies, but since the handling
of these elements is said to be unsuccessful, it is difficult to see
what the play promises in that respect.[2] The mere presence
in a few plays of certain materials may have little to do with
the author's development of a special dramatic structure and
the exposition of a master-theme. There is another considera-

tion. A play's relative success or failure as well as its promise must be posited in terms of its date. For that reason the erroneous assumption that *The Two Gentlemen of Verona* follows *Love's Labour's Lost* in date has misled critics in their estimate of the relative kind and extent of promise shown by the two plays. It is held, for instance, that *Love's Labour's Lost* is both less successful and less promising in its treatment of romantic love, and it is further believed that in *The Two Gentlemen of Verona* Shakespeare laid down the broad limits of dramatic structure he was to perfect in the later comedies. Neither notion is defensible.

Although the love-friendship conflict may have been popular in Shakespeare's age and although it reappears in some of his later plays, it is never again at the center of the action but ancillary to the main theme. In so far as *The Two Gentlemen of Verona* explores the comic handling of the love-friendship conflict, the play anticipates very little in the comedies which followed. On the other hand, *Love's Labour's Lost* deals throughout its action with the conflict of attitudes toward love, the conflict which will dominate the structure of Shakespearean romantic comedy. Nor does *The Two Gentlemen of Verona* contribute significantly to that structure in its use of cord-ladders, a friar's cell, a disguised heroine serving her beloved in his courtship of another woman, motifs which appear in the later comedies. The play's contribution is in terms of other matters.

II

As with other Shakespearean plays, the scholars have ranged widely in their assignment of dates to *The Two Gentlemen of Verona*, from 1591 to 1595, some of them adopting both dates at different times. Fleay assigned 1591 as the date of the play's first performance, with the qualification that parts of it had been written by a collaborator and that an all-Shakespeare version replaced the earlier one in 1595.[3] E. K. Chambers rejects both the notion of a collaborator and the double dates, and gives 1594-95 as the most likely date of the play.[4]

A circumstance contributing to the difficulty critics have met in dating the play is the notion that in its present form the comedy is not entirely Shakespeare's. In the opinion of its New Cambridge editors, before the copy of *The Two Gentlemen of Verona* reached the Folio printer "the theatrical people had played some strange tricks upon it."[5] These had to do, it is alleged, not only with geographical confusion but also with the "unnatural" flaw of the final scene. It is true, the argument goes, that Shakespeare was not careful about names of people or places, and some of the confusions of names may be charged to him, but it is incredible that he should have composed the final scene as it now stands. Hence the need to postulate a revision. When and why the changes is not clear. In addition to this blaming of the errors and allegedly inept parts of the play upon a reviser, there has been an attempt to demonstrate that Shakespeare made some of the changes himself upon an earlier version of his own. The theory has been advanced that the travel element in the play with the congruent changes—and confusions—in scene were added by Shakespeare to an original form of the play which dealt only with the love-and-friendship story involving Valentine, Silvia, and Proteus, a story laid in Verona throughout. To this, it is argued, Shakespeare at a later date added the Proteus-Julia story as well as new places now made necessary by that story.[6] The theory may help explain why Valentine and after him Proteus, having set out from Verona for Milan, arrive in Padua (I, v, 1), which is later identified as Verona (III, i, 81), but later still as Milan (IV, i, 19). It cannot, however, explain all the confusion, nor can it throw light upon the reasons why both Valentine and Proteus travel from Verona to Milan by water whereas Julia follows them by land.

III

The play as we have it may indeed have been revised, by Shakespeare or by another, before it reached the Folio printer, but in the absence of demonstrable evidence to the contrary, we must conclude that the comedy, including confusion of names, geographical errors, and the final scene, is Shakespeare's and Shakespeare's alone. And though one ought not to be dogmatic about its precise date of composition, it should be noted that 1594-95 draws support from the play's thematic relationship with other plays of the period. In a very general way *The Two Gentlemen of Verona* continues the theme of rivalry in love which was treated lightly in *The Taming of the Shrew*. In that connection it should be noted that Gremio the pantaloon, one of Bianca's suitors, clearly prefigures the foolish Thurio, who courts Silvia in *The Two Gentlemen of Verona*.

Other connections with *The Taming of the Shrew* may be cited. Tranio's concurrence with his master Lucentio that the latter does well to leave home for the broader experience of travel abroad, coincides with Valentine's reasons for leaving Verona:

> Cease to persuade, my loving Proteus.
> Home-keeping youth have ever homely wits.
>
> (I, i, 1-2)

The lines further repeat Petruchio's own answer to Hortensio, that he has left Verona

> To seek [his] fortunes farther than at home
> Where small experience grows.
>
> (I, ii, 51-52)

In *The Two Gentlemen of Verona* the motif is given a somewhat larger scope in an elaboration by Antonio, Proteus' father, and his servant Panthino. The latter reports that his master's brother is much concerned with the lag in the proper training of Proteus. He wonders, as Panthino reports it to Antonio,

> that your lordship
> Would suffer him to spend his youth at home,
> While other men, of slender reputation,
> Put forth their sons to seek preferment out. . . .
>
> (I, iii, 4-7)

The same motif, though with greater emphasis, opens the action of *Love's Labour's Lost,* leading the king and his courtiers to establish their own academe.

It should be further noted that act II, scene ii, of *The Two Gentlemen of Verona* recalls IV, ii, of *The Taming of the Shrew.* In the latter play the scene opens with Lucentio and Bianca seated beneath the trees reading a book, while Tranio, Lucentio's servant, and Hortensio, one of the rival wooers, come upon the pair from the other side of the square. In like manner Valentine and Silvia, seated together in a room in the ducal palace, are joined by Speed, Valentine's servant, and Sir Thurio, the foppish rival. The loving exchanges of the romantic couples in the two plays have analogous effects upon the rivals. A final and very minor point connecting the two plays might be added. In the episode in which Proteus pretends to woo Silvia in Thurio's behalf, an old host brings the disguised Julia to the scene so that, being "allicholy," she might be made merry with music and also see the man she has been inquiring about. After the song to Silvia is sung, and Thurio and the musicians have departed, Proteus proceeds to woo Silvia for himself. And while Julia listens with the "comment of her soul" to their dialogue, the drowsy host, like the drunken Christopher Sly, dozes off and minds not the wooing. And when Julia asks him to take her back, he responds in Sly's own idiom: "By my halidom, I was fast asleep." This minor reminiscence, if it may be so called, is here employed to give point to Julia's agony, and thus an episode with an inconclusive function in one play is turned into a small but meaningful incident in another. Although not striking, these contacts with *The Taming of the Shrew* suggest a chronological relationship, and as *The Two Gentlemen of Verona* is almost certainly Shakespeare's initial attempt at romantic comedy, it may well have followed the other play in date of composition.

IV

It appears that in his early plays Shakespeare was to a considerable extent bound by his sources. This is certainly true of *The Comedy of Errors* and *The Taming of the Shrew*, and it may be likewise true of *The Two Gentlemen of Verona*. But here Shakespeare's sources are much more difficult to fix. More than a half dozen works have been proposed by scholars as offering either the whole substance of the play or a large portion of it.[7] One reason for the difficulty is that among the sources proposed is the lost play, *The History of Felix and Philiomena*, performed by the Queen's Servants in 1585.[8] Whether Shakespeare adapted that play or rather based his comedy on some combination of other sources it is impossible to say.[9] The lost play very probably dealt with the lovers' separation, Felix's betrayal of his love, their reconciliation and reunion. But in the absence of the play it is impossible to know whether it included the additional theme of the betrayal of friendship. It is very well to argue that Shakespeare knew the *Diana* or some version of its story, but the *Diana* is concerned only with the Proteus-Julia-Silvia plot, and though Shakespeare may have taken the Valentine-Silvia-Proteus story from one of the other sources,[10] he could just as easily have found it in the lost play.[11]

A glance at Shakespeare's work shows that he was deeply concerned with the theme of friendship: witness the pairs or groups of friends in *The Taming of the Shrew, Romeo and Juliet, The Merchant of Venice, Much Ado About Nothing*, and elsewhere. And if the chief conflict in his sonnets is authentic he had personal knowledge of the strain the love of a woman places upon the friendship of two men. But besides this, Shakespeare no doubt was fully aware of the classical exaltation of friendship and of its continued prominence as a literary theme through the Middle Ages down to his own day. In particular, the theme of a man's sacrifice of love in favor of friendship had appeared in the story of Tito and Gisippo in Boccaccio's *Decameron,* and a later version of it in Sir Thomas Elyot's *Governour.* In Lyly's *Endymion* and his *Euphues* Shakespeare found a more recent handling of the same theme.

Whether he borrowed from a single source, such as the lost play, or combined two or more sources, what is of great sig-

nificance is Shakespeare's choice to dramatize the conflict between love and friendship. For the resolve to compose a love
comedy, what some believe to be the "earliest surviving romantic comedy of England, and almost of Europe,"[12] and to place
at its center the hero's surrender of his beloved lady involved
a contradiction. The exaltation of friendship at the expense
of romantic love in the final scene is certainly antagonistic to
the structure and movement of romantic comedy, where union
of lovers is as indispensable as general reconciliation. It was an
unfortunate choice of theme and the cause of much trouble
to the dramatist as well as his critics.

v

Whatever critical comments have been made concerning the
play's construction or characterization or verse have been made
by the way, so to speak, since the critics have been almost exclusively absorbed by the concluding scene. The play succeeds
or fails in that final episode. And the majority of critics condemn that episode emphatically, although a few of them are
unwilling to attribute it to Shakespeare. For Sir Arthur Quiller-
Couch the surrender by Valentine of his beloved Silvia is so
unexpected that "Q" feels it "like a slap in the face," and his
response is to remark that "there are, by this time, *no* gentlemen in Verona."[13] But the offense, though painful, can be overlooked, he argues, for "this most crucial blunder" cannot be
charged to Shakespeare but to one or more botchers.[14] The explanation offered is that the dramatist's own concluding scene
was ineffective when first performed and for that reason it was
rewritten by someone other than Shakespeare.[15] But would the
actors replace an ineffective scene by one which pleases so
little, and is it likely that they would wish to introduce the
somewhat esoteric motif of Valentine's surrender of Silvia to
his friend?

Another explanation, "a fanciful" hypothesis as he admits,
is offered by Parrott, namely that Shakespeare's original version
was too long for the impatient actors, who therefore insisted on
heavy cuts. Among these the most vital was of a long debate

between the two friends on the themes of love and friendship, a debate which presumably justified Valentine's behavior.[16]

In his Arden edition of the play, R. W. Bond, after reviewing a number of apologies for Valentine's conduct, reaches the conclusion that the true solution had been reserved for Dr. Batteson, who accepts the text of the episode as right, as well as Shakespearean, but believes that Valentine's couplet

> And that my love may appear plain and free,
> All that was mine in Silvia I give thee

is intentionally ambiguous. The words mean one thing to Valentine and Proteus, and another to Julia. To the two men they mean "you shall have as much interest in my heart as she"; to Julia, in her "overwrought mood," they mean that Proteus can have Silvia.[17] Hence Julia's swoon and the dénouement. But is it not clear that it is Silvia who is in an overwrought mood and that she would likewise misinterpret Valentine's meaning? Charles Lamb thought so, but went on to explain Silvia's strange silence by saying that as she was busy reviving Julia from her swoon she had no time to be offended by Valentine's overstrained act of friendship.[18]

It should be borne in mind that Proteus has already repented when Valentine offers Silvia to him; so that the only reason for the offer must be to show thereby that his love for his friend "may appear plain and free." This is what Valentine tells Proteus, but it has been suggested that the real reason is to test him, to see whether he has truly repented by allowing him "to choose for himself between Silvia and Julia."[19] But the critic hastens to add that though Valentine is taking a risk, he is so confident of the outcome that he does not hesitate to let Silvia take the same risk. But it can be argued that if Valentine is certain of Proteus' repentance, there is no need for trial. And perhaps his own reason for surrendering Silvia should be given precedence over our own opinion of his act. Furthermore, his alleged resort to stratagem here is at odds with Valentine's strongly emphasized ingenuousness.

Leaving these overstrained defenses of the episode, let us turn to what may be called substantive interpretations of Valentine's conduct. E. K. Chambers, in a spirited essay on the play, sees in the Proteus-Silvia-Valentine story a reflex of Shakespeare's own conflict between his devotion to the perjured friend and supplanting lover and his passion for the Dark Lady.[20] But the readiest explanation of the episode has been on the ground that Shakespeare was here dramatizing the classical ideal which the Renaissance had inherited from ancient times and from recent medieval exempla.[21] Professor Dover Wilson's complaint that the conflict between love and friendship "is a theme not fully understood by critics" is beside the mark.[22] For surely the critics are as well informed about the ideal here dramatized as the majority of Shakespeare's audience. What both that audience and the critics have disapproved of is the dramatic handling of that ideal. For it is one thing to read of the classical theme in ancient legends and their medieval adaptations; it is another to see it acted on the stage in a play where the hero's supreme sacrifice seems unnecessary—Proteus has already repented—and doubtfully motivated. Furthermore, the difficulty of dramatizing successfully such a theme must surely be the reason why Shakespeare never again made it the central concern in any of his later plays. If it appears at all in other comedies, it is allowed no more than a brief incident or two. Perhaps the best illustration of this is the hypothetical concern with the conflict of love and friendship in an early scene of *Much Ado About Nothing*. Claudio, having asked Don Pedro to woo Hero for him, later is convinced that Don Pedro is wooing her for himself. Whereupon he delivers this bit of wisdom:

> Friendship is constant in all other things
> Save in the office and affairs of love.
>
> (II, i, 182-83)

But Claudio is too hasty and in error, for Don Pedro has no interest in Hero: hence no real conflict. Later in the play

Benedick is forced to choose between his friendship for Claudio and his love for Beatrice. But again the conflict, at least from the audience's point of view, is hypothetical since the truth about Hero's calumny has already been discovered and will be shortly revealed by Dogberry and his watch.

VI

But if the conflict between love and friendship is never again given prominence in Shakespeare's romantic comedies, the theme of forgiveness and reconciliation most assuredly is. And in terms of this theme *The Two Gentlemen of Verona* may be said to anticipate an important element in the structure of Shakespearean comedy, romantic or otherwise. And just as the choice of the love-friendship conflict attests to the play's early date and experimental nature, as well as to Shakespeare's immaturity, so does the inexpert handling of forgiveness and reconciliation in the concluding scene. For it is certainly clear that no defense of the play has been able to remove the charge of ineptitude and awkwardness in that final episode. Nor is there any doubt that the same kind of dénouement is handled much more successfully in later comedies. The forgiveness and rehabilitation of Proteus is repeated in such characters as Oliver in *As You Like It*, Angelo in *Measure for Measure*, as well as in other characters in other plays. Indeed, the act of forgiveness lies at the center of Shakespeare's thought; and it is the ultimate measure of human achievement. It is for that reason, perhaps, that it is given its final expression in Prospero's lines:

> The rarer action is
> In virtue than in vengeance.

(V, i, 27-28)

But the capacity for such forgiveness is seldom achieved without a struggle. In *As You Like It* Orlando, though ill-treated by his brother, nevertheless risks his own life to save him. Upon finding Oliver asleep and a certain prey to the couching lioness,

> Twice did he turn his back and purpos'd so;
> But kindness, nobler ever than revenge,
> And nature, stronger than his just occasion,
> Made him give battle to the lioness. . . .
>
> (IV, iii, 128-31)

In harmony with the general tone of the play, the lines lightly report Orlando's brief struggle before choosing the "rarer action." There is no attempt to represent on the stage the struggle itself. That struggle and the fierce moment wherein the choice is made are put into action upon the stage in *Measure for Measure*. In the concluding scene of that play the Duke is "definitive" in condemning Angelo, in asking "An Angelo for Claudio, death for death!" to which Isabella seems in silence to assent. Whereupon the frantic Mariana pleads to her for aid to save Angelo's life:

> O my good lord! Sweet Isabel, take my part!
> Lend me your knees, and all my life to come
> I'll lend you all my life to do you service.

No answer from Isabella, but the Duke interposes:

> Against all sense you do importune her.
> Should she kneel down in mercy of this fact,
> Her brother's ghost his paved bed would break,
> And take her hence in horror.

One more plea from Mariana:

> Sweet Isabel, do yet but kneel by me.
> Hold up your hands, say nothing; I'll speak all.
> They say best men are moulded out of faults,
> And, for the most, become much more the better
> For being a little bad; so may my husband.
> O Isabel, will you not lend a knee?
>
> (V, i, 435-47)

And after a long, painful silence Isabella does.

Here, then, are three episodes in three well-spaced plays which deal with forgiveness, a forgiveness laying immense strain upon the one who forgives. The difference among them is obvious: in *The Two Gentlemen of Verona* Proteus' repentance is as sudden as Angelo's, but Valentine's forgiveness is far too swift and perfunctory. A little different from this, a little less perfunctory, though merely reported, is Orlando's change of heart. But in *Measure for Measure* Isabella's forgiveness of Angelo which works his salvation, and in a special sense her own, is agonizingly slow to show itself. At least it is made to seem so to Mariana and to us. And it is precisely this slowness and deliberation which we miss in *The Two Gentlemen of Verona*. Forgiveness is much slower, much more difficult to attain, than repentance. No audience, of course, objects to forgiveness as an ideal of conduct, and no audience would object to it on the stage if it came even to the noblest of men after a recognizable human effort. It may indeed be true that in the final scene of *The Two Gentlemen of Verona* "the inmost meaning of love, as Shakespeare conceived it, is displayed,"[23] but it is a meaning placed upon the incident from the outside, so to speak, a meaning displayed indeed, not experienced.

VII

The theme of forgiveness and reconciliation, appearing for the first time in *The Two Gentlemen of Verona,* became a fundamental element in the structure of Shakespearean comedy. In the romantic comedies that theme is an adjunct to the indispensable union of lovers at the conclusion of each play. And since the union of lovers as well as forgiveness and reconciliation imply opposition and strife, it is clear why the action of Shakespearean romantic comedy must express itself in conflict. What matters most here is the kind of conflict or conflicts which serve as the basis of Shakespeare's romantic plots. One of these conflicts is external, the opposition to love and lovers by antagonistic characters or circumstances, such as Proteus' perfidy or the attitude of Silvia's father toward her love of Valentine, or Don John's obstruction of the Claudio-Hero love affair in *Much Ado About Nothing,* or the strife between the two Dukes in *As You Like It.* But in addition there is the far more significant interior opposition proceeding from the lovers' attitudes toward love and each other. In all, Shakespeare dramatizes three such attitudes in his romantic comedies: the idealizing of love and its object, the realistic or matter-of-fact concept of it, and the outright rejection or disdain of love. In *The Two Gentlemen of Verona*, the stress is upon the external conflict between love and friendship, a conflict never again given such prominence in the later comedies. But the play deals also with the internal conflict, that is, with the interplay of attitudes toward love. And it is precisely here where *The Two Gentlemen of Verona* makes its most significant contribution to the emerging form of Shakespearean romantic comedy.

Though the disdain of love, the scoffing at it, is given limited scope in the play, it is nevertheless an important motif, which in such plays as *Love's Labour's Lost* and *Much Ado About Nothing* becomes the basis of most of the comic action. In *The Two Gentlemen of Verona* its role is tentative, as if Shakespeare was trying it out to discover its possibilities. Valentine scoffs at love in the opening scene, and of course upon sight of Silvia later in Milan he falls in love with her at once. And he proceeds to extol her beauty in the fashion of the Petrarchan blazon. In later plays Shakespeare will invent episodes in which the scoffer at love is mocked and will balance these with additional episodes mocking the hyperbolic Petrarchism of the scoffer now transformed into a lover. In the play before us only the latter device is exploited, and this exploitation takes us to the other and larger conflict of these plays, that is the opposition between the conventions or poetics of love and the realistic or matter-of-fact concept of it.

Early in the opening scene Valentine alludes mockingly to one of the archetypal romances which recur throughout Shakespeare's romantic comedies. When Proteus promises to pray for him, Valentine replies that if he does he will pray on

> some shallow story of deep love,
> How young Leander cross'd the Hellespont.

> (I, i, 21-22)

This passage does double duty by not only recording Valentine's mockery of love, his comic hamartia for which he will later do penance, but also by establishing the tone and general atmosphere of the lover's attitude towards his love. For Proteus is indeed in these early scenes the lover of romance, the votary of love, whom the "heavenly Julia" has completely "metamorphosed." But the hyperbolic blazon of the beloved lady is properly reserved for Valentine, the scoffer who, after seeing Silvia, is himself bitterly suffering the pains of the convention. When Proteus has joined him in Milan, Valentine tells him of it:

> I have done penance for contemning Love,
> Whose high imperious thoughts have punish'd me
> With bitter fasts, with penitential groans,
> With nightly tears, and daily heart-sore sighs; . . .
> O gentle Proteus, Love's a mighty lord
> And hath so humbled me as I confess
> There is no woe to his correction,
> Nor to his service no such joy on earth.
>
> (II, iv, 129-39)

In the fashion appropriate to romantic lovers he showers conceits upon his lady: she is a "heavenly saint," she is "divine," or

> if not divine,
> Yet let her be a principality,
> Sovereign to all the creatures on the earth.
>
> (II, iv, 151-53)

She is a "jewel," a "pearl," "pure gold." Even Proteus, himself a lover and therefore adept in the art of hyperbole, is taken aback by Valentine's "braggardism." And later on the letter Valentine intends for Silvia, which the Duke intercepts along with the cord-ladder, is of course a love sonnet, though the Duke reads only eleven lines of it. Finally Valentine's lament for his banishment, anticipating Romeo's, is in the proper self-pitying idiom of the much-suffering romantic lover:

> To die is to be banish'd from myself,
> And Silvia is myself. Banish'd from her,
> Is self from self, a deadly banishment!
> What light is light, if Silvia be not seen?
> What joy is joy, if Silvia be not by? . . .
> Except I be by Silvia in the night,
> There is no music in the nightingale.
>
> (III, i, 171-79)

Even the foolish Thurio, prompted by Proteus, courts Silvia with a "sonnet," which is presumably the song "Who is Silvia?" sung to her by his musicians. No doubt the "sonnet" is beyond Thurio's poetic capabilities, being the work of a professional "sonneteer" since it answers well the requirements set down by Proteus' "discipline." To win Silvia, Proteus tells Thurio,

> You must lay lime to tangle her desires
> By wailful sonnets, whose composed rhymes
> Should be full-fraught with serviceable vows.

And after this preliminary you must serenade her in "the night's dead silence":

> After your dire-lamenting elegies,
> Visit by night your lady's chamber-window
> With some sweet consort; to their instruments
> Tune a deploring dump.
>
> (III, ii, 68-70, 82-85)

"Who is Silvia," that "sweet-complaining grievance," though ostensibly offered by Thurio's consort, is used by Proteus to advance his own suit, and a few lines later he takes credit for it. Although "Who is Silvia?" may have been Shakespeare's first attempt to employ song in the comedies, it is clear that the attempt is eminently successful. Not only does the song reproduce and by exaggeration caricature the extravagance of the Petrarchan sonnet, but it also implies a comment upon both Thurio who addresses the song and Proteus who later appropriates it.[24] The incongruousness of the song's spirituality to Thurio's character points up the ridiculousness of his courtship; and the juxtaposition of Proteus' betrayals with that same spirituality vitiates the slightest suggestion of integrity on his part.[25]

Although the two gentlemen of Verona are shown addressing their ladies in the self-satiric conceits of the sonneteers, the ladies themselves offer a striking contrast in their protestations of love. The passionate Julia approaches much closer to the sentiments of the conventional lover, and it is she who, alluding to her intended journey to Milan, speaks of herself as a "true-devoted pilgrim" who

> is not weary
> To measure kingdoms with his feeble steps;
> Much less shall she that hath Love's wings to fly,
> And when the flight is made to one so dear,
> Of such divine perfection, as Sir Proteus.
>
> (II, vii, 9-13)

She speaks of her hoped reunion with Proteus as her Elysium, and when she is told by Lucetta that she must cut her hair if she is to dress as a page, she answers:

> No, girl; I'll knit it up in silken strings
> With twenty odd-conceited true-love knots.
>
> (II, ii, 45-46)

For Proteus is not like other lovers; he is a paragon of men.

> His words are bonds, his oaths are oracles,
> His love sincere, his thoughts immaculate,
> His tears pure messengers sent from his heart,
> His heart as far from fraud as heaven from earth.
>
> (II, vii, 75-78)

And it is Julia who later associates her own plight with that of Ariadne, "passioning" for Theseus. But if further evidence is needed that Julia is the true heroine of romance, her conduct in the episode with Proteus' letter early in the play certainly supplies it. More particularly her words to the torn pieces of that letter proclaim her as the romantic lover, a creature of artificial pathos and excessive sentiment.[26]

With Silvia it is not so. In studies of the play she is nearly always dismissed as the representative of convention, as the exemplar of the stilted words and movements imposed by the code of romance. It is true, of course, that she addresses Valentine as her "servant" and that when Proteus is introduced to her she accedes to Valentine's request that she entertain his friend as his "fellow-servant," although she gives her response a slight suggestion of the gentlest irony. And it is also true that her romantic *milieu* is confirmed by the atmospheric function of Sir Eglamour. But Silvia is a much more complex character than that, and the question in the opening line of the song addressed to her has, I believe, a just aptness easy to overlook. The answer given in the song is that she is "holy, fair and wise," but this is the view of the romantic lover, not her own nor the poet's estimate of her. Much has been made of what Silvia anticipates in the later comedies. She prefigures Juliet in the harsh treatment she receives at the hands of her father, in her flight from a marriage she detests, in her rendezvous at the friar's cell, and so on. In her flight from an angry father she anticipates also Rosalind and Celia of *As You Like It*. Like Imogen she is wooed with a song offered by a detested lover. All this may be true, but of far greater significance is what she anticipates, not in such incidents, but rather in the conception of the chief heroines themselves of the later comedies. And here, it may be said, lies one of the significant innovations of the play.

Silvia differs from Julia not merely in the color of her hair, which the poet, as will be his custom, takes care to indicate, introducing with the gentlest mockery the perverse predilection of both gentlemen of Verona for a brunette, although Julia's own hair is not only Queen Elizabeth's "perfect yellow" but also the indispensable color of the heroine of romance. What further distinguishes Silvia from Julia is that she is possessed of a sturdier nature, greater spirit and directness. And these, though necessary to the most elementary distinction between two characters of the same sex, accompany or perhaps are responsible for a special point of view, a perspective which we shall find in its final perfection in later heroines, in Portia of *The Merchant of Venice* and even better in Rosalind of *As You Like It,* as well as Viola of *Twelfth Night.* Silvia falls in love with Valentine, calls him her servant, she is associated with Sir Eglamour, she is said to be "holy, fair and wise"; but she is something else too. She is able to look at romance and its trappings with a gently ironic twinkle. Upon the insipid rivalry of Valentine and Sir Thurio and their protestations she comments directly with the line "A fine volley of words, gentlemen, and quickly shot off." In presenting Proteus to her, Valentine informs her that his friend would have come along with him to Milan

> but that his mistress
> Did hold his eyes lock'd in her crystal looks.
> *Silvia.*   Belike that now she hath enfranchis'd them
> Upon some other pawn for fealty.
> *Valentine.* Nay, sure, I think she holds them prisoners still.
> *Silvia.*   Nay, then he should be blind; and, being blind,
> How could he see his way to seek out you?
>
> (II, iv, 88-94)

To Valentine's further protestations, she adds the abrupt "Have done, have done; here comes the gentleman." What the dramatist attempts to unite in Silvia in this early study of his ideal romantic heroine is sentiment, even passion, with the ability to see both of these as well as one's self in amused perspective. In Rosalind of *As You Like It,* as we shall see, the union of the two seemingly antithetical attitudes towards romantic love and its concomitants achieves a charming equilibrium. But though that union reaches no such perfection, the attempt is made in earnest for the first time in this play, and that attempt is one of the most significant advances toward the Shakespearean comic mode. For that mode, as will be made clear later, is crystallized in the temperament of Shakespeare's later comic heroines, to whom it gives their very life and being.

But the juxtaposition of two attitudes towards love tentatively expressed in the character of Silvia is supported by the presence of different characters representing the two points of view. In this, Shakespeare is following tradition and his own practice in the earlier comedies where the servants, for instance, parody their masters' romanticism by means of antiromantic speech or action. Later on, the servants become or are replaced by clowns or village mechanicals whose function is the same. Bearing in mind the role of the Dromios in *The Comedy of Errors,* of Gremio and especially Tranio in *The Taming of the Shrew,* of Launcelot Gobbo, Touchstone, and Feste, one is astonished to come upon the assertion that "unintentionally, Launce has become the means by which the incompatibilities and the unrealities of romantic postulates are laid bare."[27] On the contrary, that function is the most deliberate reason for his being. His is an indispensable contribution to the structure of Shakespearean romantic comedy. It is true that Launce differs in ancestry from Speed and from the clown and the court fool, but his function here is approximately the same as theirs. Not infrequently in Shakespeare comic servants, the slaves of classical drama turned clowns, no longer direct the intrigues of their young masters but roundly parody the romanticism of their love affairs. Surely it is inaccurate to say that Launce "has no real right within the play, except that gentlemen must have servants, and Elizabethan audiences must have clowns."[28] The realism of Launce's stage action with his dog, his description of the milkmaid he loves—"She hath more qualities than a water-spaniel . . . she can milk . . . she hath no teeth . . . she hath more hair than wit . . ."—all these are far too pointedly relevant to the courtship of the aristocratic lovers to be taken as accidental. Launce is indispensable to the conduct and meaning of the story: he is a necessary device in the structure of Shakespeare's emerging comic mode. And where the country lout is absent, his role is assumed by the clown or jester, but the role is the same: to parody through contrasting realistic speech and action the sentimental romanticism of the main story.

In this function Launce is aided by Speed, who is of different ancestry, being an immediate descendant of the classical slave somewhat reduced in both sparkle and stature in the plot. But he does his best to give perspective to the activities of the romantic lovers. It is Speed who delivers himself of a satiric description of Valentine's love symptoms (II, i, 17-30), very like those discovered by Benedick in Claudio and by Rosalind mockingly found wanting in her Orlando. It is Speed who in the midst of his master's soulful concerns with love keeps talking of his belly. When he reminds Valentine that it is dinner time, his master, having just had a meeting with Silvia, sighs that he has dined. To which Speed responds: "Ay, but hearken, sir; though the chameleon Love can feed on the air, I am one that am nourish'd by my victuals and would fain have meat." (II, i, 177-80). Earlier in the play he informs Proteus that he has carried his letter to Julia. And having exchanged with him some lines of feeble quibbling on ship—sheep and the ubiquitous horn, he says that he, "a lost mutton," gave the letter to "a laced mutton," and she gave him nothing for his labor. What matters here is not the crudeness of Speed's quibbling but rather the introduction of the phrase "laced mutton." Its function, as the function of bawdry elsewhere in Shakespearean comedy, is simply to oppose and by juxtaposition reduce the excessive sentiment of the romantic action.[29] At least two editors of the play have been scandalized by Speed's apparent liberty, for they assume that he is here referring to Julia. But although that is the apparent meaning of the lines, Speed in fact had given the letter to Lucetta, who in the scene following brings it to her mistress.

But the use of bawdy quibbling for the purpose cited above is not reserved for the servants or even the male characters only. On the contrary, one of the most striking features in the speech of Shakespeare's great comic heroines is its bawdry, although this is not true of the heroines of *The Two Gentlemen of Verona.* Here such speech is given to Lucetta, who insists Julia must have her breeches made with a cod-piece. To which Julia at first objects:

> Out, out, Lucetta! that will be ill-favour'd.
> *Lucetta.* A round hose, madam, now's not worth a pin,
>   Unless you have a codpiece to stick pins on.
>
>   (II, vii, 54-56)

Compared to the bawdry the ladies of *Love's Labour's Lost* (for instance) bandy about, this is exceedingly feeble, but it will serve. Like Speed's laced mutton and horns and Launce's parodies, Lucetta's lines advance the claims of nature by placing them next to the claims and codes of the romantic convention. And the juxtaposition of the two extremes, faintly here but more forcefully in the later comedies, points to a more nearly balanced attitude towards the experience of being in love. It is in this attempt to base part of its comic action upon the opposition of extreme attitudes and by implication to suggest the mean that *The Two Gentlemen of Verona* can be called Shakespeare's first romantic comedy. For it is this aspect of the play's structure which Shakespeare takes up in the later plays and for which he achieves a near perfect mode in the "joyous" comedies.

Love's Labour's Lost

Chapter IV

I

The fortunes of *Love's Labour's Lost* have been nothing short of extraordinary. It is in many ways an exceptional play and in one or two points unique among Shakespeare's comedies. Of all his plays it is by general agreement the most topical, or so it appears to be. Certainly a large number of what seem like allusions to contemporary events or persons have been lost to the modern reader. It employs in fictionalized form a few events in recent French history together with the names of a few of the persons involved in that history. It seems to allude not only to characters and recent events in France but also to Raleigh, Florio, Nashe and Harvey, Essex and Southampton, and others. It is the play for a long time thought to be Shakespeare's first drama. It is believed by many to be his least substantial, the one with the weakest structure and most superficial characterization. It is the one play Hazlitt would choose to dispense with if he was forced to have a choice. And yet of this allegedly earliest and least mature play Dr. Johnson said that he found "scattered through the whole, many sparks of genius; nor is there any play that has more evident marks of the hand of *Shakespeare*."[1] The general critical approach to the play has changed in recent years. Critics have come to believe that *Love's Labour's Lost* is neither Shakespeare's earliest nor least vital comedy, and they have found in both style and plot seminal elements which prefigure important aspects of the later and greater comedies. And not a few students of the play have been converted by the "theatricality" of *Love's Labour's Lost*. They have been impressed by the "powerful effect of Mercade's entrance"[2] in V, ii, by the imaginativeness and variety of mood throughout, by its vivacity and the patterning of its structure, its speech and characterization.[3]

The play is thought to be different from Shakespeare's other comedies in another way. One critic has asserted that "what is striking about *Love's Labour's Lost* is how *little* Shakespeare used exciting action, story, or conflict, how far he went in the direction of making the piece a set exhibition of pastimes and games. The play is a strikingly fresh start, a more complete break with what he had been doing earlier than I can think of anywhere else in his career, unless it be where he starts to write the late romances."[4] Because no literary or theatrical sources for the play have been discovered, the same critic believes that Shakespeare "makes up everything himself, because he is making up action on the model of games and pastimes."[5] *Love's Labour's Lost* seems so different that according to another scholar "there is no good reason for believing either that Shakespeare originated it, or that he wrote all of it as it now stands."[6] Whether *Love's Labour's Lost* is so sharply separated, or separable, from the comedies written before and after it we shall see presently. And whether the play is Shakespeare's we need not consider at all although his author-

ship, tacitly accepted by nearly all, is brought into strange question in connection with the date of its composition. That, too,
we shall look into presently. For the moment we may note that
the opinion concerning the play in general goes to extremes:
it is a unique comedy; it is Shakespeare's worst play, it is his
least substantial, it stands apart, it is his earliest play, it may
not even be his; on the other hand it is truly Shakespearean,
it is charming, it makes a powerful theatrical impression, it
"abounds in beauties of fancy and phrase, as beautiful today as
ever,"[7] it is "a first-rate comedy of the pattern kind . . . of
permanent wit, of brilliant and entrancing situation. . . ."[8]
This in brief is the general range of comment upon *Love's
Labour's Lost.*

II

If now we look at particular aspects of the play we shall find
the same conflict of extremes in comment and considered
scholarly opinion. Concerning the date of *Love's Labour's Lost*
there has been an extraordinary debate which has ranged the
year of the play's composition between 1589 and 1598. And
the dispute shows no signs of abating.[9] The evidence for
assigning such dates to the play is almost entirely internal, the
only external facts being the dates of the first quarto (1598),
and of John Gerarde's *Herball* (1597), from which Shakespeare
took details for the spring song at the conclusion of the play.[10]
Among important aspects of internal evidence is the play's
style, especially the high proportion of rhymed lines, end-
stopped lines, and doggerel meters. Another is its structure,
which T. W. Baldwin considers the simplest, least classical,
of all Shakespeare's plays.[11] On the basis of its style and structure, then, the play has been placed at the very beginning
of Shakespeare's dramatic career. Neither of these, however,
can be accepted as conclusive evidence. Metrical tests determine
the kind, not the quality, of the verse. On the other hand the
structure of a play may depend on the story, invented or borrowed, and on the choice of a theme, or a particular aspect of it,

which the dramatist chooses to set forth. Simplicity in structure can be found in a dramatist's late as well as early work.

Of far greater import in determining the date of *Love's Labour's Lost* have been the presumed allusions in the play to contemporary French and English history, to individuals, contemporary poets and poetry, literary quarrels, rival philosophic and political cliques, to entertainments royal and aristocratic. The maze of such alleged allusions, their infinite ramifications, their agreements and conflicts, is truly bewildering. This is not the place to attempt a sifting-out of the relevancy of historical facts alleged to bear upon the date of *Love's Labour's Lost*.[12] But since the position of the play in Shakespeare's development as a comic dramatist is of singular importance, it is necessary to consider briefly the problem of dating the play in terms of its postulated references to contemporary persons and events.

The events, places, and names in contemporary French history which supplied Shakespeare with the merest thread of a story as well as the *locus* and chief characters of the comedy have to do with the conflict between Henry of Navarre and the King of France. More particularly, the visit of the French princess and her ladies to the court of Ferdinand of Navarre in the play was suggested by the visit of Catherine de Medici, her daughter Marguerite, and the famous "escadron volant" to the court of Henry of Navarre at Nerac in 1578 for the purpose of discussing Aquitaine as Marguerite's dowry and of converting the King to Catholicism.[13] It is true that the Protestant Henry's popularity in England was at its highest in the summer of 1591, when Essex, with customary tragicomic flamboyance carried ineffectual aid to Navarre in the campaign against Rouen. But English interest in Navarre was strong also in 1593, when he renounced his religion, and more so in 1595, when he realigned himself with England by making war on Spain. Shakespeare, therefore, could have employed Navarre's affairs as a broad source for his comedy in any one of those years.

Other evidence may be found in what appear to be direct allusions in the play to certain pamphlets in the Harvey-Nashe quarrel, especially Nashe's *Pierce Pennilesse* (1592) and perhaps *Have With You to Saffron Walden* (1596), and Harvey's *Foure Letters* (1592) and *Pierces Supererogation* (1593).[14] That Nashe and Harvey are alluded to in at least a few passages in the play is made almost certain by Armado's "congruent epitheton" of "tender juvenal" which he applies to Moth (I, ii, 8, 12). "Juvenal" may have been Nashe's nickname, for Francis Meres addresses him as "gallant young Juvenall" in his *Palladis Tamia* (1598). Moth, who in such a context may be thought of as Nashe, is responsible for a great many puns on purses and pennies which echo puns made by both Harvey and Nashe about the title of the latter's *Pierce Pennilesse.*

This connection between the play and the Harvey-Nashe quarrel points to a date around 1593 or later, unless we assume that the entire list of echoes and allusions to the quarrel was inserted later in the allegedly revised portions of the play. Such an assumption is indefensible, for the echo-lines are far too frequent and they are so vitally worked into the text of the play that they can scarcely be interpolations. Another allusion detected by scholars has to do with the Russian disguise of King Ferdinand and his lords in V, ii, which is thought to have been suggested by the mock embassy of a Russian dignitary and his retinue, dressed in the Russian manner, which was part of the extensive Gray's Inn Revels during the Christmas festivities of 1594. It was during these celebrations that the members of the society witnessed the performance of *The Comedy of Errors,* as was noted in an earlier chapter.[15] The likelihood of a connection is somewhat strengthened by the coincidence of two points in the play and the Revels. In both, the "Muscovites" are accompanied by "blackamoors" (they are called "Negro Tartars" in the Revels); and Rosaline's phrase "sea-sick, I think, coming from Muscovy" (V, ii, 393), with which she taunts Berowne, echoes a passage in the letter purportedly written by the "Lord of Purpoole," the chief officer in charge of the Christmas Revels. One of the many aspects of those revels was the pretended journey to Russia of the Lord of Purpoole. On his return the Lord had purposed to call upon the Queen, "to

kiss her sacred Hands, as a Tender of the Zeal and Duty" he
owes her Majesty. Being unable to do so, he writes to Sir
Thomas Heneage praying him to make his excuses to the
Queen, saying that the reason he cannot call upon her is his
illness: "I found, my Desire was greater than the Ability of
my Body; which, by length of my Journey, and my Sickness
at Sea, is so weakened. . . ."[16]

Shakespeare may very well have had in mind those festivities
when he composed the "masque of Muscovites" for *Love's
Labour's Lost*. The relation—if one is accepted—between the
two would strengthen the argument for a date of 1594-95, though
of course it cannot prove it. Besides, the masque of Muscovites
could have been suggested by a passage in an earlier work, the
second edition of Holinshed's *Chronicles*, 1587.[17] The passage describes a masque performed by Henry VIII and certain
lords, two of these dressed "after the fashion of Russia or Rus-
land." Included in the masque were six ladies, whose "faces,
necks, armes, and hands [were] couered in fine pleasant blacke
. . . so that the same ladies seemed to be Nigers or blacke
Mores."[18] In addition to this, interest in Russia was strong
during the early years of the 1590's. In 1591 that interest
was given special impetus by the publication of Giles Fletcher's
Of the Russe Commonwealth, although the appearance of the
work could scarcely have influenced Shakespeare. What it
probably did was to inspire the mock-Russian portion of the
Gray's Inn Revels. Precisely which event or source lies behind
the "masque of Muscovites" it is impossible to demonstrate,
but if one had to choose the most likely, it would be the masque
of Russians in the Gray's Inn festivities of 1594.

The same year is also suggested by another allusion to
contemporary events in England, namely to Sir Walter Raleigh
and his circle and particularly to Chapman's poem *The Shadow
of Night,* printed in 1594 and expressing the general philosophy
of that circle.[19] That philosophy, the pursuit of study, knowledge, and contemplation as opposed to an active and practical
life, seems to be precisely what *Love's Labour's Lost* in part
ridicules. And it is thus possible that in the quixotic plan

of an academe undertaken by King Ferdinand and his three
lords Shakespeare may be satirizing not only Chapman and
Raleigh but also other members of their group, Matthew Roy-
don, to whom Chapman penned an introductory epistle, and
the "most ingenious Darby, deep-searching Northumberland,
and skill-embracing heir of Hunsdon." Marlowe and the mathe-
matician Thomas Harriot round out the little "academy,"
which a 1592 pamphlet had called "Sir Walter Rawley's Schoole
of Atheisme." There can, of course, be no proof for it, but
it is highly probable that "the school of night" in the play
(IV, iii, 252) is an allusion to both that very academy and to
Chapman's poem celebrating its ideal.[20] And so this too would
tend to strengthen 1594 or 1595 as the date of the play. And
this is the date accepted by most scholars at present.[21]

III

The problem of dating the play is related to the likewise
insoluble difficulty of determining the extent and nature of
revision which is by most scholars believed to have taken place
between the time of the original composition and the printing
of the quarto in 1598. The title-page proclaims the text to be
"Newly corrected and augmented," but what precisely the
phrase means it is impossible to determine, and scholars have
provided conflicting interpretations.[22]

Whatever the final conclusion should be concerning the
time and extent of revision, our concern here is with the play
as we have it. Whether written early and revised shortly
before the quarto appeared, or whether it was originally composed in 1595 or even later and again revised before 1598,
the play precedes the joyous comedies of the final period which
it prefigures in significant ways. For the play as it has come
down illustrates Shakespeare's early handling of a particular
comic mode, a mode best suited to the theme of romantic love.
And that choice must have occurred shortly after the unsuccessful experimentation of *The Two Gentlemen of Verona*.

Although the date and the question of revision have elicited
an extraordinary amount of research and speculation, even more

time and space have been expended in the study of the play's sources, and particularly its connections with the contemporary political and intellectual scene and therefore allusions to persons and events in England and abroad shortly before the turn of the century. And the attractiveness of this connection has absorbed almost completely those who have studied the play with any degree of penetration. As a consequence, the play itself, aside from its topical connections, has been given adequate hearing by only a handful of critics.

But of course a consideration of a play's sources is necessary, for we wish to know, wherever possible, what it is that the dramatist begins with, what he chooses to base his plot on, and what he does with the materials at hand. In writing *The Two Gentlemen of Verona* Shakespeare began with at least two stories—one dealing with the unfaithfulness of a lover and the other with the devotion of a friend—which he combined into a single plot. But in so doing he followed rather closely— too closely—the details of his borrowed stories. This is of particular significance in the final and troublesome scene wherein Valentine, following the example of classical story, surrenders Silvia to his friend. In *Love's Labour's Lost* Shakespeare did something very different. To begin with, he used no sources, that is, no literary sources as such, except so far as his type-characters derive from earlier drama, but rather based the general movement of the plot on hints he may have derived from travelers recently returned from France. From these he must have received a general notion of the visit of Catherine de Medici, her daughter Marguerite, and the "escadron volant" to Henry of Navarre at Nerac in 1578.[23] But though this visit, together with the names Navarre, Berowne, Longaville, and Dumain, served as the general framework of Shakespeare's plot, it does not follow that he began with these elements. It is more likely that he began with an idea, the rejection of love, a theme he had lightly touched upon in *The Two Gentlemen of Verona* and was to treat again in later plays, including *A Midsummer Night's Dream, Much Ado About Nothing, As You Like It,* and *Twelfth Night.* In

The Two Gentlemen of Verona Valentine's rejection of romantic love is balanced by his about-face at the sight of Silvia,
and his early mockery of Proteus' devotion to Julia is countered
by the hyperbolic Petrarchism of his own courtship. But in *The
Two Gentlemen of Verona* the theme of rejection and about-
face is given limited scope and the chief concern of the action
is a conflict of another kind. In *Love's Labour's Lost* this same
theme fills the entire play.

Before pursuing this matter further we must return to the
question of sources and topical allusions on which the action of
the play is based. Reference has already been made to the broad
historical framework of the action, that is, the visit to Nerac
of Marguerite, Navarre's estranged wife, in company with her
mother and the bevy of ladies in attendance. As was proper,
Shakespeare changed the King's name from Henry to Ferdinand,
made his queen a princess, though in some speech-headings she
is cited as queen; and he made the matter of Aquitaine and
the payment of a hundred thousand crowns the chief reason
for the embassy. In addition, Shakespeare may have based
the story of Katherine's sister, who is said to have died of a
broken heart (V, ii, 14), on the death of Helene de Tournon,
daughter of one of the attendant ladies, who died of love in the
absence of her beloved, the Marquis de Varembon. It is probable that the idea for the King's academe may have been suggested by Pierre de la Primaudaye's *Academie françoise,* translated into English in 1586. But although he employed such
elements of French history, Shakespeare recreated his aristocratic characters to fit his own comic scheme. In such characterization he may have received hints from Greene's drama, as for
instance in the charm of his heroines, one of the outstanding
characteristics of the women in the comedies of the two dramatists. Another similarity, though not demonstrable indebtedness, may be seen in the attempt to integrate secondary themes
and characters with the love story, which in both Greene and
Shakespeare forms the central action.

In the ease and grace of prose dialogue of the aristocratic
characters who discourse on love Shakespeare was indebted to

the comedies of Lyly, although his borrowing was not uncritical. On the contrary Shakespeare looked to the style in Lyly's comedies as both model and satiric target, and that paradox is best demonstrated in the play under discussion. Here the manner in which characters speak or write—and there is a great deal of writing within the play—is now attractive, now ludicrous, mostly the latter. But there is far more than this in the role of language in *Love's Labour's Lost*. As we shall see later, a character's style, his way of speaking and composing, is most vitally associated with his way of loving. This, one of the most obvious themes in the play, has been curiously overlooked by critics, who have given their attention to the *kind* of speech, its background and ancestry, instead of delving into its dramatic or rather thematic significance. The influence of Lyly's style is strong in the play, in spite of Shakespeare's recoiling from its excess and indeed making that excess one of his targets. But in certain parts of the comedy he allows the clever dialogue to deteriorate until it becomes a mere exhibition of stale wit, and this without any ironic intention.

Lyly's influence in *Love's Labour's Lost* appears also in the matter of characterization, particularly of Armado and Moth, whose likeness to Sir Tophas and Epiton of Lyly's *Endymion* has been noted by critics. In spite of that likeness, Shakespeare's Armado and his page, as well as the rest of the low-comedy group, derive from characters of the *commedia dell' arte*. Professor Campbell has shown that Italian comedy of the sixteenth century had converted the braggart of classical comedy into a Spanish swashbuckler, the Capitano of the *commedia dell' arte*.[24] To that form of Italian comedy and its type-characters Shakespeare is indebted for his own transformed *miles gloriosus*, Armado, and also Moth who is his zany. From the same source are derived the rest: Holofernes is the pedant anglicized, Nathaniel the parasite, Costard the rustic fool, and Dull the stupid magistrate. Though all of these go back to Italian prototypes, Shakespeare enriched them by adding to their generic elements English details. This has been noted particularly of Armado, who is by some thought to have been conceived partly in terms of the roaring boy as well as the Elizabethan gallant who aspires to court connections.[25]

IV

But the most interesting, indeed fascinating, aspect of the sources for *Love's Labour's Lost* has to do with the nature and extent of the topical content of the play. Of this, mention was made earlier in connection with theories concerning the play's date. "Theories" is also the best that can be said of the attempts to see the meaning or secret of the play in its alleged dramatization of the rival politico-philosophic ideologies of two powerful groups headed by Raleigh and his adversary Essex. The play, says Professor Dover Wilson, "was Shakespeare's most elaborate and sustained essay in satire and burlesque. It teems with topical allusions to persons known to the original audience— allusions bound to fade. . . ."[26] This expresses the general attitude of Shakespearean commentators on the play, and it may well be accurate. The dialogue, the characterization, the allusions which seem pointed at something or someone we can no longer identify, the tantalizing phrases we come upon which send our minds to historical persons and events in search of relevancy—these matters cannot be overlooked; we cannot say that, because we have no demonstrable proof, Shakespeare intended no such allusions in the play. On the other hand, it is equally foolhardy to insist that Armado represents a particular person, say Florio, throughout. Two scholars who have studied the play with care warn against such a point of view and they propose, instead, a more judicious attitude. Miss Bradbrook believes that *Love's Labour's Lost* "was among other things Shakespeare's account of the School of Night."[27] In particular she is convinced that Armado fits Raleigh perfectly, but she nevertheless concedes that "the play is on the whole more concerned with theories of living than with personalities: the satire is not sustained and consistent."[28] Professor Campbell offers an even wiser approach. He believes that Shakespeare took care to "make his characters reminiscent of this and that person, but never fashion them into rounded portraits of anyone living or dead."[29] And "rounded portraits" is what most commentators find in the play. Not only this, but the occasion, the place of first performance, as well as the content of the play, have been identified with a special event in the life of a particular person. According to this very interesting theory, *Love's Labour's Lost* was designed and performed before the Queen as a plea for her aid in Southampton's struggle to evade the marriage proposed for him by Burleigh, who was acting as his guardian.[30]

That the insistence upon seeing in the play consistent historical portraits is inadvisable is confirmed by the number of different identifications. For instance Armado has been equated with Raleigh, Lyly, Chapman, Harvey, Florio, Antonio Perez, and Don John of Austria. No attempt can be made here to review the theories supporting the several identifications. For the correct equation, if there is one, cannot materially affect our estimate of the play. Indeed the overzealous devotion to that sort of study has deprived the comedy of the interpretive, as opposed to historical, attention it deserves. But it cannot be denied that it is of importance to know whether Shakespeare, in giving a certain speech or action to a character, even a minor one, was concerned with some historical matter or some aspect of the theme of the play. For instance, is Jaquenetta's being with child in the fifth act a glance at Raleigh's discomfiture or is it instead a motif necessary to the full expression of multiple attitudes toward romantic love? It may be that Shakespeare intended both, but unfortunately many students of the play, allured by the irresistible attraction of the historical event, have overlooked the thematic significance of the episode. And how far afield this can take us can be seen in the theory that *Love's Labour's Lost* was conceived as a satire of Raleigh, especially his poetry to Queen Elizabeth, and his predicament that, after writing love poems to her, he was found to have had an affair with one of her maids of honor.[31] This may of course be true, though it is impossible to demonstrate. But that is not the point. The point is that the love poetry satirized in *Love's Labour's Lost* is satirized also in *The Two Gentlemen of*

Verona, in *Much Ado About Nothing,* in *As You Like It,* in *Twelfth Night,* and elsewhere. What is satirized is a kind of poetic composition and the experience which underlies it. And both of these, as we have many times noted, form one of the bases of the Shakespearean comic mode.

The same can be said of the theory that *Love's Labour's Lost* is a satire of the School of Night. The members of the school were concerned with the study of philosophy, mathematics, and astronomy, and some of them, or their associates, introduced anti-feminism as a necessary adjunct to their academic endeavors. Such anti-feminism appears in three important documents composed by members or associates of Raleigh's academe. It is introduced by Chapman in his *Shadow of Night* and by Henry Percy, ninth earl of Northumberland, in an essay in which he attempts to convince his wife, Dorothy Devereux, Stella's sister, that the attractions of learning were far greater than those of any woman.[32] Furthermore, not only Dorothy Devereux but also Essex's other and more famous sister, Sidney's Stella, had already been offended by the Italian astronomer Giordano Bruno, who while in England shared a house with John Florio. In his *De gli eroici furori,* dedicated to Sidney, Bruno attacked romantic love, love poetry, and particularly sonneteering. Although the work had appeared in 1585, Bruno's attitude towards love, and indirectly his affront to Stella, were revived, the theory goes, by Florio's *Second Fruits* (1591), a manual for teaching Italian to Englishmen. The conclusion reached by some scholars, and particularly Frances Yates, is succinctly stated by the editor of the play in the revised Arden series: "Essex is insulted by Raleigh, his sisters, famous beauties, by Raleigh's friends, the members and correspondents of Raleigh's pretentious study-circle; their defence is undertaken by Shakespeare, protégé of Essex's friend Southampton. 'Women *are* stars' is the theme of the play."[33] It is a most attractive theory, and it may very well be that Shakespeare was aware of this correspondence between parts of the play and the injuries sustained by the Devereux sisters at the hands of Raleigh's academicians. Indeed it is difficult to see how he could have avoided knowing about such matters. But that he wrote the play in order to defend Dorothy and Penelope Devereux is not only impossible to demonstrate but most unlikely since the satire of those who reject love appears in most of Shakespeare's romantic comedies. It is a theme tentatively treated in *The Two Gentlemen of Verona,* as we have already noted; it is taken up in *Love's Labour's Lost,* and resumed in play after play including the so-called problem comedies. Certainly little if any topical content can be inferred in the action of these plays. But there is another difficulty. If in the King and his three lords Shakespeare is satirizing Raleigh and his anti-feminist academicians, who is being satirized in the second half of the play where the same characters, now in love, appear even more ridiculous in their sonneteering, their Russian masques, and their general romantic convolutions? Do these same characters represent different historical personalities in different parts of the play? If so, they must stand for the Raleigh faction in the first half of the comedy and for the Essex group in the second. But how can that be, since the characters in the play are mocked and satirized in both parts of the comedy? Shakespeare would thus be mocking in the second half of the play the attitude of the very group he is defending by attacking the rival camp in the first half. Furthermore, is it true that the theme of the play is the doctrine that "women are stars"? Is not this, rather, a vivid and comprehensive conceit expressing one of the most common romantic doctrines? And it is by no means peculiar to the play under discussion, for the same metaphor is given even greater prominence in *Romeo and Juliet.* Although Shakespeare must have been aware of the correspondences between certain details in the play and the Raleigh-Essex rivalry, I believe that *Love's Labour's Lost* possesses its own thematic and structural integrity, a story and a principle of its organization which are independent of their topical reference. But it must be admitted that in the speech and actions of certain characters Shakespeare could, and perhaps did, suggest persons and events easily recognizable by his first audience. This, however, is a different matter from the notion that the whole play was conceived as a historical action.[34] The mockery of philosophies and pedantic affectation in the play may be a hit at the pretensions of Raleigh's academe, but the hit is incidental to the movement and meaning of the action. The King and his lords reject the society of women in favor of study. In later plays, like *Much Ado About Nothing* and *Twelfth Night,* characters reject love for other reasons, and in these plays, as in *Love's Labour's Lost,* the rejection is satirized by direct statement, but more effectively by reversals in the action itself; those who reject love, those who mock it, fall in love and are themselves mocked by others. The rejection of love in the action of these plays is a Shakespearean, not a historical theme.

In connection with this we may note yet another point of view expressed by commentators on Shakespearean drama, namely the dramatist's personal note in the plots of these plays. Here the somewhat startling view has been proposed that in some ways Berowne represents Shakespeare. "In this character," says Walter Pater, "which is never quite in touch, never quite on a perfect level of understanding, with the other persons of the play, we see, perhaps a reflex of Shakespeare himself, when he has just become able to stand aside from and estimate the first period of his poetry."[35] Even more venturesome is the view, based on Pater's notion, that Berowne *is* Shakespeare. "It is that here," writes Professor Parrott, "for the first time, he seems to draw aside the veil that conceals his inmost self and to present, as he was later to do in the sonnets, *Hamlet,* and *The Tempest,* something that might be likened to a painter's self portrait."[36] But he adds that "Shakespeare was not trying to draw a portrait of himself in the costume of Berowne. On the contrary this character seems to express what Shakespeare wished to be."[37] The view illustrates the dangerous extreme to which the search for historical identifications may lead. It is dangerous simply because it abandons the principle, at least for the moment, of the character's dramatic integrity. And what can be said of Benedick, whose anti-romanticism, wit, and self-chosen role of scourge to the female sex are far stronger than Berowne's? If Benedick's characterization is entirely dramatic, why not Berowne's? Still, it must be admitted that Shakespeare was certainly capable of creating characters with what might be called "multiple simultaneous reference." In the present play it is more likely to find such characters in the low-comedy group, particularly Armado and Holofernes, for these are given far more individual traits, large and small, which may point to different historical persons at different moments in the play. The historical content of the play, then, French and English, is merely a backdrop, forming a recognizable background to the action.

v

We may now turn to consider the play itself as comedy, its theme and structure, and through these its contribution to the comic form which Shakespeare is developing for the accommodation of a love story. As we saw at the beginning of this chapter the weight of comment on the play has been until recently overwhelmingly unfavorable. There is no need here to review what has been said of the play in detail. It will suffice to note the general tenor of that negative comment. Although Richard Burbage thought the play excellent for its "wytt & mirthe," Dryden and Dr. Johnson, each for a different reason, are the two early critics whose adverse comment began the long list of detractors. Most of these believed that *Love's Labour's Lost* was Shakespeare's earliest comedy and therefore his least attractive; and it is possible that other critics, believing this an unsuccessful play, determined to prove that it was Shakespeare's first. But what matters here is the reason for thinking the play unsuccessful. The reason given is that it lacks both plot and characterization: the play has no clearly defined characters and it has no structure. Pater, though seeming to praise the play, suggested its lack of plot in saying that "the unity of the play is not so much the unity of a drama as that of a series of pictorial groups, in which the same figures reappear, in different combinations but on the same background."[38] This is as damaging as it is inaccurate, and it has fostered a variety of critical estimates of the play that are at best superficial. Later critics approached the play with the inherited opinion that it had no plot and no characters, that instead of these it had a park as its *locus* and a series of scenes reminiscent of a royal progress. One way of explaining what Professor Charlton has called "the spinelessness of the thing" is to see it as deliberate, to conclude that Shakespeare was not interested in a story with a serious plot, that he did not wish to lay stress on conflict in the play. "We know," says Professor Barber, "how the conflict will come out before it starts. But story interest is not the point: Shakespeare is presenting a series of wooing games, not a story."[39] Knowing how the story will come out may be true of *Love's Labour's Lost,* but it is no less true of the conflict in Shakespeare's greatest comedies, the stories of Benedick and Beatrice, of Orlando and Rosalind, of Orsino and Viola. The outcome is never in doubt in any of these stories. What makes them different from *Love's Labour's Lost* is the way in which they arrive at their predetermined conclusion. And here Professor Barber is quite right; there is more story in these than in *Love's Labour's Lost.* But there is a story with its conflict, though both are much simpler, in *Love's Labour's Lost* too. In its simple linear movement that story is similar to that of Benedick and Beatrice, with this most important difference: it lacks its absorbing complexity. An important element of that complexity is that in the later play both Beatrice and Benedick reject romantic love and each other at the beginning of the play so that the action dealing with their relationship must show not only two rejections but two conversions as well. And it should be further noted that this conversion is not simply stated as in *Love's Labour's Lost* but represented in sequent steps. The difference, then, is not in the presence or absence of a story but in the episodic fullness of the one as contrasted with the simplicity of the other. It is as if Shakespeare had believed that the conversion of four men would somehow lend weight and even complexity to a simple plot: that multiplicity of reversal would make up for the lack of complexity in the story.

Something analogous to this takes place in the concluding scene of *The Two Gentlemen of Verona* where both Valentine and Proteus change attitudes from one extreme to another in the briefest time. There is repentance and forgiveness within a dozen lines. How this repentance and forgiveness should be represented, Shakespeare showed, as we noted in an earlier section, in the final scene of *Measure for Measure*.

There is a story, then, with its conflict, and there is a structure in *Love's Labour's Lost,* but they are both of a simple sort. For Shakespeare is experimenting with a theme and he invents a story for it which turns out to be rather thin. And of course it is for this reason that in resuming that theme in *Much Ado* he again invents a story for it, the story of Benedick and Beatrice, but he gives it far greater episodic complexity, and in addition joins it to another story, the story of Claudio and Hero. And he repeats the design in *Twelfth Night*. In *Love's Labour's Lost* Shakespeare is presenting a play whose general action he develops far more successfully in later comedies. The play need not be thought to have "like opera, its conventions, which we must accept at the outset if we are not to be merely bewildered and antagonized by their apparent unreality."[40] Its conventions are those of romantic comedy, as we shall presently see, although judged by these, as it must be, the play falls far short of *Much Ado* and *Twelfth Night*. But its relationship to these is so vital that one must reject out of hand Professor Charlton's conclusion that the play "has small importance in establishing the line along which Shakespeare's comic genius grew."[41] On the contrary it lies fair in the middle of the path he trod. Aside from the successful characterization of Holofernes and Nathaniel, in whom Shakespeare may have intended incidental thrusts or mere allusions to individuals then living, the conception of Armado is a distinct achievement. In his self-inflation, his general deportment and language, and his role of commenting, through speech and action, upon the affairs of the aristocratic group—in these matters Armado prefigures Shakespeare's greatest comic character, whose exploits the dramatist was to immortalize in the *Henry*

IV plays within a year or two. But it is not only in the characterization of the non-aristocratic group that *Love's Labour's Lost* occupies an important position in the development of Shakespeare's comic genius. Much more significant is the play's experiment, admittedly not very successful, of dramatizing the conflict between the capricious rejection of love and the hyperbolic idealizing of it. And this, as we have often noted, henceforth becomes the structural cornerstone of Shakespearean romantic comedy.

Let us now turn to examine briefly the structure of *Love's Labour's Lost,* the aspect of the play which has received the most adverse criticism of commentators. Most of these assert that the play has no structure, and the reason is not far to seek. The play admittedly has a simple structure, but this is not what the play's detractors contend. They believe it has no structure whatever, and reach such a conclusion because they assume at the outset that *Love's Labour's Lost* is Shakespeare's earliest comedy, or, more significantly, they take for its theme some aspect of the plot which in truth contributes to the theme rather than being the theme itself. For instance, it is said that "literary affectations . . . are the theme of the play";[42] that "the dominant theme of this play . . . is the overwhelming event of the English language and all that had been happening to it in the last twenty years or so";[43] that the theme of *Love's Labour's Lost* turns upon "the question of what is the best way of qualifying as a poet, of achieving full development as a man. . . ."[44] Another critic believes that "Shakespeare's real interest was in the general theme of active *versus* contemplative living";[45] finally a recent commentator concludes that "the play, in both plot and subplot, is about the writing of love poetry."[46] Now if one assumes that one of the above is the theme of the play, it is not unreasonable that he should conclude that the comedy lacks both characterization and structure. But one might reach the same conclusion if he assumes that lyrical poetry is the theme of *Romeo and Juliet* or that Hamlet's incomparable mastery of the arts of language is the theme of his play. Now it is true that the role of language in *Love's Labour's Lost* is greater than in the other plays, but the difference is a matter of degree. This is particularly true if we consider for a moment the language of Claudio in *Much Ado,* Orlando in *As You Like It,* and Orsino in *Twelfth Night.* Their language, when they speak or write of love, is no less forced and extreme than that of the lovers in *Love's Labour's Lost.* The difference between the two is that, in this play, the language of the lovers and of the low comedy characters, though serving the theme, is given greater space than in the later comedies. But language, or the writing of love poetry, is not the theme of *Love's Labour's Lost* any more than it is the theme of *Twelfth Night* or *As You Like It.* One of the points in which these comedies are superior to *Love's Labour's Lost* is that in these the role of language is made properly subordinate to the theme it serves to express. This failure to subordinate means to ends can be found elsewhere in Shakespeare's drama, even in later comedies than *Love's Labour's Lost.* In *The Merchant of Venice* the bond plot, intended as a contributory action, usurps first place and for a while threatens to eclipse the love story. And of course the character of Shylock does most surely overshadow everybody and everything else in the play. And this, from the point of view of the mutual accommodation of theme and sub-theme within the plot, that is, from the point of view of the just relationship of theme and structure, may be seen as a flaw. Or this imbalance between the weight given to the theme and to the devices by which that theme is expressed can lead to a misunderstanding not only of the dramatist's intentions as revealed in the over-all structure of the plot but also of the theme of the play itself. For instance, the emphasis on satire *through* language—and we shall return to this matter later— may lead one to conclude that the play is a satire *of* language and no more, that the play's "mood [is] not of comedy but of good-natured satire."[47] This is an unjust estimate of the play's mood, and it would be inaccurate to reach the further conclusion that the play is a satire rather than a romantic comedy,

albeit one in which the necessary satiric devices are given unduly extensive scope. Satire is not the theme and aim of the
play: it is romantic love. Satire is a means to dramatizing that
theme, as it is in all Shakespeare's romantic comedies.

Such misunderstanding of the play's theme, then, may be
in part responsible for the conclusion that the comedy lacks
structure, or that its structure is different from that of any other
Shakespearean romantic comedy.[48] Not infrequently one finds
a favorable comment about the plot-structure, namely the
startling entrance of Mercade near the end of the final scene.
It is indeed a *coup de théâtre*, and Professor Dover Wilson has
stressed the "extraordinary impression left upon the audience
by the entrance of the black-clad messenger. . . ."[49] And he adds
that Mercade's entrance taught him two things: " (a) that however gay, however riotous a Shakespearian comedy may be,
tragedy is always there, *felt*, if not seen; (b) that for all its
surface lightness and frivolity, the play had behind it a serious
mind at work, with a purpose."[50] The observation is just, and
the general attitude towards the play which Professor Wilson
expresses in his comments is like fresh air stirring the cob-
webs. But although striking, Mercade's entrance upon the
scene of courtship and revel is not in itself an outstanding or
praiseworthy element of the plot; it fails to vindicate the play
against the charge that it lacks plot and structure. For the
episode is sudden, unexpected, external. Mercade is like a *deus
ex machina*. His sudden appearance to announce the death of
the Princess' father interrupts the progress and possible consummation of the love affairs, and by so doing it weakens the
more organic or internal obstacle to that consummation,
namely, the conviction on the part of the ladies that the expressions of love they have received from their respective lovers
have been too facile, expressed in such exaggerated language
that they cannot be accepted as the witness of a love that alters
not "when it alteration finds."[51] And so, the widely acclaimed
and theatrically effective episode with Mercade is yet another
symptom of the play's structural deficiency.

But structural deficiency, as already noted, is not characteristic of *Love's Labour's Lost* alone among Shakespeare's comedies. What is of interest here is that the play employs a new theme-structure which, though not fully successful, becomes the basis for the construction of later comedies. What, then, is this comic structure of Shakespearean romantic comedy? The principle which organizes the events of the play is analogous to that of tragedy. It is the committing by the chief characters of a comic error, which in turn leads to reversal and recognition. The error is of two kinds: one is the rejection of love, the other the exaggerated idealizing of it. After the experiments of the early comedies Shakespeare seems to have concluded that romantic comedy could best be based upon these two antithetical errors which express contrasting attitudes towards love. But there is a third element in this comic structure, one that brings about changes and reversals in the other two, and that is truth of human nature, what man really is, not what he is said to be by either those who reject love or those who idealize it.

In the first half of the play the King and his lords, as well as Armado, forswear love and the society of ladies in order to devote themselves to study and contemplation. This vow is their initial error, which immediately becomes the target of relentless satire both in the main action and in that of the non-aristocratic characters. That vow redounds most awkwardly upon them, for it is broken on the very day it is taken; at the first sight of the French ladies these "brave conquerors," as the King calls them, fall in love, lowering their colors "at the first summons from a troop of petticoats." And even as he presents them in love Shakespeare introduces the subject of the second half of the play, which is the extravagant idealizing of romantic love. In this second half, then, the chief action presents the satire of the extreme Petrarchism of the lovers, particularly as it is expressed in their language. Thus the two parts of the action mock first the rejection of love and then its opposite, the romantic idealization of it. And though Shakespeare does not state it directly, the intention or end of the action is to lead, by the juxtaposition of the two extreme attitudes, to a middle point of view. The King and his lords move from one extreme to the other, and though the play ends inconclusively on the surface, our inference is that at the expiration of the year of penance, they will have achieved the balance in their attitude toward love which they lack at present.

We might note here that *Love's Labour's Lost* introduces another structural principle, namely, the change from one extreme attitude towards love to the other in the same character or characters, instead of presenting the extremes in different characters, as in *The Comedy of Errors* and *The Taming of the Shrew*. What Shakespeare is doing, then, is to replace the juxtaposition of characters representing opposite attitudes with the juxtaposition of such attitudes within the same individual. And this very clearly leads to a more careful conception of character. In the play before us, with the exception of Berowne, the attitudes juxtaposed do not produce the tension we find in such characters as Benedick and Beatrice, and the reason is that one attitude replaces the other too swiftly: what we have is really the replacement of one attitude by another, instead of their juxtaposition. Even in Benedick and Beatrice the integration of the two attitudes is imperfect, that perfection being achieved only in the conception of Rosalind and Viola in the last two of Shakespeare's romantic comedies.

Though satire is a much over-worked device in the play, it is a device, a means serving a larger structural and thematic principle. In an earlier section mention was made of Shakespeare's choice to express his comic vision in terms of conflict which leads to reconciliation. And it was noted there that the conflict was to be between the rejection of love and the romantic or sentimental idealizing of it. And in addition we saw that there was a *tertium quid,* the indispensable motif acting as agent of the reconciling process: the truth of human nature, the sober, non-sentimental, balanced approach to the human condition. This is, then, the reducing ingredient which aims satire against the two extreme attitudes. In *Love's Labour's*

Lost the King and his lords choose philosophy instead of love
and in their vow they violate the very nature of their being.
But the choice of contemplation over love has been taken by
many critics to be the theme of the entire play, the consequence being a bewildering accumulation of studies, theories,
and opinions concerning topical allusiveness, the question of
the School of Night, and so on. The comic error of these
characters is not the choice of philosophy or contemplation
but the rejection of love, the resolve to isolate themselves from
the normal processes of life, to "study, fast, not sleep"! As
Berowne tells them after they have broken their vows:

> Let us once lose our oaths to find ourselves,
> Or else we lose ourselves to keep our oaths.
>
> (IV, iii, 361-62)

They fall in love, for nature will not allow them to lose themselves long; the vows are broken on the day they are taken, and
they are broken because man is not what the King and his lords
had supposed him to be: certainly *that* philosophy, that sort of
self-knowledge, was deficient. And this is the chief source of
the comic in the first half of the play. Now if we glance for a
brief moment at their oaths as romantic lovers, oaths implied
or stated in their professions of undying love, may we not
anticipate also the possibility of their violating those vows as
well since they, like the earlier ones, take scant note of man's
true nature, his flesh and blood, his instincts and affections?
And is this not precisely the reason why the ladies must reject
their suit and must ask them instead to wait till they have
achieved more of self-knowledge?

Now the second movement of the plot has to do with this
non-realistic rush to the opposite extreme of romantic idealization of both the experience of love and of the beloved ladies.
And this part of the plot-structure occupies a much larger
portion of the story. The change of the lovers from rejecting
love to writing Petrarchan sonnets is swift, too swift, as we have
already noted. Indeed the satire aimed at them inheres in the
very speed of their transformation. In the second movement of

the story, the satire of the lovers' Petrarchism, particularly as this is expressed in terms of language, occupies most of the play. And again the wide scope Shakespeare gave such satire has led commentators to suppose that language or linguistic affectation is the theme of the comedy. It is not so. The satire of linguistic pyrotechnics is there, but it is not the chief idea of the play. That idea is to mock or satirize *attitudes* toward love, not simply the language in which those attitudes are expressed. It is true that the play satirizes the language of wooing, both in the sonnets and other protestations of the aristocratic lovers as well as in Armado's missive to Jaquenetta. And it is also true that here Shakespeare devotes a large part of the action to this satire, but he does the same in *Much Ado, As You Like It,* and *Twelfth Night.* In the later comedies that satire is not quite so persistent because the stories in these plays are by design more complex so that the episodes satirizing the lovers' Petrarchism are fewer and more widely spaced. But the *kind* of satire in these episodes is the same as in *Love's Labour's Lost.* Again, the difference is in degree, not kind. And here, too, it may be added, *Love's Labour's Lost* shows a deficiency, a lack of economy in both the amount and quality of the satire needed to express effectively the play's theme.

VIII

This satire of romantic attitudes and of the language which records them begins early in the play, but perhaps a good place to note is Berowne's description of Rosaline to Costard, who is to carry Berowne's love letter to her. How is Costard to find her? Berowne tells him:

> When tongues speak sweetly, then they name her name,
> And Rosaline they call her. Ask for her,
> And to her white hand see thou do commend
> This seal'd-up counsel.
>
> (III, i, 167-70)

But Berowne is no ordinary sonneteer. He will write love sonnets, but he knows what he is doing and can see himself in self-mocking perspective. And in this he of course stands apart from the King and the others and historically anticipates not only Benedick and Beatrice but also the heroines of the other two "joyous" comedies, Rosalind and Viola. For indeed he "runs with the hare and hunts with the hounds."[52] The difference between him and these heroines is that he is too concerned with the tension between his two points of view and that he has much to say about it. And in this he is closer to Benedick. For suddenly Berowne discovers himself in love, though he can scarcely believe it, and for good reason:

> And I, forsooth, in love! I, that have been love's whip;
> A very beadle to a humorous sigh;
> A critic, nay, a night-watch constable; . . .
>
> (III, i, 175-77)

But in love he is, and all the "maladies of hereos" are upon him:

> And I to sigh for her! to watch for her!
> To pray for her!

And yet underneath all this there is a reservation simultaneously expressing not simply his incredulity at his change but also his earlier attitude towards love. That reservation is revealed in both matter and manner in Berowne's concluding couplet.

> Well, I will love, write, sigh, pray, sue, groan:
> Some men must love my lady, and some Joan.
>
> (III, i, 206-7)

When he writes to her, however, he composes as a romantic sonneteer, no longer like an "obstinate heretic in the despite of beauty." In his misadventured sonnet to Rosaline he tells her:

> Well learned is that tongue that well can thee commend,
> All ignorant that soul that sees thee without wonder;
>   Which is to me some praise that I thy parts admire.
> Thy eye Jove's lightning bears, thy voice his dreadful thunder,
>   Which, not to anger bent, is music and sweet fire.

> Celestial as thou art, O, pardon love this wrong,
> That sings heaven's praise with such an earthly tongue.
>
> (IV, ii, 116-22)

Though earthly, Benedick's tongue calls Rosaline "celestial" and likens her to Jove also. Though he is forsworn in loving her, he assures her that to her he will "faithful prove." The King's poetic effusion is more literate, containing a complex, Donnesque conceit of tears which may have some connection with "A Valediction: of Weeping." He, too, admits that he lacks the skill necessary to extol the beauty of the Princess.

> O queen of queens! how far thou dost excel
> No thought can think, nor tongue of mortal tell.
>
> (IV, iii, 40-41)

And how does Longaville describe Maria? He speaks of the "heavenly rhetoric" of her eye, she is a goddess, she is "heavenly love," she is the "fair sun," she is "a paradise." Dumain's beloved is a "most divine Kate," and the "ode" he has composed to her concludes in this manner:

> Thou for whom Jove would swear
> Juno but an Ethiop were;
> And deny himself for Jove,
> Turning mortal for thy love.
>
> (IV, iii, 117-20)

This and much more "painted rhetoric" is expended by the lovers in the praise of their loves. And thus in their about-face and in their very protestations of love, the lovers employ language and express attitudes which expose them to further satire. Berowne voices the meaning of breaking their vow even as he had predicted its necessity, its inevitability:

> Sweet lords, sweet lovers, O, let us embrace!
>   As true we are as flesh and blood can be.
> The sea will ebb and flow, heaven show his face,
>   Young blood doth not obey an old decree.
> We cannot cross the cause why we were born.
>
> (IV, iii, 214-18)

And this is nothing less than the record of their recognition of what had been a comic illusion; love they cannot avoid, for it is as necessary and unavoidable as the truth of their own being. In loving they are as "true as flesh and blood can be." But the directness and simplicity of this gives way to a different attitude, already manifested in their "sonnets," and it will be expressed, appropriately enough, by Berowne in his long and comprehensive declaration. For he is the one lover who has throughout shown the temperament necessary for both experiencing and expressing simultaneously different and even opposed points of view.

In that declaration Berowne sets down the romantic conception of love, not only in harmony with the "sonnets" of the four lovers, but going far beyond them in its Petrarchan hyperboles. And it is precisely in these hyperboles, in this overstating the case for romantic love, that Berowne admits into his effusion the self-critical element of exaggeration. His wit is too much for him; it is his only real love, and it appears that Berowne's ecstasies have much more to do with this love than with the other. And this is his second comic error, which is treated in the second portion of the play. It is well for Berowne to say that

> To fast, to study, and to see no woman

is nothing short of

> Flat treason 'gainst the kingly state of youth.
>
> (IV, iii, 292-93)

Nor can we object to his vigorous assertion that

> . . . love, first learned in a lady's eyes,
> Lives not alone immured in the brain;
> But, with the motion of all elements,
> Courses as swift as thought in every power,
> And gives to every power a double power,
> Above their functions and their offices.
>
> (327-32)

But presently Berowne's rhetoric runs away with him:

> A lover's eyes will gaze an eagle blind;
> A lover's ear will hear the lowest sound
> When the suspicious head of theft is stopp'd. . . .
> For valour, is not love a Hercules,
> Still climbing trees in the Hesperides?
> Subtle as Sphinx; as sweet and musical
> As bright Apollo's lute, strung with his hair;
> And when Love speaks, the voice of all the gods
> Make heaven drowsy with the harmony.
>
> (334-45)

And he concludes that, for "wisdom's sake" or "love's sake," or "men's sake," or "women's sake," they should lose their oaths in order to find themselves.

> Or else we lose ourselves to keep our oaths.
> It is religion to be thus forsworn.
>
> (362-63)

It is all lovely and vigorous and persuasive and overdone. This last is its important structural feature, for as we have said a large portion of the play is devoted to exposing and satirizing wit and rhetoric or rather their abuse, the emphasis on the word rather than the thing or idea it conveys. But before we leave the scene, it is interesting to note that Berowne's role of seeing both sides simultaneously is not vitiated by the hyperboles of his long declaration. On the contrary, one suspects that Berowne is conscious of his "painted rhetoric"—his own phrase. And the dramatist, as always eager to guide our understanding, gives him this composite line at the end.

> Allons! Allons! Sow'd cockle reap'd no corn!

Even in his homeliest idiom Berowne affects the French![53] He is never so clearly sophisticated as when he is trying to be plain.

The satire of wit is fundamental to the theme-structure

of *Love's Labour's Lost,* and it is carried on in both actions of
the plot, the aristocratic story and the story of Armado and
Jaquenetta, Nathaniel and Holofernes. By means of wit the
King and his lords try to declare their love but in so doing
they express something less than their true selves and their true
loves. Indeed they fail to communicate with the objects of
their love, for they address them in language which disguises
instead of revealing. Rosaline tells her friends that in his
verses to her, Berowne calls her "the fairest goddess on the
ground," and that she is therein "compar'd to twenty thousand
fairs." Katherine interposes that she has "some thousand
verses of a faithful lover," and Maria protests that Longaville's
"letter is too long by half a mile." And the Princess has received from the King

> as much love in rhyme
> As would be cramm'd up in a sheet of paper,
> Writ o' both sides the leaf, margent and all. . . .
>
> (V, ii, 6-8)

The lords' fascination with their own wit is their undoing,
for, as the Princess declares,

> None are so surely caught, when they are catch'd,
> As wit turn'd fool.[54]
>
> (V, ii, 70-71)

When the disguised "Muscovites" call upon the Princess and
her ladies in the park, Rosaline, impersonating the Princess,
demands of Boyet to know of them:

> What would these strangers? Know their minds, Boyet.
> If they do speak our language, 'tis our will
> That some plain man recount their purposes.
> Know what they would.
>
> (V, ii, 174-77)

She learns that they wish peace and gentle visitation, which she
grants and then asks that they be gone. To which the King
interposes:

> Say to her, we have measur'd many miles
> To tread a measure with her on this grass.
>
> (184-85)

And Rosaline:

> It is not so. Ask them how many inches
> Is in one mile: if they have measur'd many,
> The measure then of one is easily told.
>
> (188-90)

As Hamlet says of the grave-maker, "how absolute" these ladies of France are! Wit, alas, tends to cloud and hide the matter. And when the Princess and her ladies hint to their lovers that their wit had indeed betrayed them, Berowne again voices his recognition of their comic folly and offers to amend his ways:

> O, never will I trust to speeches penn'd,
>   Nor to the motion of a schoolboy's tongue,
> Nor never come in vizard to my friend,
>   Nor woo in rhyme, like a blind harper's song!
> Taffeta phrases, silken terms precise,
>   Three-piled hyperboles, spruce [affectation],
> Figures pedantical. . . .
> Henceforth my wooing mind shall be express'd
>   In russet yeas and honest kersey noes.
>
> (V, ii, 402-13)

To woo in "russet yeas and honest kersey noes" is perhaps a little too much for Berowne, who starts to woo Rosaline anew, but not without some remnants of what he calls "the old rage."

> And, to begin, wench,—so God help me, la!
> My love to thee is sound, sans crack or flaw.
>
> (414-15)

"Sans sans, I pray you," she retorts!

But the folly of wit, of the placing stress upon words rather than the things they stand for, is mocked more consistently in

the action of the non-aristocratic characters. Here are a few
lines from Armado's love letter to Jaquenetta: "By heaven, that
thou are fair, is most infallible; true, that thou are beauteous;
truth itself that thou are lovely. More fairer than fair, beautiful than beauteous, truer than truth itself. . . ." (IV, i, 60-64).
According to Holofernes, Armado "draweth out the thread of
his verbosity finer than the scope of his argument." And what
of Holofernes and Nathaniel? Theirs is the more particularly
bookish rhetoric, with its ridiculous alliteration—"The preyful
princess pierc'd and prick'd a pretty pleasing pricket"—its
strings of synonyms, its incorrect Latin, obstacles all to communication. In these two what is ridiculed is their language,
whereas in Armado, who is one of the lovers in the play, what
is satirized is not simply language but a lover's language. It is
as if Shakespeare thought of speech or style as a metaphor
whereby a lover reveals himself: as a man speaks so he loves.
A lover's mannered and overwitty speech betrays shallowness
of feeling. No wonder that such characters as Henry V and
Hamlet are, as the latter says, "ill at these numbers." And it is
precisely this wit in Berowne and the rest that a year's probation
is intended to eliminate, as Rosaline tells her lover:

> To weed this wormwood from your fruitful brain,
> And therewithal to win me, if you please,
> Without the which I am not to be won,
> You shall this twelvemonth term from day to day
> Visit the speechless sick and still converse
> With groaning wretches; and your task shall be
> With all the fierce endeavour of your wit
> To enforce the pained impotent to smile.
>
> (V, ii, 857-64)

And this is precisely the same censure obliquely addressed to
Benedick and Beatrice by those taking part in "one of Hercules'
labours . . . to bring Signior Benedick and the Lady Beatrice
into a mountain of affection. . . ." The reason Hero gives for
not telling Beatrice of Benedick's love for her is that she fears
Beatrice will scorn that love with some witty word:

> Disdain and scorn ride sparkling in her eyes,
> Misprising what they look on, and her wit
> Values itself so highly, that to her
> All matter else seems weak.

If I tell her of Benedick's love, says Hero,

> she would laugh me
> Out of myself, press me to death with wit.
>
> (III, i, 51-54; 75-76)

It would be the same with Benedick. But what is to be noted here is that in the later play Shakespeare assigns to wit no more space than is necessary to stress that aspect of his theme.

In *Love's Labour's Lost* the lovers fail to win their ladies at the end of the play because they have fallen in love too suddenly, too soon, before they have had the opportunity to know them, indeed before they have known themselves. And they betray all this in their language, in their excessive use of wit. At the end of the play, as earlier, the dramatist underscores his point. When the Princess resolves to return to France because of her father's death, Navarre addresses to her a speech of some dozen lines imploring her to reconsider. But the lines are so brimming with metaphor that the speech brings from the Princess the emphatic response:

> I understand you not.[55]
>
> (V, ii, 762)

To which the ever-ready Berowne adds his own (and presumably the other lords') recognition of the folly of their wit and rhetoric:

> Honest plain words best pierce the ear of grief.
>
> (763)

And here we may observe the lovers' second recognition, if we wish to apply the principle suggested earlier in this chapter. But that recognition is not synonymous with profound change and for that reason "Jack hath not his Jill." Their sport, says Berowne, is made "a comedy." And the reason is that both in their rejection of love and the swift about-face and subsequent Petrarchism—in both of these—the lords took no notice of the facts of human nature. It is that truth of human nature which brings about the two reversals, first their yielding to the human impulse to fall in love, and second their failure to consummate that love. In falling in love they were "as true as flesh and blood can be," something they had wholly overlooked; in their expressions of love, in their very concept of that love, they again left flesh and blood far behind. Of that neglect they are reminded obliquely by the mocking of the French ladies but more bluntly by two episodes in the final scene of the play. The high point in the play of "The Nine Worthies" is reached when Armado enters as the all-conquering Hector, who "far surmounted Hannibal." Whereupon Costard, who is onstage, brings into the "play" these startling circumstances:

> *Costard.* The party is gone, fellow Hector, she is gone; she is two months on her way.
> *Armado.* What meanest thou?
> *Costard.* Faith, unless you play the honest Troyan, the poor wench is cast away. She's quick; the child brags in her belly already. 'Tis yours.
> *Armado.* Dost thou infamonize me among potentates? Thou shalt die.
>
> (V, ii, 678-85)

Is not this the most shocking revelation to be made in the presence of the romantic lovers? How bluntly Costard thrusts upon the spiritualities of romantic love the irresistible force and claim of the flesh! Into the midst of mounting sentiment created by the declarations of love, Costard's communication introduces the reducing ingredient of fact and truth to nature with the result that the atmosphere of the scene is brought to a lower, middle region, a mean between the idealism of romance and the realism of nature. To this same end is employed the quite large incidence of bawdry in the play.

The second episode through which Shakespeare places the life of flesh and blood by the side of its idealization by romance is the entrance of Mercade upon the scene of courtly proceedings. His appearance is sudden, unprovided for, external to the inner necessity of the plot, and for that reason aesthetically unsatisfactory, though theatrically effective. But its purpose is clear. The excessive idealism of the romantic scene is thus reduced by the two episodes and brought to a view of life more compatible with both fact and sentiment, neither as it is idealized by romance, nor yet as represented exclusively by the bluntness of nature. In this mutual accommodation of the real and the ideal, the scene implies, lies the very path towards happiness in this workaday world.[56]

That this is the theme of the play, the heart and meaning of its story, is confirmed by the concluding songs of Spring and Winter. These, as other elements of this widely misunderstood and underestimated play, have been subjected to much detailed study yielding a diversity of opinion. Some critics see no thematic relevance in the songs and dismiss them as mere tags to the play.[57] On the other side are those who find in the songs a connection with the play but disagree as to the nature of that connection. One view of the songs of the cuckoo and the owl is that one is "a reminder of the flesh, the other of death."[58] Professor Bronson's interpretation of the songs is that they express the idea that the "sum of vernal delights but serves to remind husbands of their fears of infidelity in their wives"; and that the "sum of winter's annoyances but intensifies one's sense of well-being (given fire and a pot)."[59] Another critic holds that the two songs contrast youth (Spring) and adulthood (Winter), with the admonition that "in the winter of life a person must live fully. He should be married and at home, living in the midst of life and not afraid of or repelled by it."[60] Somewhat related to this view is the notion that the songs are "an expression of the going-on power of life."[61] Though these views contain helpful elements, most of which are mutually compatible, they do not relate the songs vitally to the theme of the comedy. Richmond Noble, in his study of Shakespeare's songs, came very near hitting the mark, although at the critical point his comments glance off the target. He sees the content of the two songs much more clearly than their thematic significance, and this for a very good reason. "Both," he says, "are Elizabethan comic songs, without any serious intention whatever."[62] To this conclusion he may have been led a priori by his belief that the play "is a conversational satirical comedy, a forerunner of *Sir Fopling Flutter* and *The Way of the World*, and it is absolutely devoid of any serious intention."[63] Having said this of the play, he was not likely to see serious thematic content in the two songs. And yet this is what he does discover, although he fails to relate it in any way to the play. Of the first song he has this to say in part: "All the learned men's idealism of the meadow flowers, the shepherds' piping on oaten straws and the merry larks waking the ploughman is dissipated by the fear of the woeful tragedy with which, as the cuckoo's habits remind them, married men are threatened in the Spring. . . ." Of the Owl Song he says that "in the first stanza romance is contrasted with reality, the picturesque with the disagreeable. . . ."[64] But is not this precisely what the whole play does, and is not the function of the songs to crystallize in a few verses the theme of the entire comedy? There is spring and winter in love and life, even as there is both beauty and ugliness in both spring and winter. As Spring and Winter in their symbolic opposition yet borrow in transverse fashion of each other so that each in turn and both together represent a wholeness, so love and all life partake of the spirit and of the flesh, of the ideal and the real, of mind and body. It is in the springtime, with its beautiful flowers, its daisies and violets and larks, symbols all of romantic love and idealism, that the cuckoo sends out its fearful note to married men. And it is likewise in the midst of the cold and ugly scene of winter, with its foul ways and sights, highlighted by greasy Joan and "Marian's nose . . . red and raw," that the owl nightly sings its "merry note." We may, if we like, take the last phrase as ironic, in which case the Owl Song expresses the raw uncomeliness of winter in opposition to the loveliness of spring.[65] The second view may find support in the concluding line of the play: "The words of Mercury are harsh after the songs of Apollo." Thus the broad opposition of Winter and Spring is reinforced by that of the two gods, one the patron of commerce, the other the patron of music and poetry.[66]

A Midsummer Night's
Dream

Chapter V

I

By universal consent *A Midsummer Night's Dream* is Shakespeare's first success in the comic mode. It is by most critics believed to be near perfection, a perfection all the more startling when we consider the flaws in the comedies immediately preceding it in composition. Although, as we shall presently see, its date is not altogether easy to fix, it may be assumed that *A Midsummer Night's Dream* follows such plays as *The Two Gentlemen of Verona* and *Love's Labour's Lost*. What aids us in part in placing the play after the other two in date is the fact that *A Midsummer Night's Dream* takes up and develops further, and more successfully, certain motifs found in the earlier plays. From *The Two Gentlemen of*

Verona it takes an important portion of its main action, that is, the betrayal by Demetrius of Helena in favor of Hermia, who loves Lysander instead, and the ensuing conflict between the two friends. Though different in important details, and in the manner of its resolution, in its main substance this is a version of Proteus' betrayal of his Julia in favor of Silvia and the conflict between love and friendship which forms the chief action of *The Two Gentlemen of Verona*. From *Love's Labour's Lost, A Midsummer Night's Dream* borrows the use of a minor plot which culminates in the device of acting, by a group of humorous characters, a playlet before a critical audience made up of the characters of the main plot. And as in the case of resolving the conflict in the main plot, so here, too, the integration of the playlet with the main action is much more successful in *A Midsummer Night's Dream*. In addition to its close relationship with these two comedies, *A Midsummer Night's Dream* must have been composed very shortly before or, more likely, after *Romeo and Juliet,* for it shares with it an important element of its story: Hermia's dilemma is very much like Juliet's in loving one man while she is wooed by another who is preferred by her father. And like Juliet she takes action in pursuing her own choice. Furthermore, the burlesque of the tragic resolution of *Romeo and Juliet* by the Pyramus and Thisbe playlet in *A Midsummer Night's Dream* may very well be an instance of Shakespeare's ability to see himself and his drama in perspective. But it must be borne in mind that that inference loses little by the assumption that *Romeo and Juliet* may have followed *A Midsummer Night's Dream* in date of composition instead of preceding it.[1]

II

Precisely in what year *A Midsummer Night's Dream* was written it is impossible to say, and though it would be valuable to know that date, it would not change significantly our estimate of the play's position in the process of Shakespeare's development. This is said partly in the conviction that neither of the two extreme dates suggested for the play is likely to be

confirmed through external evidence.[2] The date 1590, proposed
by Elze and Kurz, has received no support from scholars, but
1592, first cited by Malone in 1790, was recently revived by the
editors of the New Cambridge Shakespeare in their edition of
the play in 1924. At the other extreme is 1600, proposed by
Steevens in 1773, which has received no more support than
1590.

What makes dating the play not an easy matter is the lack
of sufficient external evidence. All we possess is the date of the
first quarto, 1600, and the reference to the play by Francis
Meres in 1598. In the absence of further evidence of this sort,
various dates have been proposed on the basis of internal evidence.[3] For our purposes it is sufficient to note that most students of the play have agreed that it was written some time between 1594 and 1596, that it is contemporary with *Romeo and
Juliet* and *Richard II,* that it was written later than *The Two
Gentlemen of Verona* and *Love's Labour's Lost,* and very probably before *The Merchant of Venice,* thought by most scholars
to be a maturer play than the comedies we have considered,
including *A Midsummer Night's Dream.*[4]

Another problem closely related to the matter of date
has to do with the text of the play and the question of its
alleged revision once or twice before the first quarto was printed
in 1600. It is again very difficult to be certain about the exact
relationship of the received text and what may have been
earlier versions of it.[5] But although we are uncertain about
such details, we can be reasonably sure that the play as we have
it was substantially the version acted some time in 1594-96, a
conclusion to which Professor Wilson's theory can pose no
serious objections. In that version of the play are to be found
the three plots and their special relationship, through which
the dramatist attempted to express a fundamental comic vision.

III

Far more significant than the questions of date and revision
is the poet's choice of his materials, where he found them and
what he did with them in writing his comedy. Important as

the particular place or places are from which the dramatist drew
the components of his plot, what is of far greater significance
is the reason why he chose those elements or stories and whether
and why he changed any details. For instance, why did Shakespeare choose the Theseus-Hippolyta story, why did he employ
it as he did to provide a frame for the story of the young
lovers? Why did he change so drastically the character of the
historical Theseus, or why did he retain such a change if he
had found it in his sources? Both the choice and modification
of the individual stories as well as their final relationship were
most assuredly dictated by a concrete artistic impulse, the desire
to compose a love comedy in which certain themes or ideas were
given appropriate emphasis, to create a total form or merely
to employ in final or experimental associations elements of a
particular comic structure.

Any speculation concerning the overriding idea which dictated choice and treatment of particular materials should begin with the play's connections with earlier comedies, that is
to say, with identifying motifs and ideas and devices in earlier
plays which Shakespeare might be attempting to employ in a
more effective way in *A Midsummer Night's Dream*. In terms
of its immediate theme and the action it calls for, *A Midsummer
Night's Dream* is closest to *The Two Gentlemen of Verona*
among the earlier comedies. Both treat of inconstancy in love,
a theme most tentatively adumbrated in *The Comedy of Errors*.
This then was Shakespeare's point of departure: how to treat
in a fresh but comprehensive way that particular aspect of his
great theme of love. It was an aspect to which he returned
again and again in both comedy and tragedy. Here, in this
play, at this moment in his dramatic development, Shakespeare
presents the theme of inconstancy in love in a comic mood, in
the context of moonlit woodlands and fairies, in a mood of
ease and lightness but neither superficial nor completely free
of the hint of the darker areas of human nature. But though
the immediate theme, which gives body and direction to the
plot, is inconstancy in love, the larger idea of which that theme
forms a part is one which we have seen in the earlier comedies

and will see again in the comedies which follow. And that idea, the heart and soul of Shakespearean romantic comedy, is the rational or judicious, we might call it the ideal, attitude towards love, the attitude which will bring maximum contentment and felicity in this world of ours, a world where men love and hate, make and break vows, where men fall in and out of love, a world of Titanias as well as Bottoms, a world at once of dreams and diurnal drudgery.

The theme of inconstancy in love, the violation of vows offered in the hyperbolic idiom of romantic lovers, lay close to the center of Shakespeare's dramatic consciousness. In the mid-1590's it must have been the very center itself at least in terms of its suitability for comic or tragic treatment. For besides the brief insertion of that theme in *The Comedy of Errors* and its more substantial role in *The Two Gentlemen of Verona,* constancy or inconstancy in love receives the poet's attention in *Love's Labour's Lost,* especially in the repeated vows by the king and his courtiers that though they have broken one oath they will keep another. And the year's probation imposed upon them by their beloved ladies is but a test of their constancy. But the theme of constancy in love is given its supreme expression in *Romeo and Juliet,* a play inseparably connected with Shakespeare's romantic comedies of the period. Like his other tragedies it is but the extension and dramatic fulfillment of one element in the larger comic conception of the human circumstance. What gives *Romeo and Juliet* special relevance here, what separates it from Shakespeare's other tragedies, is that its tragic action derives in great part from the very ideal towards which romantic comedy aspires. But this tragic treatment does not place constancy in love in opposition to the larger comic apprehension of human experience. The death of Romeo and Juliet, though they contribute to it through their own acts, is brought about in the main by forces outside the lovers: the family feud, symbol of the darker areas of human passion, controls the action and in the end strikes the lovers down in spite of their devotion to the ideal. And it is because he discovered that in such a context the lovers, by the very nature of the ideal to which they clung, could not be charged with the necessary tragic responsibility that Shakespeare abandoned for a while the treatment in tragedy of that ideal. *Romeo and Juliet* is the most moving tragedy of young love in all literature, but it is not tragic in the manner of Shakespeare's later and greater tragedies. Even Shakespeare could not make the love and constancy of Romeo and Juliet, in spite of hastiness and much impulsive action, part of a tragic hamartia. Instead, he was forced to generalize the concept of tragic error through the feud, that is, to place it outside the chief characters. In tragedy this would not do. And though the lovers' constancy serves the larger comic conception, of which tragedy is but a part, by reconciling the feuding families at the conclusion, as a tragic theme it was abandoned. The story of Romeo and Juliet, their constancy unto death, is instead transformed into the tragical mirth of "Pyramus and Thisbe," which in turn may have suggested to the dramatist not merely a more detailed treatment of that theme than he had heretofore given it in comedy, but also the choice of a story. For the archetypal "Pyramus and Thisbe" fable is roughly reproduced in the love story of Hermia and Lysander.

There is no claim here that Shakespeare approached the materials of *A Midsummer Night's Dream* in this or that sequence. Such a claim would be a presumption and it could scarcely achieve either demonstration or conviction. What is presented here is mere speculation as to the reasons for Shakespeare's choice of the chief elements of his plot. Shakespeare went to the story of Theseus and Hippolyta because their courtship and union could provide both thematic continuity as well as structural framework. Their royal wedding, announced as imminent in the opening scene and consummated in the last, is more than a background against which the adventures of the lovers and the gambols of artisans and fairies are framed. In Shakespeare's conception of the play the story of Theseus is thematically made an integral part of the other stories or plots. Like Lysander and Demetrius and Titania, and unlike Pyramus and Thisbe, Theseus had been an inconstant lover in his youthful days, and his inconstancy is most carefully and pointedly referred to by Oberon when he and Titania hurl accusations of inconstancy at each other. Titania charges Oberon with love for Hippolyta while he accuses her of being in love with Theseus.

> Didst thou not lead him through the glimmering night
> From Perigenia, whom he ravished?
> And make him with fair Aegle break his faith,
> With Ariadne, and Antiopa?

> (II, i, 77-80)

And of equal importance to the chief idea in the comedy is Theseus's present attitude towards love, what might be called, if not an ideal point of view, a judicious attitude, one reached after romantic escapade, including inconstancy. And it is to this attitude that the Athenian lovers are brought at the conclusion of their strange adventures in the woods beyond Athens. But these matters in the life of Theseus were not the only reason why Shakespeare chose the story of Theseus and Hippolyta for his plot of *A Midsummer Night's Dream*. These matters merely confirmed the choice, which may have been dictated by something else. It is quite possible that the initial impetus for writing a play on Theseus and Hippolyta and the Athenian lovers came to Shakespeare from his having seen the lost play *Palamon & Arsett,* which according to Henslowe's *Diary* was acted on September 17, October 16, October 27, and November 9, 1594.[6] It is quite possible, in turn, that the play sent Shakespeare to Chaucer's *Knight's Tale* and perhaps to other tales and poems, especially to the *Merchant's Tale* which could have provided not only a close parallel to Oberon and Titania in Pluto and Proserpina but also offered a further hint in its reference to Pyramus and Thisbe (ll. 2128-30).[7]

The tale of Palamon and Arcite in its broader limits held an analogy to the story of Montemayor's *Diana,* which Shakespeare had already dramatized in *The Two Gentlemen of Verona.* There were, of course, important differences, especially the addition in the play of a second lady. Indeed the *Diana* itself contained a variant tale wherein two pairs of lovers act very much as Shakespeare's Athenian lovers do in *A Midsummer Night's Dream*.[8] The love of two men for the same woman is at the center of all of these stories; and Shakespeare had already made the love of one of the men turn upon inconstancy. What he added to that story here is not only a second woman but also analogous or related tales in the story of Theseus and Hippolyta, Oberon and Titania, and Pyramus and Thisbe. For all of these, though not appearing together in a single source, had been associated in Shakespeare's consciousness through contact with them in books as well as the theatre. If he began with the resolve to write a comedy dealing with inconstancy in love, it is likely that behind that resolve lay the notion of modifying the sort of story he had dealt with in *The Two Gentlemen of Verona*. He might have turned to that theme if the impetus to write such a comedy had come from a detached view of *Romeo and Juliet*. Such a view might well send him to the comic treatment of love and constancy as in the Pyramus and Thisbe story. That story had been told so many times that by Shakespeare's day it was, as Madeleine Doran suggests, ready for parody.[9] Here parody was not Shakespeare's chief end, or at least not literary parody, although it must be admitted as an incidental element.[10] But parody *is* one of the purposes of the Pyramus and Thisbe playlet, that is, parody or satire of the romantic and sentimental approach to love which earlier versions of the story had expressed. And more to the point, the playlet is intended to reflect upon the romantic and sentimental story, very much like that of Pyramus and Thisbe, of Hermia and Lysander. The parody then is dramatic, rather than literary, achieved by the tone of the playlet and especially the incongruity of the actors presenting it on the stage.

For the details of the related story of Pyramus and Thisbe, aside from its connection with the derivative tale of Romeo and Juliet and its incidental mention in the *Merchant's Tale*, Shakespeare went to Ovid's *Metamorphoses,* in the original as well as in Golding's translation, in whose account certain

parts were somewhat ludicrous; he may have also seen the story
in a ballad by J. Thomson which appeared in *A Handfull
of Pleasant Delites* (1584), and another version in *The Gorgious
Gallery of Gallant Inventions* (1562). Another rendering of
the story, now lost, was by Dunstan Gale, and still another by
Thomas Mouffet in his poem *Of the Silkwormes, and Their
Flies* (1599), believed to have been first printed in 1596. The
same story had been told in Lydgate's *Reson and Sensualyte,*
in Gower's *Confessio Amantis,* and Chaucer's *Legend of Good
Women.*[11] How many of these versions Shakespeare had read
it is impossible to know, but he was clearly struck by the often
unintentional ludicrousness in both the Ovidian original and
more especially in the numerous post-Ovidian, greatly amplified
renderings.[12] So vulnerable was the "tragedy" of the two lovers
in the versions available to him that Shakespeare's use of it in
the manner he chose was inevitable. Indeed we may speculate
that it was this failing of the story to achieve pathos which led
him to oppose it, so to speak, to his own recent and much more
successful experimentation with the cognate story of *Romeo
and Juliet.*

In addition to Theseus and Hippolyta, the Athenian lovers,
and the playlet of Pyramus and Thisbe, the comedy contains
two more sets of characters representing opposite poles in the
structural as well as thematic scheme of the play. And here
again, as before, the idea or theme Shakespeare is trying to convey dictated the choice of those two extremes. For Shakespeare,
the juxtaposition of extremes was, both early and late in his
career, a structural necessity. *A Midsummer Night's Dream*
and *The Tempest,* a play it prefigures in important ways, share
the distinction of illustrating better than any other plays
Shakespeare's device of juxtaposing extremes for the purpose
of indicating a golden mean. But Bottom's adventure with the
fairies is not a mere mechanical device but an integral
part of the construction, having to do with both the immediate
theme of the play, that is, inconstancy in love and also the
larger, all-encompassing idea of the comedies: the proper attitude, shorn of extremes, to love and life generally.

For Bottom and his fellow artisans Shakespeare needed no literary source since he doubtless found them in the villages of his native shire, the source which had already provided Launce and Christopher Sly and was to yield the Gobbos, the watch in *Much Ado About Nothing* and the recruits Justice Shallow offers Falstaff in *2 Henry IV*. But Bottom's transformation, aside from hints provided by witch-superstitions in the country, could have been suggested to Shakespeare by a variety of sources, including Reginald Scot's *Discovery of Witchcraft* (1584) and the *Golden Ass of Apuleius*.[13]

For details concerning the third group of characters, the fairies, who are contrasted with Bottom's mechanicals, Shakespeare may have gone to a number of sources. The general hint may have come from a lost play identified by Nashe simply as *The King of Fairies*.[14] But the presence of such creatures who were to symbolize certain ideas and attitudes was inevitable, for Shakespeare had already represented those ideas and attitudes in human characters in earlier plays. Here it was necessary to embody attitudes in characters of automatic and instantaneous symbolism, hence Bottom and the ass's head and Titania and her fairies. The world of nature in its most immediate and realistic aspects and the world of romance and fancy, earlier represented by different human characters, or by the same at different points in a play, are here contrasted by means of characters drawn literally from different worlds, yet characters who are shown together and who under special circumstances see no difference between themselves.

Shakespeare may have taken the name of Oberon from *Huon of Bordeaux*, translated by Lord Berners in 1533, although the name had appeared much later in Greene's *James IV*. Titania, the fairy queen, whom Shakespeare elsewhere calls Queen Mab,[15] is the epithet given by Ovid to Diana in the *Metamorphoses* (III, 173). For information regarding Puck as well as the fairies Shakespeare could have turned to Reginald Scot's *Discovery of Witchcraft* (1584), and he doubtless knew of the treatment given the fairy-world by Chaucer and Spenser. The names Peaseblossom, Cobweb, Moth, and Mustardseed are

Shakespeare's own. Though he owed much of his conception of the fairy-world to popular tradition, Shakespeare made two important and very necessary changes: he reduced the size of some of the fairies, and he made them all benevolent and amiable.[16] But Oberon and Titania as well as Puck are conceived somewhat differently, both with respect to size and character. Puck retains the size and some of the mischievousness attributed to him in popular tradition, whereas Oberon and Titania, though fairies symbolic of the world of romance and fancy, are endowed with human frailties and passions and motives. To this part of the play and its significance we shall return later. For the moment it may suffice to say that these are the main sources for the fairy-world of the play as well as Shakespeare's chief changes of detail in his presentation of the principal characters of that portion of the plot.

IV

What, then, is the principle which organizes the seemingly incongruous stories into what most critics believe to be a "stability of structure."?[17] For the happy management of its multiple plots has led nearly all critics to extravagant praises of the play's form, and in at least one or two cases to a similar praise of its characterization.[18] Professor Charlton is surely right in insisting that the "three separate worlds are moulded into one by a controlling point of view, by an idea, not a philtre." And he adds that "*A Midsummer Night's Dream* is not Shakespeare's first masterpiece because in it he is technically more expert than hitherto in such qualities as deftness in structure; it is because in it he has seized more securely on the vital temper of his generation and embodied with it more of the essential spirit of his time."[19] England, he writes, had by Shakespeare's time become the land of romance. "The poet's world of fairy and the lover's rural England are indistinguishably one."[20] The Elizabethans "clamoured for romance, because they themselves had become romantic."[21] And it is because Shakespeare resolved to give them that romance in *A Midsummer Night's Dream,* it is argued, that he is able to achieve for the first time comic unity in a play. There is much truth in Professor Charlton's interpretation, particularly when he sets aside his general view of the controlling idea and examines individual elements in the play. But his notion of that controlling principle can be applied equally to Shakespeare's earlier romantic comedy and especially *Love's Labour's Lost*, which Professor Charlton places at the very beginning of Shakespeare's career. In that play the controlling idea of which Professor Charlton speaks is surely embodied in Berowne's famous speech on love. It is present also in *The Two Gentlemen of Verona* as well as in the wooing of both Katherina and Bianca in *The Taming of the Shrew*, and it appears for the first time in *The Comedy of Errors* both in Adriana's reminiscence of her romantic wooing and Antipholus of Syracuse's courtship, brief though it be, of Luciana. The resolve that love and romance should be his comic theme was made by Shakespeare at the very outset of his career. What he achieved gradually was not the resolve, but the means by which to create a dramatic form which would accommodate that theme. The importance of *A Midsummer Night's Dream* resides primarily in its own artistic integrity irrespective of its relation to the sequent steps Shakespeare followed in perfecting his comic form. But it nevertheless indicates one of those steps, for though successful the play does not represent Shakespeare's final achievement in romantic comedy.

First of all *A Midsummer Night's Dream* differs from both earlier and later romantic comedies in employing an explicitly symbolic action which is repeated most clearly in Shakespeare's romances at the end of his career. From this it follows that the over-all artistic aim is to present an idea, for which characters and action are selected, but the idea controls all. Consequently, character delineation suffers and is indeed inferior to what we have seen in earlier plays. The main idea here is not, as Chaucer says, that

> A man moot nedes love, maugree his heed,
> He may not flee it, thogh he sholde be deed.

That had served as the overriding theme of *Love's Labour's Lost,* as it would of *Much Ado About Nothing* and *Twelfth Night,* and in part of *As You Like It.* In *A Midsummer Night's Dream* Shakespeare creates a plot which deals not with *whether* man falls in love but with whom and why. To this he was led by the desire to explore further the theme of inconstancy which he had treated in earlier plays, particularly *The Two Gentlemen of Verona.* But inconstancy could be explored only by delving into its cause, that is to say, the lover's choice or choices, his falling in love and his betrayal of that love in favor of another. The play would thus extend the theme of inconstancy by dramatizing the mysterious attraction between this man and that woman and not another, or first with one and then another, the inexplicable caprice of choice, the very blindness with which Cupid shoots his fateful shafts. This is the central idea of the play but it is not the only important one. Allied with it is yet another theme which in other comedies occupies the central position, both structurally and thematically, and that is the way to love, the ideal attitude towards the experience of being in love.

v

Earlier in this chapter it was argued that Shakespeare began work on the play by first selecting the idea he wished to dramatize and then choosing fables and then characters accordingly. But since that idea, the *why* in the lover's choice, could not be dramatized in direct objective terms, Shakespeare chose to express it by means of a fairy-story. But the fairy-plot, particularly its *locus* and atmosphere, serves the other theme of the play as well, that is, the juxtaposition of opposed attitudes toward love. The world which romantic lovers in Shakespeare's earlier comedies had created through their fancy, the spirituality which they had attributed to their loved ones, the otherworldliness which they had seen in the angelic features of their ladies—all these *A Midsummer Night's Dream* presents in the persons of the fairies in the enchanted woodland beyond Athens. Though not the most important characters in the play, the fairies occupy a pivotal position in the multiple relationships of the stories. They have come to Athens to honor the Theseus-Hippolyta wedding; they have to do also with the lovers as well as Bottom and his artisans. They are here to bless the royal wedding; they tangle and then untangle the love affairs; and they meet the artisans in direct and meaningful interaction. Here the world of immediate fact blends with the world of fancy: as the fairies, ethereal spirits though they are, are given human passions—they exhibit love and jealousy as well as inconstancy—so Bottom dreams a dream and with his mechanicals puts on a playlet of love and constancy; and thus his role in the play is as symbolic as that of the fairies. And the golden mean to which the placing together of these extremes points is represented by the love of Theseus and Hippolyta, whose attitude towards romance is the norm, the ideal, to which men may be admitted in this world. It is to this attitude that the extravagance of the four lovers is reduced at the conclusion of the play.

This, then, is the pattern, and these the parts and their relationships in the structure of *A Midsummer Night's Dream*. It seems as if Shakespeare had felt some impatience with his own hitherto partially successful comedies, as if he here chose to make explicit his comic idea. For the play shows an extremely careful joining together of three plots, thus exhibiting a diagrammatic formality which can be easily expressed in intellectual, one could almost say mathematical, terms. And this is precisely the single weakness of the play. The importance given to the symbolic aspects of the plot reduces its comic possibilities by removing immediate human responsibility from the target of the comic spirit. There is consequently no profound development or comic recognition on the part of the lovers at the end. Related to this is the need, mentioned earlier, to keep realistic characterization at a minimum, at least among the four Athenian lovers. At no point in the play, unless it be the final scene, do we laugh either with or at them. Instead the target at which the comic spirit aims its arrows is transferred to another part of the woods where Titania embraces Bottom, both of whom are secondary characters, though of course very important ones. In this sense the comedy fails to achieve the final integration we observe in *As You Like It,* for instance, where character, in a sense, becomes plot, where the thrust and direction of the action proceeds from character, where character, finally, embodies the idea of the play. But we must bear in mind that such minor inferiority of *A Midsummer Night's Dream* is a matter of choice in the kind, not the execution, of its structure.

It may appear strange to speak of weakness or inferiority in *A Midsummer Night's Dream,* but the terms are used only in viewing the play against the later and greater comedies. In structure the play far surpasses earlier comedies not simply because it employs more successfully devices which had already appeared in the comedies which preceded it. For instance, *A Midsummer Night's Dream* achieves superior integration of song and action, an achievement comparable only with that of *As You Like It,* according to a student of Shakespeare's songs.[22] This is particularly true of the song with which her fairies sing Titania to sleep. The song is provided for very naturally. It is not decorative or intended merely for entertainment; it is part of the action itself. Titania not only calls for the song in her opening line but also anticipates part of its content in the things she commands her fairies to do while she is asleep. In setting, atmosphere, in content, and in function, the song is an integral part of the scene.

Another example demonstrating the superiority of *A Midsummer Night's Dream* over earlier plays is its successful use of the play-within-a-play. The general plan of enclosing one dramatic action within another was very clearly one of Shakespeare's favorite dramatic devices. It provided him with the means of presenting action in a double perspective which could create the illusion of reality. It could also serve as a sort of subplot or at least it could be made to perform an important function of the subplot, namely to reproduce the broad lines of the main action but in a wholly different tone. In *The Comedy of Errors* the story of Egeon

and Emilia at the beginning and end of the play illustrates
a simple device employed in other plays as well, including *A
Midsummer Night's Dream*, where the story of Theseus and
Hippolyta serves as the framing action. As we observed earlier,
the Theseus-Hippolyta plot is thematically as well as structurally made part of the main story. In *The Taming of the
Shrew* Shakespeare employed the device of the play-within-a-
play for the first time. But the arrangement or rather the
relationship of the two actions was so awkward that he very
probably dropped the framing action in mid-play. The reverse scheme of presenting a short playlet within a longer
action was far more satisfactory. And Shakespeare promptly
employed it in *Love's Labour's Lost*. But whatever success the
play of the Nine Worthies achieves is due not to the playlet
itself or its relation to the rest of the play but rather to the
performance of the individual "actors" and the incongruity
of the roles they are acting.

In *A Midsummer Night's Dream* there is far greater integration of the playlet with the rest of the comedy. In the won-
derful economy with which the two actions are fused, the play-
within-a-play here compares very favorably with the one in
Hamlet. Although Quince's players have no direct connection
with the two pairs of Athenian lovers, although their respective
stories are merely brought together in the final scene, there is
a connection of theme and tone between the play and the playlet. The artisans act in a play reproducing in part the story
of the lovers, and one of the artisans suffers a change by virtue
of the same agency which transforms the loves of Lysander
and Demetrius. And the ludicrous lament of Thisbe over her
dead Pyramus recalls by its contrast the grave tone of the
melancholy and self-pitying speeches of the forsaken Helena.
But these connections between the artisans and the story of
the lovers are of secondary significance. What is most brilliant
in the economical use of the artisans and their part of the plot
is the fact that Bottom plays the role of two lovers in the play,
first with the ass's head upon him as the lover of Titania, and
then as the tragical Pyramus. And of course it is this double

role which elevates Bottom to a position of exceptional significance among the *dramatis personae* of the play. And if his roles, or rather the acting of them, were to be meaningful, his own character had to be revealed with ready clarity and precision. For the success of his two roles, their significance in themselves and in relation to the entire play, depends on the poet's conception of Bottom's own character. Titania falls in love not merely with a man with an ass's head but with Bottom, the weaver who is to play the comico-tragic role of Pyramus, the man who dreams a dream, who sees nothing unusual in being beloved by the queen of fairies. He can both be and play the lover of Thisbe and of Titania with equal aplomb, and he would act the role of Thisbe, too, and of the lion and everything else. He is the most down-to-earth mortal in the play, the one most devoid of fancy, the most literal in what he sees and says and does. Is it not utterly unthinkable that he should be beloved of Titania and that he should impersonate Pyramus, for whose love Thisbe slays herself? The dramatist's conception of Bottom, a distant and more fully developed cousin of Christopher Sly, is that he should possess at once Sly's earthiness and the pretence to the sort of misplaced sophistication that is far worse than no sophistication at all. Sly very properly is unaffected by the alien world of the play acted for his delectation; he would it were over after the initial scene, and indeed sleeps through the rest of the play. Bottom is so fascinated by the tragedy of Pyramus and Thisbe that he would act all its parts, but his conception of the play is more ludicrous than Sly's attitude. For Bottom the enactment of the "tragedy" will be so successful that he is apprehensive lest the tender among the aristocratic audience should take the action at its face value and be most painfully frightened by it. He is convinced of the reality of the role he is acting in the playlet, a reality no different, as he apprehends it, from that of his role as Titania's lover. Both roles of Bottom as lover represent the ultimate incongruity or contrast, seen here in close juxtaposition in two separate scenes, between the real and the ideal, the factual and the romantic, the world of drudgery and the world of dreams. And as we have seen, this juxtaposition is the cornerstone in the structure of Shakespearean romantic comedy, and it appears prominently, indeed centrally, in any scene or episode dealing with love, whether in comedy or any other genre in the Shakespearean canon.

VI

In *A Midsummer Night's Dream* the expression of the chief ideas is made so clearly in terms of principle rather than of realistic human experience that the symbolic structure of the comedy has been weighted with a variety of meanings by critics. It is the sort of structure which invites over-interpretation. For instance, it was inevitable that over-interpretation should discover elemental aspects of being in the adventures of Bottom with the fairies. Thus the entire play has been read as a symbolic representation of "a primal scene night in the life of a child,"[23] or as "a restitutive gesture towards mother," elucidating the psychosexual development of women.[24] This sort of approach employs the play to explain esoteric scientific terms and concepts and thus has nothing to do with the interpretation of the play as a work of literary art. It is, to be sure, an extreme point of view. But over-interpretation, that is, seeing far too much recondite significance in the symbolic structure of the play, appears in literary approaches to the play as well.

The literary critic who comes to the play after reading the comedies we have so far considered at once realizes that this is the first comedy in which Shakespeare utilizes an extra-human agency which appears to control human action.[25] In this connection the notion has been expressed that the play is prophetic in the sense that it announces the theme of the great tragedies —the supremacy of the "unseen world" over the world of sense.[26] How accurate all this is we cannot be certain, but there is no denying that *A Midsummer Night's Dream* does indeed include episodes which demonstrate a measure of seeming influence by the invisible world upon human destiny. But the immediate point of view is other than that of the great tragedies, for here the agents of the invisible world are not merely endowed with human emotions but also beset with human limitations. Indeed some bungle their assigned tasks, whereas others surrender themselves to a ridicule far greater than do the human lovers whose actions the unseen agencies are said to control. Nevertheless their influence is ultimately benevolent; they are, says Oberon, "spirits of another sort." It is even less secure to venture more particular interpretations of the characters of that unseen world. It is certainly not possible to demonstrate that "the king and queen of the woods dramatize the two poles of the scale of values which gave meaning to marriage. They are types of the forces of Reason and Passion which in a more complex and human manner move through Theseus and Hippolyta respectively."[27] It is equally difficult to demonstrate the same critic's notion that Oberon is a figure of grace and that Titania is a symbol of earthly love. Nor is it clear how the woods can "signify the confusions which beset the earthly life," since they are the habitat of both Oberon and Titania.[28] But perhaps the strangest and least satisfactory comment is the notion that "to move from the city to the forest is to choose madness."[29]

If the principle of moving from city to forest in the other comedies is the same as here, then its meaning cannot be the choice of madness over reason. It is far more likely that the opposite meaning is intended in such plays as *As You Like It, The Merchant of Venice* with its Belmont as opposed to the Rialto, and *The Tempest*. But there is reason in the play itself why the woods cannot be construed as representing madness. Although the Lysander-Hermia love affair suffers briefly in the woods, it is here that both pairs of lovers are reunited. And in the comedies cited above, the woods or Belmont or the enchanted island, in contrast with the city or the court, are the place where love finds fruition, where lovers are united or reunited, enemies are reconciled, where a happy conclusion of the story of the plays is worked out. "The woods," Professor Barber writes, "are established as a region of metamorphosis, where in liquid moonlight or glimmering starlight, things can change, merge and melt into each other. Metamorphosis expresses both what love sees and what it seeks to do."[30] And *A Midsummer Night's Dream* is the first comedy, among those so far considered, which impresses that particular aspect of design upon the general comic mode with which Shakespeare henceforth will dramatize a love story. We may even go so far as to say that this aspect of design is one of the chief contributions made by the play to the development of Shakespearean romantic comedy.[31]

At the other extreme and opposing the view that Oberon and Titania are allegorical characters representing Reason and Passion respectively, is the notion that they should be viewed in human terms and that in so viewing them we should apply to their actions our own moral, material, and psychological laws. It has been argued, for instance, that the reason Titania will not yield the changeling to Oberon is that she has made the boy her lover.[32] As noted earlier, Shakespeare very carefully attributes to his fairies human emotions and limitations, but that is not quite the same as having them act like humans, nor does it follow that Titania has made a human her lover. Certainly it would be absurd to conclude that she is enamored of Bottom in the same sense. And it is going too far to say that Shakespeare pursued the paradox of making Titania, whose name is Ovid's epithet for Diana, a licentious goddess of chastity. If the fairies represent agencies of the invisible world, then their own strictly individual acts are far less emphasized than the meaning they carry. Those beings and their actions are prominent not in themselves but in their relation to the story of the human characters. What Shakespeare emphasizes is not so much the detailed nature of the invisible world as its relationship to the course of human affairs. Indeed the precise nature of that other world must necessarily remain shadowed, for through it Shakespeare not only forecasts human events, but also, and more significantly, points to the mystery surrounding them. If the fairies of *A Midsummer Night's Dream* are a part of that world, then their actions, whether they affect the fairies themselves or influence or merely reveal human destiny, are compact of that mystery which human reason encounters in essaying to penetrate first causes. Doubtless the most striking examples of this in Shakespeare are to be found, besides *A Midsummer Night's Dream,* in *Macbeth,* where quite different agencies of the invisible world assume a ponderous note. And it might be added that in Shakespeare's drama the impenetrable mystery in the revolutions of human destiny is presented to our imagination by the absolute opposition between the fairies of *A Midsummer Night's Dream* and the witches in *Macbeth.* It was Shakespeare's way to allow a measure of vagueness and indeterminateness about the creatures of the unseen world. This was part of the design in *Hamlet,* where the ghost is the subject of much question in the play. And the same is true of the witches. Banquo and Macbeth are baffled by the appearance of the weird sisters:

> You should be women,
> And yet your beards forbid me to interpret
> That you are so.

So also the creatures of the unseen kingdom in *A Midsummer Night's Dream.* Their natures and their actions can have meaning only if they remain just beyond human understanding: one of their chief functions is to point to the limitations of that understanding.

VII

Looking back over what has been said about Shakespeare's materials and his fusion of them into a successful play, we may set down certain broad conclusions. The dramatist was evidently led to the choice of those materials by the resolve to produce a play in which his chosen comic themes might be more clearly and more forcefully dramatized than he had hitherto achieved in the earlier comedies. To do this he had to treat the same themes in a new way, with a new structure or perhaps a more sharply outlined structure than he had used in the past. And it was thus inevitable that he should select a symbolic action as the agency of the comic process, for only through such action could he record in unmistakable fashion his own discoveries about themes that were to receive chief emphasis in the plays to follow. Thus all the elements of the play are presented in their extreme form. More than that, the success of that symbolic action led Shakespeare to make it, in milder form, an element of the comic mode he was gradually evolving. It is for these reasons that the play has been called the "diagram and parable of its type."[33] Certainly *A Midsummer Night's Dream* is more than a "skilful re-working of parts and devices for an acting company which had already proved these parts and devices dramatically and theatrically valid in the performance of *Love's Labour's Lost*."[34] *A Midsummer Night's Dream* is a new kind of comedy. And although none of Shakespeare's other comedies are quite like it, a familiarity with it is indispensable to an understanding of the others.

As already noted, the play combines elements of startling contrast, a contrast made necessary by the dramatist's resolve to compose a play presenting sudden conflict between lovers as well as antithetical attitudes towards love. The choice to write such a play entails grave risks, for the disparity in its stories and especially in the sets of characters tends to make their blending difficult and the achievement of unity, if not impossible, certainly highly improbable. And yet Shakespeare, meeting the challenge head-on, was able to create an extraordinary degree of unity. How did he do it?

The story of Theseus and Hippolyta, though not directly connected with the story of the lovers, is certainly bound up with the fairy plot and the "Pyramus and Thisbe" playlet. Theseus is not the character of classical legend although he retains many of his Plutarchan attributes. Shakespeare's conception of him adds to the classical outline some of the features of Chaucer's "duc Theseus" and, more significantly, traits of the Renaissance Prince.[35] On his legendary side the character of Theseus admits association with the fairies, while his Renaissance features make it easier to accept his connection with native characters of Shakespeare's Warwickshire. In addition,

Theseus and Hippolyta are to end their military conflict with marriage. Like that conflict and reconciliation, the king and queen of the fairies have their own quarrel and reunion. The connection between the Athenian lovers and the royal pair is achieved by a similar thematic parallel. All six are lovers, all three men show inconstancy—Theseus, too, had been an inconstant lover—and all are united in a triple wedding. Finally the artisans put on a love tragedy to celebrate the royal wedding, and one of them is transformed by the same agency which transforms the Athenian lovers and Titania. Furthermore, the love tragedy they enact is a comico-tragic version of the Lysander-Hermia story.

These are the broad relationships of the stories making up the plot of *A Midsummer Night's Dream*. But there are other lines of connection in the weaving together not only of the stories but of individual episodes and scenes. These are addressed to both our conscious and subconscious awareness of the detailed process of the play. For instance, Shakespeare creates a special atmosphere, a special and congruent quality in the scene before us. He creates it by placing before our eyes, and by calling upon our own imaginations to evoke, the moonlit woods and its fairies with their lullabies and utterly unpredictable ways; he evokes a scene suggestive of unreality, a strange place where incredible things can happen to humans. And he intensifies this impression of unreality in the scene by his innumerable allusions to the moon and moonlight, symbols of change and mystery. Furthermore, the feeling that much of what is happening may not be real is created by the ubiquitous allusion to dreams, by the puzzled self-reassurance of certain characters that what they have done or seen or even what they have been during the night in the woods was a dream. In continuing contrast to the dreamlike atmosphere surrounding the events of the night in the woods is the normal world of everyday life, with its natural as well as social processes. With this world the play begins and to this same world it returns its human characters in the end.

In addition Shakespeare employs other less obvious details

which contribute to the impression of unity in the play. The strangeness of the events of the night is anticipated by the strangeness of the Athenian law which would put Hermia to death if she married Lysander. The strife of Oberon and Titania anticipates the strife of the four lovers, and all are anticipated by the former strife between the royal pair. Anticipation and retrospect become in this play an indispensable device which Shakespeare will employ for the creation of supremely ironic effects in later plays, particularly his tragedies. The device addresses itself to our subconscious, supplying it with impressions later to be periodically recalled for the purpose of ironic recognition. Francisco's " 'Tis bitter cold / And I am sick at heart" is the readiest example. Commenting on Cawdor's defection, Duncan editorializes as follows at the very moment Macbeth enters the stage:

> There's no art
> To find the mind's construction in the face.
> He was a gentleman on whom I built
> An absolute trust.

Although in *A Midsummer Night's Dream* the device in no way achieves the startling effects it creates in *Macbeth,* its appearance in the earlier play is no longer an experiment but a confirmed and necessary element of dramatic construction.

In the opening speech Theseus alludes to the moon and complains of its slow waning which lingers the interim before his wedding. And in her own initial speech Hippolyta tells him that the intervening four nights "will quickly dream away the time." Upon entering the stage a moment later Egeus accuses Lysander of interchanging love-tokens with Hermia, that he has "by moonlight at her window sung." "Moon" and "dream" fill the lines of the opening scene, projecting in broad terms the general atmosphere of the central scenes we are about to witness in the woods. The young men's inconstancy there is anticipated by Lysander's allusion to Demetrius' betrayal of Helena, calling him "this spotted and inconstant man." Hermia on her side stresses the same incon-

stancy in men by alluding to Dido's death, "When the false
Trojan under sail was seen." Then after Hermia and Lysander
have vowed to meet in the woods "Tomorrow night, when
Phoebe doth behold / Her silver visage in the wat'ry glass,"
Helena, left alone on the stage, reflects upon Cupid's unpredictable ways. She alludes to Love's blindness and irrationality,
both of which cause it to be beguiled and perjured.

> Love looks not with the eyes but with the mind,
> And therefore is wing'd Cupid painted blind.
> Nor hath Love's mind of any judgment taste;
> Wings and no eyes figure unheedy haste;
> And therefore is Love said to be a child,
> Because in choice he is so oft beguil'd.
> As waggish boys in game themselves forswear,
> So the boy Love is perjur'd every where.
>
>   (I, i, 234-41)

The passage anticipates the strange events of the following
night, and Helena points to them more directly by adding that
if she tells Demetrius of Hermia's intended flight, he will follow
her to the woods, whither she, Helena, will pursue him.

   In the second scene the artisans prepare for a rehearsal of
the play they will act in honor of the royal wedding. The theme
of their play is constancy in love and as noted earlier the plight
of Thisbe and Pyramus—though not their death—parallels
the troubled love of Lysander and Hermia. Finally the artisans
plan to rehearse "by moonlight" in the palace wood beyond
the city. In the next scene the woods, the night, and the moonlight are upon us, described and sustained by the presence
of the fairies. And though the scene is in sharp contrast to the
preceding episodes, the three sets of characters are held together
by the announcement earlier that both the lovers and the
artisans intend to meet upon the very plot where the fairies
have met. Furthermore the heated exchange between Oberon
and Titania recalls the conflict between Demetrius and Helena
and at the same time anticipates the more violent strife to come
among the four lovers. And Oberon's description of "Love-in-

idleness," with its power to make "or man or woman madly
dote," recalls Helena's allusion to Cupid's blindness and lack
of judgment. In the same scene Demetrius turns upon the
pursuing Helena with words clearly intended to be ironically
recalled in a later episode.

> Tempt not too much the hatred of my spirit,
> For I am sick when I do look on thee.
>
> (II, i, 211-12)

In the following scene Lysander on his side protests his deathless love to Hermia, and his words are likewise intended for
ironic retrospect later. Hermia in maidenly modesty asks that
they sleep some distance from each other:

> So far be distant; and, good night, sweet friend.
> Thy love ne'er alter till thy sweet life end!
> *Lysander.*   Amen, amen, to that fair prayer, say I;
> And then end life when I end loyalty!
>
> (II, ii, 60-63)

Lysander's protestation is supported by Hermia shortly thereafter when upon awakening she discovers that he is gone. And
her faith in his constancy is maintained in words matching,
indeed overgoing, his own declaration:

> The sun was not so true unto the day
> As he to me: would he have stolen away
> From sleeping Hermia? I'll believe as soon
> This whole earth may be bor'd and that the moon
> May through the centre creep and so displease
> Her brother's noontide with the Antipodes.
>
> (III, ii, 50-55)

When Demetrius awakens, after receiving in his sleep the

> Flower of this purple dye,
> Hit with Cupid's archery,

he sees the forsaken melancholy Helena before him. But her
presence no longer makes him ill.

> O Helen, goddess, nymph, perfect, divine!
> To what, my love, shall I compare thine eyne?
> Crystal is muddy. O, how ripe in show
> Thy lips, those kissing cherries, tempting grow!
>
> (III, ii, 137-40)

Lysander's change is as great and equally ironic, for now having fallen in love with Helena, he turns in violence away from the puzzled and incredulous Hermia:

> Away, you Ethiope!

Enough has been said to show that such passages of anticipation and retrospect contribute to the unity of the play, but of course the passages have other functions as well. The irony they produce is intended to underscore both the nature and extent of the change in the affections of the lovers, and even more important they demonstrate the *idea* of change, of inconstancy, of the unreason and blindness of Love's choice. And thus the devices employed for achieving structural unity are not mechanical and external but rather internal and organic, for they express aspects of the central idea of the play.

And now let us turn in conclusion to that idea, and the meaning of *A Midsummer Night's Dream*. For meaning it possesses although some scholars have, strangely enough, failed to see it. It is, for instance, difficult to follow Peter Alexander's conclusion that "there is no deep significance in the magic juice, no profound interpretation of life in the adventures of the lovers."[36] It is true that the play "conveys a sense of people being tossed about by a force which puts them beside themselves," but it is going too far to say that the change "is presented simply, with little suggestion that it involves a growth in insight—Demetrius is not led to realize something false in his diverted affection for Hermia."[37] Although deeply puzzled by the change he experienced during the strange night in the woods, the one thing Demetrius does realize is that there was something false in his affection for Hermia and his rejection of Helena:

> To her, my lord,
> Was I betroth'd ere I saw Hermia;
> But like a sickness did I loathe this food;
> But, as in health, come to my natural taste,
> Now I do wish it, love it, long for it,
> And will for evermore be true to it.
>
> (IV, i, 175-80)

Demetrius understands the meaning of his brief change, though not its cause.

Another interpretation of the play sees it as a literary satire, arguing that in following Chaucer, Shakespeare produced "the lightest and gayest satire on medieval romance."[38] As we have said earlier, the play's chief aim is not literary satire, though such satire is present in an incidental role. In any case the play's primary concern is with the theme of romance, not its literary expression, and the aim is not ultimately satiric: it is not satire for its own sake. As we have seen in earlier plays, Shakespeare's satire of romance is a device, not an end in itself, and it is so here. The ultimate concern of the play is positive, and one scholar has identified that concern in this manner. " 'What is Love?' or rather, 'What is the place of love in life?' is the question underlying *A Midsummer Night's Dream*."[39] It is quite clear that the play poses the first question in Professor Charlton's definition, and it is equally clear that the answer given is that there is no certain and positive answer. But Professor Charlton's second question, though central in other Shakespearean comedies, is tangential in *A Midsummer Night's Dream*. That Professor Charlton is thinking about other plays in which the question is at the very center of the plot is strongly suggested by the following comment. "At all events," he writes, "in *A Midsummer Night's Dream*, wedlock and house-keeping are imposed on man for his advantage; and the advantage as a social being he gains thereby is made patent by setting beside him the undomesticated irresponsible beings of fairyland."[40] Professor Charlton's comment is an accurate estimate of the theme of such plays as *Love's Labour's Lost*,

Much Ado About Nothing, and *Twelfth Night.* In *A Midsummer Night's Dream* alone among these comedies there is no rejection of love: no characters here oppose love as the king and his lords do in *Love's Labour's Lost* or as Benedick and Beatrice do in their play. There is no Phoebe here mocking the love of Silvius, nor Olivia spurning all thoughts of love in favor of a seven-year mourning. The question here is not *whether* to love, but *whom.* How do lovers fall in love, what is the cause and secret of their choice? "What is love?" is indeed the oblique query to which *A Midsummer Night's Dream* offers its oblique answer. It is the question asked directly at the most critical moment in the chief love affair of the play we shall consider next, *The Merchant of Venice;* it is asked by Nerissa in the opening line of her song even as Bassanio makes his choice.

It was not Shakespeare's way to define but rather to suggest, and his favorite device of doing so, whether he was dealing with love or honor or valor, was by means of juxtaposing different—often antithetical—attitudes or points of view. In the comedies he chose to place side by side the romantic and realistic concepts of love and in so doing to point to a middle ground, to a golden mean. In the play before us Shakespeare not only employed this device but he presented it in the strongest possible terms, in symbolic terms. In the world of the fairies he represents the extremes to which the lovers' fancy takes them in the contemplation of their loves. The dream world is the strange country created by the lovers' "seething brains," the imagined land far removed from our own real world. It is the world Mercutio describes as the product of Queen Mab's machinations, and in that sense it is true that his speech belongs to *A Midsummer Night's Dream.* And although we may agree that it "is a play in the spirit of Mercutio," and that the dreaming in it includes the knowledge "that dreamers often lie,"[41] *A Midsummer Night's Dream* deals with much more than that. Dreamers may "often lie" but not always. And their dreams, though seeming to belie truth, may lead to it. Shakespeare does not, either in *Romeo and Juliet* or *A Midsummer Night's*

Dream, share Mercutio's final view of the matter. But Mercutio's attitude defines that other extreme, which in the play before us is represented by the matter-of-fact world of Bottom. But is it not meaningful that Bottom, like the lovers, had "dreamed a dream," and that he should be the one to make the most significant comment in the play? For it is Bottom who says that man "is but an ass, if he go about to expound his dream." It may be true that "cool reason" comprehends things as they are, but among these love is not one. Theseus is convinced that the lovers' romanticism is but the work of fancy even as the world of the poet is, but Theseus is not given the final comment on the matter. And Hippolyta's reply remains unanswered, and for Shakespeare no doubt unanswerable:

> But all the story of the night told over,
> And all their minds transfigur'd so together,
> More witnesseth than fancy's images,
> And grows to something of great constancy;
> But, howsoever, strange and admirable.
>
> (V, i, 23-27)

The dream is indeed inexplicable. It is so strange, says Bottom, that "the eye of man hath not heard, the ear of man hath not seen. . . ." But to say that a dream, the dream of a lover, is inexplicable is not to place a moral judgment on it; nor is it true that one like Bottom, "neither born to be a great lover nor destined to utter a line of verse, may from his own life realize the harm of poets' and lovers' qualities."[42] This is precisely what Shakespeare's Bottom does not realize. On the contrary, Bottom's drab existence receives its single magic illumination from contact with at once the poet's and lover's world.[43] No doubt Shakespeare saw man's reason as the means of distinguishing bears from bushes, but it is not at all certain that he considered it the single agency of ultimate truth. Nor does he in the comedies laugh at "men without cool reason, who are the sport of seething brains and of the tumultuous frenzies of fancy and of sentiment," and neither does he consider them "the victims of the world, and the butts of its comedy."[44] Lovers do indeed exaggerate, and their words fly beyond the bounds whereto cool reason may reach; their words, born of fancy, may seem to impeach their own truth through Petrarchan hyperbole. But this is so only to us who see, not to the lovers who feel and imagine.[45] For Mercutio, all maids must be taught

> to bear,
> Making them women of good carriage.

For Romeo one such maid is a "bright angel," a "winged messenger of heaven"; she is a "dear saint," for whom he will be "new baptiz'd." And here, as well as in similar passages in the later comedies, the conceit of the sonneteer, a stylistic device which is self-conscious and even false, becomes the idea itself. To the lover love has become the agency of salvation, the way to the "high heavens, temples of the gods," as Spenser calls them in his *Epithalamion*. This is the poet as lover speaking, and his speech is the speech of Shakespeare's romantic lovers. Cool reason may object, but the lover, whether Spenser or anybody else, believes that the high heavens for which he longs can be attained only through love. And it is precisely at this point that the Platonic concept of love replaces Petrarchism. In Shakespeare the Petrarchan attitude towards love may be mocked but never the Platonic. Petrarchism has to do with describing the beauty of the beloved, the pains of the lover, the cruelty of the one and the sufferings of the other. The Platonic concept has to do with the meaning of love itself, from the desire to enjoy beauty to the topmost step on the ladder which leads to the bosom of God.

All this is much more directly expressed in *Love's Labour's Lost* and *The Merchant of Venice* than in *A Midsummer Night's Dream*. The Platonic concept of love is implicit in Berowne's *credo* and in Lorenzo's lines on music in the final act of *The Merchant of Venice,* as well as in Portia's appeal to Shylock for mercy. But we have touched upon the subject here in order to show that Shakespeare's attitude towards lovers' dreams is not moral but psychological. What matters most is not whether those dreams are factual, whether they can be accepted and approved by "cool reason," but rather whether lovers dream. Nor is Shakespeare concerned to separate those dreams from what we call actuality. In *A Midsummer Night's Dream* he is especially anxious to eliminate that line of demarcation between them. And the mastery of fusing the disparate elements of the plot contributes to that impression. And thus the structure of the play, this blending of diversity, reflects this most significant idea of oneness. The world of dreams, the world poets and lovers create, is an aspect of our world in that it is a world wherein men long to be. It is for that reason that the world of romance cannot be called false and that it cannot be considered in moral terms. What is of moment is that the poet and the lover create such a world and that in imagination they inhabit it. That is the supreme truth.

The Merchant of Venice

Chapter VI

I

*T*he *Merchant of Venice* takes up and develops further certain motifs attempted in some of the earlier comedies. One of these themes has to do with two large aspects of love, romantic love and what might be called love in the social sphere, the love guiding and controlling human relationships, love expressed in friendship, love as the basis of ideal justice, justice qualified by mercy. Having dealt with the love-friendship conflict in *The Two Gentlemen of Verona* and in a smaller way in *A Midsummer Night's Dream*, Shakespeare proposes here to present the ideal relationship of friendship and love. In *The Comedy of Errors* and *The Taming of the Shrew*, on the other hand, he had attempted to express somewhat indirectly the proper relationship of wealth to love and to suggest the importance to a harmonious social organism of that relationship. On the dramatic and artistic side he had employed the idea of wealth, gold in particular, as a way of describing human associations and especially love. In *The Merchant of Venice* he carries all these matters to their final presentation in his comic drama. Most important of all, *The Merchant of Venice* resumes a theme indeterminately treated in some of the earlier plays, a theme made central to the action of *A Midsummer Night's Dream*. It is the theme of choice, a lover's falling in love with this woman and not another, the basis of attraction between two lovers, the question Shakespeare had essayed to answer by means of the mysterious operation of the fairies in the earlier play. Why Lysander and Demetrius suddenly discover what they call a deathless love for Helena and why one of them as suddenly transfers that love back to Hermia—why these things happened the lovers cannot tell. And their only explanation is that it was all a dream, and a dream, according to Bottom, cannot be explained.

These are the chief matters with which *The Merchant of Venice* is concerned, and if the reader or audience holds to these as the main concern of the dramatist, then the questions raised by the play, including Shylock's role, may prove somewhat less perplexing. One of the reasons for those questions is that because Shylock dominates certain scenes he is thought to be the most important character and his fortunes the chief concern of the play. Of his emotional impression upon the reader and audience there can be no doubt. But in terms of the play's structure in expressing the themes cited above he is not the chief character, and though his own individual destiny is absorbing, it is not that destiny that matters most in the play. What matters is Shylock's immediate as well as symbolic representation of an attitude, a point of view which is by the dramatist opposed to another point of view, this one represented by the Venetians in general but expressed most pointedly by Portia.

In thus taking up and further developing these themes

The Merchant of Venice must by necessity follow certain of Shakespeare's comedies in date of composition. Certainly the quality of its verse and the mastery of its construction suggest that it follows *A Midsummer Night's Dream*; and in delineation of character, at once exhaustive and economical, it far surpasses anything we have considered so far in this study. The majority of scholars agree with E. K. Chambers in setting the autumn of 1596 as "a very probable date for the play," his reason being the play's style and its links with other plays and the sonnets.[1] A few of the earlier critics seemed unable to fix a date for the play, saying merely that it was written early or late in the decade. Others, including Malone, believed 1594 was the year. That early date has been revived by J. Dover Wilson, who argues that in that year, because of the popularity of Marlowe's revived *Jew of Malta* and also because of the trial and execution of Dr. Roderigo Lopez in June of 1594, Shakespeare, taking advantage of public feeling, provided for his company a play with a Jew by recasting an old play entitled *The Jew,* to which Stephen Gosson had alluded in his *School of Abuse* (1579).[2] In the absence of weighty external evidence, Dover Wilson's date cannot be positively rejected. The only external evidence available is two-fold: the play was entered in the *Stationers' Register* on July 22, 1598, and it was mentioned by Francis Meres in September of the same year.[3] Although there may be a connection between *The Merchant of Venice,* and particularly Gratiano's reference to "a Wolf, hanged for human slaughter," and Dr. Lopez,[4] the play need not have been written while the trial of Dr. Lopez was in progress, as Dover Wilson insists. The line would have had relevance a year or so later, and of course it is quite possible that Shakespeare intended no such relevance at all.[5]

Unless evidence can be produced which demonstrates an early date like 1594 for the play, the opinion that it was written in 1596 or 1597 will stand. For that date there is support of an unusual kind in the line "And see my wealthy Andrew dock'd in sand." "Andrew" has been explained as a reference to the Spanish vice-admiral, the *St. Andrew,* which was captured by the English at Cadiz in 1596.[6] The line is particularly significant because the *St. Andrew* was captured after she had run aground in the harbor.[7] The news of the ship's capture reached the Court in the summer of 1596 so that the line, if it alludes to the Spanish ship, and perhaps the entire play must have been written in that summer or shortly thereafter. What is probable, then, about the date of *The Merchant of Venice* is that it must be after the summer of 1596 and before the autumn of 1598.

II

But there is a further question, namely the notion offered by the Clarendon editors and expanded by J. Dover Wilson that the text as we have it is the result of Shakespeare's revision, some time before the printing of the first quarto in 1600, of his own recasting of the old play *The Jew* in 1594. Although Gosson's allusion to *The Jew* as "representing the greediness of worldly chusers and bloody mindes of usuerers" has been thought to point to the Bond and Casket stories, it is by no means certain that it does so.[8] But even if a connection between the old play and *The Merchant of Venice* should be demonstrated, that connection would in no way confirm 1594 as the date of Shakespeare's comedy. Nor would it support Dover Wilson's elaborate theory concerning the history of the received text.[9] That Shakespeare revised portions of the play is not impossible, although Dover Wilson's bibliographical evidence is not convincing. Others have detected differences in style and characterization within the play and these they attribute to revision by Shakespeare some time before 1600.[10] Since dramatic exigencies may dictate the use of different styles within the same work, variety of styles in a particular play can scarcely be accepted as conclusive evidence of revision. The Clarendon editors believe that there are in the play "indications which would lead us to suppose that its first composition was earlier than 1598, such as the many classical allusions, the frequent rhymes and occasional doggerel verses."[11] This testimony Dover Wilson adduces in support of his own bibliographical evidence for an early composition and multiple revision of the play.[12] Rhymes and doggerel appear in late as well as early plays, and the same can be said of classical allusions. In *The Merchant of Venice* such allusions appear in force in the fifth act and they are concentrated in the opening episode with Jessica and Lorenzo in the Belmont gardens. Their exchange, wherein reference is made to Troilus and Cressida, Thisbe, Dido, Medea and Aeson, is written in blank verse, the verse used also in Lorenzo's description of the floor of heaven with its "patines of bright gold" and the orbs "quiring to the young-ey'd cherubins." Lorenzo then commands the musicians to "wake Diana with a hymn," and as the music begins he turns to speak of its "sweet power" to Jessica, affirming in witness of that power that

> the poet
> Did feign that Orpheus drew trees, stones and floods. . . .

All this is expressed in what most readers believe to be the best and maturest blank verse in the entire play. And yet these passages with their great blank verse contain more classical allusions than the rest of the play. The fifth act, then, must be thought as part of the early version because of its classical allusions, and at the same time part of the final text because of its blank verse. Clearly this will not do. Nor can we say that the passages with classical allusions belong to the original version and that those with the blank verse were added in the revised text, for the allusions and the blank verse are to be found in the same passages. The theory of an early date and multiple revision is yet to be demonstrated.

III

The question of Shakespeare's sources for the play has relevance in our study because the poet's choice and blending of his materials is to a great extent controlled, even dictated, by his concept of comic form, a concept taking firm shape at this stage of Shakespeare's development. As in *A Midsummer Night's Dream,* the question is of particular interest here as the stories chosen are of such disparate nature that their special fusion and the emphasis placed upon certain parts of those stories must reveal the overriding idea directing the poet's dramatic energy. For such an overriding idea most assuredly exists and it can be readily seen in the very consistency with which Shakespeare holds fast to the treatment of his chosen themes. Here, whether he received the bond and the casket stories in combination or whether he combined them himself, what is of moment is the way in which he fused them in his own play, the way in which he pressed the two disparate tales into mutual comment, the way in which he selected for emphasis those aspects of the tales through which he might explore, as he had done in earlier plays, aspects of his master-theme of love. For the bond plot is concerned with that theme no less than the casket story, while the latter, by its very insistence on defining love in terms of choice between gold (or silver) and lead, depends for final significance upon the counterpointing story of the usurer.

For us it is impossible to know precisely whence came the impetus to compose a play in which a story of usury with a bond for a pound of flesh is combined with a story of romantic love. Some believe the impulse was not artistic but resulted from Shakespeare's deliberate choice to respond to the events of the hour.[13] It may be so. It is quite possible that Shakespeare was led to choose the story for his play by the affair of Dr. Lopez. But it is equally possible that the impulse was a literary one, namely the success of earlier plays which have materials in common with *The Merchant of Venice*. Among these were Marlowe's *Jew of Malta* (1589) recently revived, the *Venesyon Comodye*, acted in 1594, and Dekker's *The Jew of Venice*, a play of uncertain date. In addition there was *The Jew*, an older play, but in all probability closer in content to Shakespeare's comedy than any of the others.[14] One or more of these may have supplied Shakespeare with both the impulse to write his play as well as with the material for it. The only play extant among them is *The Jew of Malta* and it is thus the only one whose influence upon Shakespeare we may determine.

A few general characteristics of Marlowe's Barabas may be reflected in Shylock, but their resemblance is not significant. As its title proclaims, Marlowe's play is about the Jew Barabas: he is the central character, eclipsing all others in the play. *The Merchant of Venice,* on the other hand, is not a play about Shylock. He may be the most absorbing character in it, but it is not his play.[15] However, the story of Abigail may have provided Shakespeare with some hints for the story of Jessica and Lorenzo, although of course he may have found this portion of the plot, like the rest, in one of the lost plays cited above.

The only extant work which may have provided most of the episodes for Shakespeare's comedy is Giovanni Fiorentino's *Il Pecorone,* written around 1378 and printed for the first time in 1558. The reason *Il Pecorone* is Shakespeare's pre sumed source is that it is the only extant work which combine the bond story with the wooing of a Lady at Belmont.[16] It bond story deals with a friend's bond to a Jew for a pound o flesh, and furthermore the Lady of Belmont intervenes in th disguise of a lawyer, saves her husband's friend from death, and begs a ring from him as a fee. Since it is impossible to say how much of this had been dramatized in the earlier plays we have cited, we must presume that Shakespeare went directly to *Il Pecorone.* In dealing with the two plots thus combined by Fiorentino, Shakespeare made important changes, dictated either by the nature of the stories themselves or by his own commitment to certain motifs or ideas. For instance, in *Il Pecorone* the lover is his benefactor's foster son. Shakespeare changed that relationship, making Antonio and Bassanio friends, and his purpose doubtless was so that he might deal once again with the theme of friendship and its relationship to romantic love; in the present play he raises that relationship to the ideal, presenting in perfect balance, as we shall see, the claims of the two themes. In *Il Pecorone* the Lady of Belmont tricks her suitors by giving them especially prepared wine which puts them to sleep. And this in turn causes them to lose all, for the agreement is that if they can possess the lady during the night, they shall win her and all that is hers; if not, they shall forfeit their possessions. Here Shakespeare made far-reaching changes. He completely recreated the Lady of Belmont, who in *Il Pecorone* is a widow, so that Portia represents those qualities of character which approach the ideal. And since the bedroom scenes of the source were inappropriate to her, he replaced them with the story of the caskets which he probably borrowed from the *Gesta Romanorum*.[17]

But why choose the story of the three caskets? "What," one critic asks, "in the name of all dramatic propriety and relevance are the casket scenes doing?" "They are," he believes, "irrelevant to the plot, and, apart from this negative needlessness, they are, from the point of view of the characterization of Bassanio, a positive nuisance."[18] On the contrary, Bassanio's test, his very choice, as well as his exposition of its meaning, define his character, but far more important that choice is opposed to the assumed choices which underlie Shylock's words and deeds. It is, of course, plain that Bassanio's trial is most immediately contrasted with Morocco's and Arragon's, and that contrast possesses its own relevance, but the choice of lead over gold and silver has a far wider application. We may add a further detail here which involves yet another change made by Shakespeare. In *Il Pecorone* in the evening of the third trial, Gianetto is warned by a maid against drinking the drugged wine which would have again put him to sleep. This aid to the lover on trial Shakespeare eliminated for the reason that he wished Bassanio to be fairly tested. The chief function of Nerissa's song is not to guide Bassanio, as some believe, but rather to contribute to the play's thematic unity by making the connection between love and gold, that is to say, by defining the true basis for choice, in love as well as in any other human activity.

IV

To this we shall return presently. For the moment we may look briefly into the related question of the play's dramatic unity. If it is true that the plot of a play is its controlling metaphor,[19] then whatever statement the play projects is expressed by the nature and relationship of the parts of that metaphor. But, like a metaphor, the plot must possess cohesion, its parts must be so related that they are mutually complementary, its various episodes must comment upon each other. In this special quality of its plot *The Merchant of Venice* testifies to Shakespeare's startling advance in dramaturgy. For here he achieves a cohesion of parts and a unity of the whole which far surpass what he had attained in his earlier comedies.

How is that cohesion attained in a play wherein the disparity of motives in the two main portions of the plot seems greater than that in any other Shakespearean comedy? How, that is, is the dramatist able to unify a plot combining the negative but powerful action of Shylock and his Rialto with the positive story of Portia and her Belmont? It has been said that romantic comedy places its emphasis upon the latter action whereas satiric comedy gives pre-eminence to the former, emphasizing the action of the antagonist, the force which obstructs and for long prevents the happy resolution which concludes the comic action.[20] Shakespearean romantic comedy in general does indeed minimize the role of the antagonist, scarcely defining his character and merely hinting at his motive, and throwing the forces of dramatic interest upon the lovers and their relationship. But in *The Merchant of Venice* this is not so, for it is plain that the antagonist here is the most forceful character in the comedy. His personality and motive are explored with far greater care and penetration than those of any other analogous character in the rest of Shakespeare's comedies. How, then, does Shakespeare manage to create a balance between the force and power of Shylock's role and the rest of the play? How does he achieve unity?

Since the problem facing the dramatist was unusual he brought to it an unusual solution. In other plays of two or more plots, he begins with the two plots in the opening scene, separates them in subsequent episodes, and in the concluding scene joins them together and brings the chief characters on the stage for a final happy reconciliation. In *The Merchant of Venice* the action begins in Venice with the two stories together: Bassanio, the lover on his way to Belmont, borrows from Antonio who borrows from Shylock; the play ends in Belmont without Shylock. The two plots come together not in the fifth act but in the fourth, where the mighty opposites confront each other for the first time. But here Portia plays the role required by the Shylock action, and the whole trial scene is concerned with the defeat of the antagonist, that is, with the negative motive of the play. As Act IV is laid in Venice and is concerned primarily with the antagonist, so Act V is laid in Belmont and is concerned with the protagonist and what she and Belmont symbolize.

In terms of content and location, the scenes of the play are arranged in a way which tends towards close interweaving and unity. The first act begins in Venice, takes us to Belmont in the second scene, and in the third returns us to Venice. The second act, following a reverse pattern, begins and ends in Belmont, with the middle scenes laid in Venice. The third act begins in Venice, moves to Belmont, returns to Venice, then ends with two scenes in Belmont. The fourth act is laid in Venice, the fifth in Belmont.[21] In the first three acts the action in Venice alternates with the story at Belmont, the two actions reaching a turning point at approximately the same time: the bond matures and is forfeited at the time of Bassanio's test at Belmont. News of Antonio's forfeiture and imminent danger reach Bassanio a few moments after he chooses the lead casket. The fourth act, though it brings together the two plots and their chief characters, deals with the antagonist's opposition to union and harmony in the social sphere, not with romantic love. The force of Shylock's part is so great that, with the exception of oblique allusions to the love theme, it requires the exclusive concentration provided by the fourth act. And when the antagonist has been disposed of, the fifth act concludes the play by stressing the union of lovers and the triumph of love, with one or two allusions to the Shylock theme.

This arrangement of the two actions, each operating in the main in its own *locus* but with thematic cross-connections, tends towards cohesion by maintaining an important relationship between the two themes. That relationship is, of course, one of contrast, a contrast symbolized by the opposition of Venice and Belmont. In the course of the action we are led to associate Venice with the Old Law, justice, commerce, and the public life; with Belmont we associate the New Law, mercy, love, and the private life.[22] But though these two possess individual integrity, they achieve significance in the play by being juxtaposed, for Shakespeare's ultimate aim is not to contrast them nor to keep them separate, but rather to bring them together so that their union represents the triumph of the values which underlie the romantic action.

In addition to this strategic disposition of contrasted scenes, the play utilizes contrast in the conception of characters and their relationships. Here the dramatist has accomplished an extraordinarily complex arrangement. Shylock is opposed to Antonio and Portia, and he is likewise contrasted with Jessica and Tubal; Antonio, besides opposing Shylock, is contrasted with Bassanio, who in turn is contrasted with both Gratiano and Lorenzo; the bond between Antonio and Bassanio is contrasted with the love of Bassanio and Portia; Bassanio and Portia are contrasted with Lorenzo and Jessica, and with Gratiano and Nerissa; Portia is contrasted with both Nerissa and Jessica. In these contrasts we note differences in the cast of mind and habit of thought, in the attitude towards certain values and ideals; and we note also significant differences in the mode of speech, in the idiom as well as the rhythm of language. Shylock speaks a direct, immediate, lucid prose and a staccato verse, innocent of metaphor, and his delivery in both prose and verse varies from soothing gentleness to driving, hammer-like violence.[23] Antonio's speech is quite different, less intense, more metaphorical, with a regular, not to say conventional, movement. Bassanio's speech is the most elegant, Gratiano's the most vulgar in the play.

Besides contrast between scenes and characters, the play

achieves unity through another device, that of similarity or analogy of parts or episodes. For instance the law of Belmont limiting Portia's role as lover is as severe as the Venetian law countenancing Shylock's bond. The letter of the bond is balanced by the letter of Bassanio's promise concerning the ring. As Antonio gives his all for Bassanio, so Bassanio vows he would sacrifice his life and all he cherishes, including Portia, and parts with the ring, symbol of all he possesses, to save Antonio. As Antonio responds to the claims of love by giving his all to aid Bassanio in winning Portia, so Portia responds to the claims of friendship and through her wealth and finally through her own mediation wins Antonio back for Bassanio. The laws of Venice countenance Shylock's bond, but they also condemn to death and confiscation of goods any alien proved to have intrigued against the life of a Venetian. Shakespeare added the latter so that in dealing with Shylock Portia might be able to show mercy by following the spirit instead of the letter of that law.[24]

These, then, are a few of the devices through which the dramatist achieves unity of structure and therefore of impression, that is, a proper emphasis in the statement of his theme, his chief idea or complex of ideas he has chosen to dramatize. The statement of that theme in dramatic form attains clarity and force in proportion as the structure achieves unity. In the present play, it is clear, Shakespeare has taken extraordinary pains to relate closely the parts of the plot or plots, the more so as the stories he found together in his sources, or combined himself, are not of the kind that can be easily joined. A critic of Shakespeare's play to whom we alluded earlier is annoyed by the presence of the casket scenes, which he considers irrelevant. His objection, though betraying a somewhat superficial view of the play, is understandable only if one considers the story of the bond as the chief concern of the play and everything else as unrelated episodes introduced for their own limited and isolated impression. But the main idea in the play cannot be expressed by either plot alone, even as the main idea in a play like *Henry IV* cannot be expressed without the contribution of its subplot. What Falstaff says and does in *Henry IV* is most carefully calculated by the poet for its comment upon the main action, and this comment is the chief reason for Falstaff's presence in the play. It might be added that his role bears some analogy to Shylock's not only because of their most necessary contribution to the poet's statement of his theme but also because of their excessive vitality, a vitality which threatens to throw off balance their respective plays. But what relates Falstaff and Shylock even more significantly is that in the structure of their plays they are not the chief characters; they are instead contributory, representing values or attitudes which bear a most pressing relevance to values or attitudes represented by the chief agents in their plays. It is Bassanio and the Prince, not Shylock or Falstaff, who must make the significant choices, and this fact establishes the relative importance of the four characters in the scheme of their plays. The analogy may be carried further. Both Bassanio and Prince Hal at first seem to incline towards the values represented by Shylock and Falstaff respectively, but both gradually change and finally reject those values in favor of a nobler point of view.[25] And if "change" is an inaccurate term, we might substitute development or better still revelation of character, a revelation brought about by the force of events and the pressure of experience. The analogy should not and need not be carried too far, but it is clear from what has been said that there is a general correspondence in the roles of the two pairs of characters, and that these were conceived and deployed in accordance with the same principle of dramatic structure and for the same general dramatic effects.

But the similarity in the roles of Falstaff and Shylock is a general one, and there are some important differences. Certainly Shylock is given a part which has a more immediate influence upon the fortunes of the hero. His role is more direct, more concentrated, especially as he must act in the narrower compass of one play instead of two. But both Shylock and Falstaff are the antagonists, deriving from the same parent theatrical stock; they are variations of the morality-vice of medieval dramatic tradition. And thus Shylock, like Falstaff, in spite of his great vitality, is not the hero of the play, that is to say, his role, though the most absorbing, must not tempt us into seeing the play as his tragedy, or even as his play. And it is a grievous error to disregard those parts of the comedy in which Shylock does not appear. In his essay on *The Merchant of Venice,* Professor Charlton makes no reference to the casket scenes, his chief concern being a defense of Shylock against Shakespeare's alleged bigotry. One is shocked to read that Shakespeare "planned a *Merchant of Venice* to let the Jew dog have it, and thereby to gratify his own patriotic pride of race."[26] What one objects to is not the notion that Shakespeare shared his contemporaries' bigotry concerning Jews, which may be true. What must be objected to is the critical judgment that Shakespeare planned his play for the purpose of attacking the "Jew dog" and thereby gratifying his "patriotic pride of race." Such a judgment is concerned with matters outside the play, for within the play Shylock acts a role designed exclusively for the exposition of certain attitudes which are opposed to those of the Venetians. Shylock's role is dramatic, part of a play dealing with the conflict between love and hate, mercy and justice, not with the conflict between Britons and Jews. Again, let it be borne in mind that such an attitude towards the play prevents one's seeing the comedy as a whole and leads instead to a defective consideration of only a portion of it. Certainly the casket scenes are as vital to the play as the trial scene of the fourth act; without Bassanio's test in Belmont there would not have been a trial scene at all, and this is meant not only in structural terms but also, and more importantly, in terms of theme. Nor can Bassanio's conduct in his choice of the lead casket admit his being called a subordinate character of "thick-skinned arrogance."[27]

This is neither detracting from Shylock's importance in the scheme of the play nor laying undue emphasis on Bassanio's. Shylock remains the most vital character, opposed to all the rest, an extraordinary dramatic creation, a creation far more powerful and affecting than the "role" intended for him strictly required. For that reason we shall return to him in a later section. Here it is enough to suggest that in terms of the play's structure he is a vital character but not the central one, a powerful antagonist, but not the hero of the comedy.[28] As we shall see, the attitudes represented by Shylock, greed, hate, insistence on the sterile letter of the law, distrust of revelry and music—all these must be rejected and replaced by their opposites before the action of the play can resume the projected fulfillment of the love story. For as in most of Shakespeare's comedies, so here, the culmination of the romantic story is a sort of metaphoric representation, a reflex of the triumph of love and harmony in the larger social sphere.

v

Having thus examined briefly the structure of *The Merchant of Venice,* we may now proceed to a consideration of certain important questions concerning the nature and meaning of the play. What sort of play is *The Merchant of Venice*? What is it about? What is Shylock's contribution to the exposition of its theme? And finally, what is the play's position in Shakespeare's search for a comic form which would best accommodate a love story?

Mindful of the play's powerful emotional impression, the most celebrated historian of Elizabethan drama called *The Merchant of Venice* a tragicomedy.[29] He thought it a play of "divided purpose," and believed that in its final impression "it is the emotional and not the critical attitude towards life which predominates."[30] The penetration with which Shakespeare looked into Shylock tends to justify the judgment that the play contains elements which distinguish it from Shakespeare's other comedies. But those elements differ from analogous matter in *Much Ado About Nothing* and *As You Like It* in degree, not in kind. And the success with which Shakespeare adjusted the force of Don John's and Oliver's actions in those plays is the reason why the two later comedies are more successful than *The Merchant of Venice.* The difference then lies in the improper balance between the romantic love story and the story of social or national or international strife which supplies the secondary, non-romantic interest in Shakespearean romantic comedy. Although Shakespeare placed exceptionally great stress on the non-romantic tale, the play nevertheless is a comedy of romantic love, its main action being the love and final union of Bassanio and Portia. It differs from the joyous comedies only in the degree of stress placed upon the antagonistic, non-romantic opposition to the love motive. For instance the love and union of Bassanio and Portia form the same kind of action as the love and final union of Orlando and Rosalind. The difference lies in the relative stress placed by the dramatist on the actions and influence of Oliver and the usurping Duke. The same can be said of the relationship between the love and final union of Claudio and Hero and the machinations of Don John in *Much Ado About Nothing*.

The *Merchant of Venice* is not a play on a race theme, though many critics have thought so, and although there can be no doubt that the Elizabethans showed distrust and dislike for the Jew the play is not necessarily directed towards prejudice. It is not "a drama of economic theme" although Bassanio shows momentarily a concern for Portia's dowry.[31] Nor is it a play about money or gold although these are given a significant role.[32] We must also reject the notion that what has been called the "realistic theme" of Shylock's bond story "portrays the downfall of hated usury and the triumph of Christian charity in the person of a princely merchant."[33] Christian charity is opposed to something much more powerful than usury, and that charity is not represented by the merchant Antonio even though he is willing to show some evidence of charity at the conclusion of the fourth act. And although it is true that in *The Merchant of Venice* Shakespeare "most faithfully conjures up the life and soul of an Italian city," it is going too far to say that "Venice herself is the protagonist."[34] *The Merchant of Venice* is about love, and in blending the bond story with the story of the caskets it enforces the Virgilian conviction that *Omnia vincit amor,* that in the romantic as well as the social sphere, love is the only means of achieving harmony and happiness and salvation. And this is the master-theme of all Shakespeare's comedies; it is the thought which underlies his whole work. Here in *The Merchant of Venice* the principle is crystallized in Portia's declaration that human action shows most god-like when it is tempered by mercy. In *As You Like It* the same concept is expressed in a different way by Hymen during the wedding ceremony:

> Then is there mirth in heaven,
> When earthly things made even
> Atone together.

Hymen's song is cited here to show that Shakespeare's comedies, though not sermons, express fundamental moral convictions. The song celebrates the wedding of the four couples by associating romantic with general love, by suggesting that the union of lovers represents—that it symbolizes—the conversion of Duke Frederick as well as Oliver's change of heart and reconciliation with Orlando. Beyond their own immediate union, the wedding of the lovers stands for a general atonement to be achieved through love; the wedding is the festive symbol of love's triumph, individual as well as social. That this is what *The Merchant of Venice* is about is made clear by Lorenzo's taking up the theme and expressing it in somewhat different terms in the garden scene of Act V.

But though the play is not primarily concerned with usury or race or religion, these form, nevertheless, significant thematic units employed by the dramatist in order to state his central idea. It must be added that usury or the love of money, one's attitude towards accumulating and possessing gold, is of far greater importance in the play than the race theme, although the latter has been raised by both critics and actors to a position of eminence unwarranted by the play. Because these subthemes contribute to the central idea, the student of the play needs to know what the Elizabethans thought and did about them. However, it would be an error to attempt an analysis of the play by relying exclusively on what we can learn of these two questions as the Elizabethans knew them. Our analysis—

our understanding—of the play may take account of contemporary problems which are reflected in the play, but it must ultimately be based on the lines within the play itself. Furthermore, Shylock is far more than a usurer. His ultimate concern is not with the interest on the loan he has made to Antonio but with Antonio's death. Shylock is not simply unwilling to forgive or cancel; he is most passionately seeking revenge for the losses he has suffered through Antonio's generous commercial practices.[35] The usurer in him ultimately becomes an avenging would-be murderer, a man driven by hate, a term often upon his tongue. The desire for profit through interest drives Shylock to seek Antonio's death. There are other motives such as Antonio's spurning him and spitting upon his Jewish gaberdine, but as Shylock himself admits the chief motive is that with Antonio out of the way he can make what profit he pleases.

Usury in Elizabethan times and its relation to contemporary literature has been the subject of much study, and the student may receive detailed information from a number of sources.[36] For our purpose it is enough to record some general conclusions about the matter. Speaking in broad terms we may say that the attitude of the Venetians in the play towards usury reflects the contemporary point of view. Both by tradition and recent experience the Elizabethans objected violently to usury, but although they opposed it in principle many were obliged to yield to it in practice. Not only the classics and the Bible but also recent and contemporary Church and government decrees stood utterly opposed to the practice of taking interest.[37] And yet it had been found necessary in 1545 to legalize 10 per cent interest, though that law was repealed by Edward VI shortly thereafter. In 1571 the need to impose some control on the outrageous rates exacted by usurers forced Elizabeth to legalize the same rate of 10 per cent, but the Queen's law nevertheless declared usury a sin. The need to borrow, both by the individual and the government, admitted usury in practice, but that admission was accompanied by violent attacks upon the principle of usury.[38]

Evidence of the violence with which usury was opposed is to be found in contemporary literature. Among popular writers whose work reflects bitter disapproval of the practice of usury are Stubbes, Nashe, Lodge, Greene, Chapman, Rowlands, Jonson, Middleton, Dekker, and others.[39] In the drama of the period the usurer is a common target of the dramatists' satire, and one scholar has counted seventy-one plays from 1553 to 1637 in which such satire can be found.[40] Shakespeare's own attitude towards usury is made clear in scattered passages throughout his work, from an incidental allusion to "forbidden usury" in Sonnet VI to the "pernicious usurer" in *1 Henry VI*[41] and the more persistent attacks in *Timon of Athens* and *The Winter's Tale*.[42] In short, Shakespeare's feelings about usury were no different from those of his fellow Elizabethans. And he may have shared the general concern of contemporary writers for the two groups which suffered most at the hands of usurers and pawnbrokers: the very poor, and the young gentlemen, prodigals easily gulled by unprincipled money-mongers.[43] Curiously enough, Shylock calls Antonio a prodigal,[44] and both Bassanio and Lorenzo associate the term with their own fortunes.

Whether Shakespeare was aware of the irony in the Elizabethans' (and Venetians') disapproval of usury in principle and their enforced practice of it cannot be inferred from his failure to explore such irony in the play.[45] Certainly Antonio is willing to borrow from a usurer although he passionately deplores Shylock's profession, and of course he cannot defend his inconsistency on the grounds that he is to pay no interest. Antonio has a far better defense than that, the need "to supply the ripe wants of my friend." In addition to evincing the sort of flexibility which Shylock utterly lacks, Antonio's willingness to "break a custom" is another mark of his devotion to Bassanio: borrowing from a usurer is one of the concessions he is willing to make so that his bosom friend may pursue his courtship of Portia. And on the other hand, Portia herself may appear to accede to the principle of usury when she tells Bassanio to pay the usurer six times the amount borrowed.[46] But in thus freely

offering her wealth she is simply providing the means of re-
leasing Bassanio's friend, "The semblance of my soul" she calls
him, from Shylock's bond; her offer is one of the sacrifices she is
willing to make to balance Antonio's sacrifice and not a concession to usury. There is, then, much less irony in the
Venetians' attitude towards usury than in the Elizabethans'
unrealistic point of view. But this is not the only reason why
Shakespeare did not pause to explore such irony. A far more
important reason is that he was intent upon stressing ironies
of a different sort in the world of the Venetians.[47] Furthermore, usury is not Shakespeare's chief concern in the play.
Shylock's profession and the related theme of accumulating
gold, the sterile possession of wealth—these matters, though of
deep interest to the Elizabethans, are employed by Shakespeare
as a metaphor, the correlative means of expressing the chief
idea in the play. The love of gold not only points to Shylock's
inability to love anything else but also identifies the kind of love
Nerissa defines in the song she sings while Bassanio contemplates the caskets. In another section we noted that in *Love's
Labour's Lost* Shakespeare seems to suggest that "as a man
speaks so he loves." In *The Merchant of Venice* one's attitude
towards gold tends to define his capability for love.

VI

We may turn now to the other sub-theme which critics have
emphasized somewhat unduly, the fact that Shylock is a Jew.
Why did Shakespeare make his usurer a Jew? One answer, of
course, is that he found him in the sources. The money-lender
in *Il Pecorone* is a Jew. And there was Marlowe's *Jew of Malta*.
But there is another reason and that is that by presenting a
Jewish usurer Shakespeare could enforce the point that the
usurer seems utterly different from the Venetians and that
his attitude towards gold, love, mercy, and the rest appears completely foreign to theirs. Shakespeare was intent upon presenting a pointed contrast between those within a society held
together by certain traditions and attitudes and the usurer who
stands outside it. It was for such a reason that Shakespeare

stressed Richard III's deformity and Edmund's illegitimacy. Now the most significant aspect of Shylock's character is that he is a usurer, and a usurer was thoroughly hated and continually vilified by the Elizabethans; he was a man beyond the pale. Not much different from this was the Elizabethans' attitude towards Jews. These were little known to Shakespeare's contemporaries, having been expelled from England in 1290. Although a few converts or pseudo-converts to Christianity had remained in England and although a scattering of others may have secretly entered the country in the sixteenth century, their number was far too small to offer the Elizabethans an opportunity of either firsthand knowledge or dislike of the Jewish character. For practical purposes Jews were strangers, exiles, alien to English society. And it may be true, as some scholars have suggested, that the word "Jew" had come to mean someone very different or strange, a dissenter, a foreigner, even a Christian usurer.[48] And this seems to be the chief meaning placed by Shakespeare upon the term and the character in the play. As a usurer and as a Jew, Shylock would thus be most pointedly contrasted not only with Antonio and the rest of the Venetians but also and most especially with Portia, who in the trial scene propounds ideal attitudes towards wealth and love and mercy which may be called Christian. This comes very near to saying that Shakespeare opposes the Jew and the Christian and that the play deals with the conflict between races and religions. It cannot be denied that any moral conflict can be referred to religious principle. But though Shylock's attitude as usurer and would-be murderer is opposed to the Christian-like charity and communal harmony enforced by the play's conclusion, it is not Shylock's race or religion that prompts his attitudes; his race and religion are nowhere on trial in the play. It is not Shylock's race that matters but what he says and does. The contrast between "devilish Macbeth" and the "most pious Edward" has nothing to do with the fact that one is Scottish and the other English. And the same can be said, and with more point, of the contrast and conflict between the Moor and Iago.[49]

This then is the significance of the Jewish usurer in the comedy. Shakespeare was far more seriously concerned with the dramatic function of Shylock's race and more especially his profession than with these matters *per se*. But at the same time we have seen that in order to make the two motives function successfully in the comedy Shakespeare had to take account of their meaning in his own society, the society for which the play was intended. For that society Richard III's evil nature was symbolized by his ill-formed body. Upon his entering the stage he elicited an instantaneous response of a special sort. Upon this conventional response no doubt Shakespeare depended for making certain important points concerning his hero. It is the same with the "Jewish usurer." The phrase had acquired a predictable impression upon an audience, even without special details of physiognomy or dress, details which the actor can very easily abuse. If it is true that the play is primarily concerned with the conflict between love and hate, we are bound to conclude that Shylock, who represents the latter, must be so conceived that the audience shall receive an instantaneous impression of both the nature and force of his representation. For that reason he is made a Jewish usurer. Or to turn it around, that is the reason a Jewish usurer is selected by the dramatist as the antagonist of Portia, the heroine of a love story.

This interpretation of Shylock's function can be demonstrated only by recourse to the lines of the play, and to these we shall go presently. But since his function is the basis for his characterization, we shall be considering the two together. Before doing so it is well to take note of at least a few of the many views expressed by critics concerning Shylock's character. And our comment on many of these views will be made together with the attempt to defend our interpretation of both Shylock's function and the characterization it calls for.

The brief mention of a few critical judgments concerning Shylock may begin with the notion that Shakespeare created two Shylocks in the play: the Shylock "of whom the Elizabethan pit, and Shakespeare amongst them, made such hearty mockery" is the one the dramatist intended; the other, the Shylock who "wrings the withers of a modern audience," is what he became through Shakespeare's "unconscious dramatic instinct."[50] The critic believes that this is precisely what took place in the composition of *Paradise Lost,* which, contrary to Milton's intention "emerges almost as a paean to Satan."[51] The analogy from *Paradise Lost* may be sufficient comment upon the interpretation it is intended to support. However, it may be added that although characters change most profoundly in Shakespeare's hands, their change or development appears on the whole to be part of the poet's conscious and deliberate plan. But this is not what takes place here, for Shylock does not change; he merely affects audiences in different ways. The interesting thing is that there is one Shylock for Shakespeare's original audience and another for a modern one. But since the critic and his modern audience object rather violently to the first Shylock, is it not possible that Shakespeare's initial audience would object with equal vigor to the second? There are indeed two audiences but one Shylock. Or, if there seem to be two of them, they must surely be the product of deliberate design. That a Shakespearean character may affect an audience —a single audience—in two ways is not difficult to demonstrate. One of the readiest examples is the way in which an audience responds to the actions of Richard II and Bolingbroke in *Richard II.* In the first half of the play the audience's sympathy goes to Bolingbroke, while Richard II elicits whole-hearted disapprobation. From the middle of the play to the end there is a complete reversal. Furthermore, an audience's simultaneously conflicting responses to a hero's conduct is one of the most obvious features of Shakespearean characterization. Thus it is with Henry V, Hamlet, Caesar, Lear, Brutus, and Coriolanus, to name only a few. It is the same with Shylock. For it is not true, as some would have it, that Shylock is exceptional in being the only Shakespearean character who fails to elicit sympathy.[52] There is no warrant in the play for the interpretation of a Shylock who "wrings the withers of a modern audience"; but there can be little doubt that in certain well-known passages Shylock for a brief moment or two evokes, if not our full sympathy, at least our understanding of his motives. This does not include our approbation of his thirst for revenge. But there is another way whereby an audience's adverse attitude towards Shylock is momentarily modified, and that is by ironic overtones in the words or actions of the Venetians. For instance one of the pointedly ironic passages about Jessica is spoken by Lorenzo while she is making ready to elope with him. She calls to him from above:

Jessica. I will make fast the doors, and gild myself
With some moe ducats, and be with you straight.
Gratiano. Now, by my hood, a Gentile and no Jew.
Lorenzo. Beshrew me but I love her heartily;
For she is wise, if I can judge of her,
And fair she is, if that mine eyes be true,
And true she is, as she hath prov'd herself. . . .

(II, vi, 49-55)

Launcelot's reasons for leaving Shylock's household to take service with Bassanio create further, though again limited, sympathy for Shylock. Launcelot chooses to transfer his services because no man in Italy, he says, has a "fairer table" than Bassanio, and also because his household offers Launcelot greater opportunity for illicit affairs with the maids, one of whom he gets with child before the play's end.[53] Another device for creating some sympathy for Shylock is the abuse he receives at the hands of the Venetians, particularly Gratiano.

In presenting Shylock, Shakespeare aimed at suggesting, if not justifications for his thirst for revenge, at least some of the motives; and to this he added an ironic criticism of certain actions and attitudes of the Venetians. The result is that there are moments in the play when we are made to see why Shylock is what he is and why he pursues Antonio's life. But it must be added that at no time in the course of the action are we intended by the dramatist to approve or even feel sympathy for Shylock's thirst for revenge. In the play as we have it, then, there is one Shylock, a complex being, but a single character, not two.

It would be unwise and profitless to comment further upon or even cite more than a few critical judgments on Shylock's character. Briefly, then, here are some of those judgments. Shylock is a "forthright man, fearless and high-minded,"[54] tricked by Portia who, knowing that he is an alien, "leads Shylock on to refuse the money . . . , then making that beautiful but tainted plea for mercy."[55] Another view insists that we cannot blame Shylock for scheming revenge against Antonio.[56] Shylock's proceedings show little cunning, another critic argues.[57] And when Salarino says that if Antonio should forfeit the bond, Shylock would not take his flesh, Shylock in reply "is moved to a revelation of his profound humanity, his sense of the community of Jew and Gentile. . . ."[58] But how far the same critic has misunderstood Shakespeare's conception of Shylock is shown in the following. There "are a few moments in each day," says Professor Charlton, "when [Shylock] can withdraw into the secluded domain of his own spiritual life, and in the sanctuary of his own house, protect himself from profanation by the Gentiles. . . ."[59] In yet another passage we read that "ducats are more to Shylock than mere material possessions. They are the only means by which, in an alien world, he preserves a refuge for the true life of his own spirit."[60]

These judgments are cited here to show the extent to which a "romantic" or sentimental interpretation of Shylock can distort the play's integrity. If this is Shylock's true character, what is his function in the play? Why is he opposed by Portia in the trial scene? How can a person with Shylock's alleged profound humanity and spiritual life conduct himself as Shylock does in his confrontation with Portia? How can we adjust this conception of Shylock's character to these lines in the play?

> I hate him for he is a Christian.
> But more for that in low simplicity
> He lends out money gratis, and brings down

The rate of usance here with us in Venice.
If I can catch him once upon the hip,
I will feed fat the ancient grudge I bear him.

(I, iii, 43-48)

How can Professor Charlton's Shylock be reconciled with the
man who would use Antonio's pound of flesh "to bait fish
withal"? It is strange indeed that the sentimental interpretation of Shylock has persisted in spite of Stoll's demonstration, a
half century ago, that such a conception is both unhistorical
and extra-dramatic.[61] But in opposing the view which inter-
prets Shylock as a pathetic figure, Stoll, in the same essay,
went to the opposite extreme in seeing him as a comic figure,
a comic villain. Another critic offers the related theory that
Shylock is conceived in the tradition of the Pantaloon of the
commedia dell' arte: the absurd old man on whom the clown
plays his tricks.[62] No doubt there are superficial or accidental
similarities, and it is true that little boys in Venice jeer at
Shylock in the streets, but these details do not make him a
comic character. He is far too serious a conception, and his
passion is "so confused / So strange, outrageous, and so vari-
able" that the dramatist's intention could scarcely have been
comic. But it must be admitted that although in the total view
Shylock is not a comic villain, there are brief episodes which
exhibit him in a comic light. By common consent the scene
with Tubal is the best and perhaps sole significant illustration
of such comic action. Professor C. L. Barber has expressed
with precision the principle involved here, namely the flat
presentation of a Shylock reduced to the rigidity of mechanism.
Tubal, by giving him good news about Antonio's losses and bad
news about Jessica's squandering his ducats, causes Shylock to
dance "like a jumping jack in alternate joy and sorrow as
Tubal pulls the strings."[63] Although the episode represents
most successfully Shylock's rigidity, there are other instances
of it, for example his unbending opposition to revelry and
music, his conscious banishing of all imagery from his speech
("Water-thieves—I mean pirates," "my house's ears, I mean

my casements"), his iterative, echo-like, and persistent fixity upon the cold letter of the law. His is the sort of rigidity which some theoreticians associate with laughter. But the laughter in one or two episodes and in the general conception of the character is not hilarious; the force of Shylock's passion reduces to a minimum both laughter and the occasional note of pathos which Shakespeare adroitly introduces into his lines. Shylock is far too menacing to be laughed at long or heartily, and he is not sufficiently grotesque to be ridiculous. In short the comic is an incidental detail, a by-product of certain episodes, not a fundamental aspect inherent in Shakespeare's conception of the character.[64] A comical Shylock would scarcely need to be opposed by so grave and compelling an attitude as underlies Portia's speech on mercy. Again, as in all of Shakespeare's comedies, the structure of the play dictates the function of character, which in turn determines characterization.

Shylock's function in the play is to oppose and directly threaten the harmony represented by Belmont. If this is admitted, then Shylock's characterization must be so fashioned that he will most effectively furnish such opposition and threat. For this neither a pathetic nor a comic Shylock will do. But neither will an inhuman villain, for such a character would fail to provide opposition in human or credible terms. Nowhere in the play is Shylock shown to be bent on some evil act for its own sake; he is after revenge, and revenge is a human response to a human stimulus.[65] Revenge he seeks with terrifying singleness of mind, and in that passionate search he rejects mercy, that is, he refuses to be swayed by love in disposing of Antonio's bond. In this rejection and refusal, like many another villain or tragic hero in Shakespeare—but like no comic character—Shylock would violate his human nature. For evil, in this instance desire for revenge, is antagonistic to and a violation of the natural law inherent in man's being. That this is what happens—that Shylock would violate that law within his being—is made clear throughout the play but most pointedly in the trial scene. And the most telling expression of it is provided by the imagery, the very imagery we meet in the passages which define evil in Shakespeare's tragedies.

Early in the scene in his editorial comments the Duke recalls for Shylock and the court the general conviction that it is "brassy bosoms and rough hearts of flint" that will not be "touch'd with humane gentleness and love." Shylock, a few lines later, is made to associate his "lodg'd hate" for Antonio and his thirst for revenge with the serpent. Then Antonio himself gathers together the most striking images in the scene and through them points the extent to which hatred and lust for vengeance have violated Shylock's nature:

> You may as well go stand upon the beach
> And bid the main flood bate his usual height;
> You may as well use question with the wolf
> Why he hath made the ewe bleat for the lamb. . . .
>
> (IV, i, 71-74)

These images are repeated by Gratiano, who in a single line calls Shylock's desires "wolvish, bloody, starv'd, and ravenous." (l. 138) These are not merely the sort of images we find in Shakespearean tragedy; they are its central images. Whether employed in describing "these hard hearts" of Lear's daughters or the dark purposes of Edmund or Macbeth and his "fiend-like queen," these images become Shakespeare's indispensable means of pointing to the enormity of man's self-violation through evil. For Shakespeare that self-violation is the lapse into the subhuman, the bestial, into the uninstructed blind forces of elemental nature. In this very context Shakespeare places his Shylock, and a Shylock fit for such context can, in the total view of him, be neither pathetic nor noble nor comic. He must be one representing hate and through it revenge, that is, those forces in the dark depths of man's consciousness which oppose love and mercy and forgiveness.

The action of the play presents the conflict between love and its antithesis, and whereas the latter is represented in the main by a single character, the former is acted out by a number of persons. In Shylock the dramatist represents in their utmost concentration the thirst for revenge, the lust for possession, the neither giving nor forgiving, the complete rejection of what are called "human values." What keeps Shylock from seeming an abstraction are the human motives we referred to above, motives which, be it remembered, may explain his acts without justifying them. On the other side at least three characters represent giving and forgiving. That theme is dramatized by Antonio's generosity to Bassanio as well as to those to whom "he lends out money gratis"; it is expressed also in Bassanio's choice of the lead casket, which is preceded by a formal exposition of the principle which underlies it; and it is most forcefully stated by Portia in the trial scene, wherein she sets down the principle of love, of giving, and merciful forgiving in contrast to Shylock's insistence on revenge.[66]

Now the opposition between Shylock and Antonio in the early scenes of the play and between Shylock and Portia in the trial scene has to do with the bond story, with love or its opposite as it operates in social intercourse. But there is another conflict in which Shylock is involved, though not directly on the stage, and that is the scene of Bassanio's trial. As we noted earlier, here the obvious contrast is between Bassanio's giving and hazarding all for love and Morocco's and Arragon's failures: Morocco confuses external show with truth and beauty, whereas Arragon "assumes desert," that is, he insists upon receiving what he believes he deserves. Bassanio rejects both the insistence on receiving and the choice on the basis of external show, and thus indirectly demonstrates through the choice of the lead casket that he is Portia's true love. But the choice of gold and silver by Morocco and Arragon, and the choice of lead by Bassanio are made to recall and comment upon Shylock's love of gold and his insistence upon receiving instead of giving. In this scene, then, he is presented in opposition to Bassanio, and the conflict between them is far more significant than that between Bassanio and the other suitors. Whereas the latter conflict serves to give meaning to Bassanio's choice, the implied conflict with Shylock has a structural as well as thematic significance, for it contributes to considerable unity of impression, a desideratum for a successful play second to none. That impression can be expressed simply by saying that Bassanio's choice would not be Shylock's. The link between the two is enforced upon our consciousness not only by the attractiveness and external worth of gold and silver, which Bassanio rejects, but more directly through the scrolls within the gold and silver caskets. That in the gold casket reads in part:

> All that glisters is not gold;
> Often have you heard that told.
> Many a man his life hath sold
> But my outside to behold.
>
> (II, vii, 65-68)

And in the silver casket:

> Some there be that shadows kiss,
> Such have but a shadow's bliss.
> There be fools alive, iwis,
> Silver'd o'er; and so was this.
>
> (II, ix, 66-69)

It is clear that aside from their immediate relevance the passages serve as comments upon the usurer's most absorbing preoccupation.

But although Bassanio's trial has relevance to the bond story, his chief role is as a romantic lover, whose "choice" must carry significance in matters of romantic love. The burden of his speech before choosing is stated in the second line: "The world is still deceived with ornament." Bassanio is not so deceived and indeed chooses "that within which passeth show"; he is eager not merely to receive but also to give. These are his very words when, after his choice, he is instructed by the scroll to claim his lady "with a loving kiss":

> Fair lady, by your leave;
> I come by note, to give and to receive.
>
> (III, ii, 140-41)

The relevance of Bassanio's choice to matters of romantic love, implicit in that choice and the words which accompany it, is stated directly in Nerissa's song.[67]

> Tell me where is fancy bred.
> Or in the heart or in the head?
> How begot, how nourished?
>   Reply, reply.
>
> It is engend'red in the eyes,
> With gazing fed; and fancy dies
> In the cradle where it lies. . . .[68]

Though beauty is first carried to the lover's consciousness by the eyes, he must not choose by the view, for that is not true love's way. For love as the attraction based on the external dies and is forgotten in its infancy. Love is not love which thus begins and shortly ends. True love begins with the eyes but proceeds to consider the beloved with the eyes of the mind, whereby in a series of steps guided in turn by sense, reason, and understanding, it may reach the state of perfect happiness which in Shakespeare is usually symbolized by music. In turn the lovers' happiness or harmony is but the analogue to a universal union and harmony, the harmony which is at one with the music of the spheres, that is to say, the harmony implicit in the Divine. For expressing this union of Christian and Platonist conceptions Shakespeare provided Lorenzo with one of the most lyrical passages in the play:

> Sit, Jessica. Look how the floor of heaven
> Is thick inlaid with patines of bright gold.
> There's not the smallest orb which thou behold'st
> But in his motion like an angel sings,
> Still quiring to the young-ey'd cherubins.
> Such harmony is in immortal souls;
> But whilst this muddy vesture of decay
> Doth grossly close it in, we cannot hear it.

(V, i, 58-65)

The music of the spheres which echoes within man's immortal soul can be heard only through love, the true love which unites man and woman, and that other larger union of all men into a universal communion.

Shylock seems far from this, but, though absent, he is not utterly banished from Belmont. His absence is, of course, most significant, but the humanity which Shakespeare gave him, though self-violated, may reassert itself and thus respond to that same harmony which he had earlier rejected. This is not interpolating the dramatist's intentions: it is stated in Lorenzo's lines on the power of music:

> For do but note a wild and wanton herd,
> Or race of youthful and unhandled colts,
> Fetching mad bounds, bellowing and neighing loud,
> Which is the hot condition of their blood,
> If they but hear perchance a trumpet sound,
> Or any air of music touch their ears,
> You shall perceive them make a mutual stand,
> Their savage eyes turn'd to a modest gaze
> By the sweet power of music; therefore the poet
> Did feign that Orpheus drew trees, stones, and floods;
> Since nought so stockish, hard, and full of rage,
> But music for the time doth change his nature.
>
> (V, i, 71-82)

The bestial, then, with which Shylock was associated by means of imagery in the trial scene, can be elevated and brought back to the human through music, that is, through love.

And here we may pause briefly to note that the contrast between Shylock and the Venetians is not absolute: it is not expressed in sharp and clear-cut opposition of black and immaculate white. The reason for this is that Shakespeare sees both sides not as static but as potential principles, and "potential" is the term which best describes the ending of Shakespearean romantic comedy. In such comedy what the happy and harmonious conclusion of the story or stories represents is not an attempt to record actuality. What it represents is the imaginative fulfillment of what is possible and desirable in human experience: the perfection or ideal which Shakespearean comedy projects is a potential, not a fact. The world of the Venetians is not perfect, though it is potentially so, and it attains perfection after it has been transferred to Belmont. Thus Belmont is a symbol not of what is but of what is achievable if men will allow love and charity and mercy and forgiveness to guide their actions. Professor Wilson is surely right in insisting that Portia's speech on mercy, though addressed to Shylock, is not intended for him or his beliefs alone. It was composed, Professor Wilson believes, "to knock at Christian hearts."[69]

That the Christians of Venice, though contrasted with Shylock, are not perfect is clearly an important theme in the play, although it is treated mainly in indirect and ironic fashion. Shylock's speeches defending his thirst for revenge suggest that the conduct of his opposites is not always defensible. Antonio is too violent in his spurning and bespitting him, Salarino and Salerio too callous in their jeering him, Gratiano too strident in his taunts. In addition, Shakespeare hints at the imperfection of the Venetians in ironic passages, some of them alluded to earlier. But perhaps the clearest example is the brief passage between Jessica and Launcelot:

Jessica.   I shall be sav'd by my husband. He hath made me a Christian.
Launcelot. Truly, the more to blame he; we were Christians enow before; e'en as many as could well live, one by another. This making of Christians will raise the price of hogs. If we grow all to be pork-eaters, we shall not shortly have a rasher on the coals for money.

(VIII, v, 21-28)

In his lines on the music of the spheres and the harmony within "immortal souls," Lorenzo, or rather Shakespeare through him, admits no racial or religious distinctions in his comment that

> . . . whilst this muddy vesture of decay
> Doth grossly close it in, we cannot hear it.

The contrast between Shylock and the Venetians is there but it is not absolute, and this is the reason why over-schematic interpretations of that contrast can be misleading.[70] Nor is Belmont the symbol of an exclusively Christian paradise, although Shakespeare associates it with prayers and holy men, for along with these the final act brings to the speeches of Jessica and Lorenzo the most concentrated classical allusions in Shakespearean comedy. In these lines, as well as in Bassanio's trial, there is a happy union of Christian and Platonic ideals, but they are ideals for the Venetians as well as Shylock. Shylock's narrow world may be contrasted with the freer world of the Venetians, but there is an even more significant contrast between these two on the one hand and Belmont on the other. The achievement of Belmont is far more significant than Shylock's enforced conversion.

Belmont is also, and more immediately, the symbol of that perfect happiness achieved by the lover whose love transcends the attraction of external beauty. But this Neoplatonic projection is likewise an ideal towards which the lover aspires. And as in his other comedies, so here Shakespeare adjusts that longing for the ideal to human imperfection. To this he gives over much of the final act of the play, particularly the affair of the rings. Earlier in this chapter we alluded to the structural function of the ring episode, namely that it enables Bassanio to give his all for Antonio, which he does by sacrificing the ring, the token of his possession of Portia and all that is hers. The episode also offers Portia the occasion for insisting, briefly and in a happy context, on the letter of Bassanio's promise never to part with the rings. But the action involving the rings serves another purpose, a purpose never absent in Shakespearean comedy. That purpose is to introduce realistic, here bawdy, motifs into the romantic atmosphere of Belmont, and by so doing to qualify the idealized union of the lovers.

Shakespeare begins this "reduction" of idealized love in the

opening scene of Act V, in the classical allusions to lovers' betrayal, fickleness, frailty, and even tragedy. This is the important function of the lines telling about Troilus's sighing
his soul "toward the Grecian tents / Where Cressid lay that
night." And those other lines about Dido and Medea and
Thisbe—unhappy lovers all—are brought into the splendid
scene of romance for the same purpose. And after this introductory and oblique statement of the motif Shakespeare resumes the story of the rings, and in its conduct he makes Portia
and Nerissa first accuse their husbands of infidelity, then pretend that they themselves had violated their vows and that they
received their rings back by lying with the doctor and the
"scrubbed boy, the doctor's clerk." In all this a strongly bawdy
context is maintained by the double-entendre of the ubiquitous
ring. And the two motifs of fickleness and bawdry are united
in Gratiano's concluding fling:

> But were the day come, I should wish it dark,
> Till I were couching with the doctor's clerk.
> Well, while I live I'll fear no other thing
> So sore as keeping safe Nerissa's ring.

The Merchant of Venice is the last comedy before the climactic triad, the so-called joyous comedies, and in that position
it seems to conclude the long experimental period. Though
like *A Midsummer Night's Dream* it demonstrates an extraordinary advance over earlier plays in both structure and characterization, its central idea is not perfectly implicit in its structure. The reason for this is that Shylock and the bond story
cannot be completely assimilated into the comic conclusion;
the link between the bond story and the rest of the plot—one's
attitude toward or use of wealth—that link offers only a partial
analogy to the romantic theme. We noted earlier that Bassanio's choice is structurally and thematically related to Shylock's attitude towards gold, and that the relationship can be
stated in this manner: Bassanio's choice would not be Shylock's. But Shylock's choice is between gold and human values
whereas Bassanio's has to do with the conflict between external

appearance and inner worth as the guide to true love. Shylock's choice leads him to self-violation, whereas Bassanio's leads him to self-realization. Between the two choices there is of course a connection, but the two cannot be identified, and the division between the Rialto and Belmont, in spite of the many structural links, remains to the end. Even Portia's symbolic journey to Venice and her confrontation with Shylock cannot completely bridge that division. Although both ultimately argue for the letter of the law, neither is really concerned with it but rather with something else. Shylock calls upon the law to sanction his plea for revenge, whereas Portia turns to the same instrument to justify her desire for mercy: revenge and mercy are their chief concerns. Furthermore, it should be noted that Shylock never meets Portia, never hears of her, never discovers the identity of the young doctor who defeats his designs upon Antonio, and the reason for this (other than the need of the ring episode for Portia's disguise) must have been the dramatist's unwillingness to identify Portia with the bond story. Portia is needed in both plots, but her two roles, though related, are very different. As she does not really belong in the bond story—she appears in it disguised—so Shylock, as we noted earlier, cannot be made part of the romantic tale of Belmont. A comparison of *The Merchant of Venice* with *Measure for Measure* reveals the latter's superior integration of thematic components. Here Angelo is not only intent upon the letter of the law, refusing to admit mercy into his judgment of Claudio, but he is himself a man who on the one hand has rejected the love of Mariana and on the other has committed the same act for which he has doomed Claudio to death. And in the trial scene of the play he is saved by the interposition of both Isabella and Mariana, both of whom, in act or intention, he has wronged.

In spite of such minor imperfections, *The Merchant of Venice* marks an advance in Shakespearean romantic comedy by virtue of its treating, and therefore in a sense disposing of, certain themes which Shakespeare had attempted in earlier plays. One of these themes is the use of wealth as a metaphor for the expression of human relationships, a metaphor employed, as we have seen, in *The Comedy of Errors* and more extensively in *The Taming of the Shrew*. That motif receives its ultimate statement in *The Merchant of Venice*. Another motif given a final expression in the play is the question with which Nerissa opens her song during Bassanio's test. The nature of true love, directly described in the sonnets, is here obliquely defined by its opposite, superficial and short-lived fancy based on externals, and also by Bassanio's choice as well as by his exposition of its meaning. But the whole episode has a theoretical quality, for Bassanio's choice of the lead casket and his comment upon it are not made relevant to his own falling in love, his own election of Portia. Nevertheless his speech, together with Nerissa's song, provides a reply to the question raised in *A Midsummer Night's Dream*. The attraction effected through the eyes alone—and these are susceptible to the errant influences of magic juices—is love which "alters when it alteration finds." True love, as Nerissa's song and Bassanio's speech imply, is based not on external beauty alone but on attraction from within as well. By refusing to be guided merely by the eyes, that is, by the appetite of sense, and by turning from sense to reason and the understanding, the lover may hope to move from the immediate experience of physical attraction to the mystic realm of oneness with the divine. This is the clearest expression so far achieved by Shakespearean comedy of the Neoplatonist concept of love. And reinforcing this statement by Nerissa's song and Bassanio's choice is yet another Platonic concept, the notion that, like love, virtue may enable mortal man to break through "the muddy vesture of decay" and, like the "youngey'd cherubins," at last hear the mystic harmonies of the moving spheres. This idealization of love is never absent from Shakespearean romantic comedy. Whether stated or merely implied, it is the object of men's longing, of their aspiration towards ultimate perfection and purification, in short, the realization of man's angelic possibilities. But Shakespeare stresses the longing, not the state itself, and moreover he unfailingly presents that longing against human limitation: hence the juxtaposition of romantic sentiments with bawdry, fickleness, frailty, betrayal, greed, hate.

These, then, are the points wherein *The Merchant of Venice* records an advance in Shakespeare's development of his peculiar comic mode. Although its structure is managed with great skill, the play fails to achieve perfect unity of impression. In this one respect *The Merchant of Venice* is inferior to *A Midsummer Night's Dream*. It is superior in structure, in the penetrating conception of Shylock's character, and in its verse. And in addition it records Shakespeare's preoccupation with certain motifs which henceforth will appear in his later comedies as contributory elements, not as subjects of exploration. That exploration is conducted in *The Merchant of Venice*.

Much Ado About Nothing

Chapter VII

I

Of the three "joyous" comedies *Much Ado About Nothing* has been called the least perfect by reason of its alleged failure to integrate successfully the two stories which make up its plot. Strangely enough in this particular point it is thought to be less perfect than *The Merchant of Venice,* although in truth it far surpasses that play in excellence of structure and unity of tone, as well as in the relative emphasis it places upon the love story and the antagonistic motive represented by Don John. In *The Merchant of Venice,* as we saw in the preceding chapter, unusually heavy emphasis is placed on that part of its plot which deals with strife and conflict, that is, with the ab-

sence of love in human relationships, a theme Shakespeare
made indispensable in his comic structure. But in the proportion of that emphasis the romantic theme of the play seems
to suffer relative neglect. For instance there is wooing in *The
Merchant of Venice* but the only extensive instance of it occurs in the opening of Act V, and by that time Lorenzo has
won the heart of Jessica; for that reason their scene in the
gardens of Belmont, though one of wooing, has the air of recapitulation. If we now turn to the Bassanio-Portia love story
we shall find something very similar to this. Their wooing consists of a brief encounter before Bassanio addresses himself to
the caskets. In the whole scene Portia's role is completely passive, while Bassanio's great speech preceding his choice has the
air of semi-formal definition. It is true that in addition to defending the choice of the leaden casket the speech extends the
idea of Nerissa's song and thus suggests the nature of true love.
But in truth Bassanio's own courtship has scant occasion to
mature an external attraction into the ideal attachment which,
as he says, is based on inner beauty and worth. What is crucial
here is Bassanio's reason for his choice. And although the
speech further insists that in love also choice should be based
on something more than external beauty, the idea is not made
part of Bassanio's own experience of falling in love with Portia.
Bassanio wins her without wooing her, and although she had
given him "fair speechless messages," there is a cold, almost
mechanical quality in his winning her. In short, she is not won
through wooing, and this in a romantic comedy must be
accounted a deficiency. But it is a deficiency the dramatist will
not allow us to notice in the acting of the play, for he engages
our interest in absorbing action of one sort or another, including an elopement, which in a love comedy is a great asset.

Now love based on external attraction only is taken up in
Much Ado About Nothing and made part of the Claudio-Hero
story, where Claudio, having seen Hero, wishes to make her his
wife but is unwilling to woo her and instead enlists Don Pedro
to do his wooing for him. And here it appears we have yet
another motive which one would find alien to the spirit of

romantic comedy. But there is wooing enough in the play, though of a special sort, in the love affair of Benedick and Beatrice. The point here made is that *Much Ado About Nothing* has rather strong and intriguing connections with *The Merchant of Venice,* at least with its romantic action. Furthermore, we may note that the play takes up a theme attempted in *Love's Labour's Lost* but here given a fuller treatment both in scope and quality. This is the rejection or pretended rejection of romantic love and wedlock by Benedick and Beatrice, a theme repeated in Phoebe's attitude in *As You Like It* and Olivia's in *Twelfth Night.* It is indeed a fundamental, an indispensable, motive of Shakespearean romantic comedy, and its absence in *The Merchant of Venice* is a further deficiency of its romantic action. Finally, *Much Ado About Nothing* carries further than any other comedy before it the attempt to elicit from its audience highly complex responses to its stage action, something Shakespeare had achieved in good measure in *The Merchant of Venice.*

II

As with the other two "joyous" comedies, the question of dating *Much Ado About Nothing* is not a difficult one. The date of its composition must be 1598-99, since Kempe, who played Dogberry, left Shakespeare's company in the spring of 1599,[1] and since the play is not included in the list of Shakespeare's plays cited by Francis Meres in his *Palladis Tamia,* which was completed in September, 1598. Furthermore, on August 4, 1600, *Much Ado About Nothing,* together with three other plays of the Chamberlain's Company, was ordered "to be staied," and since one of those plays was *As You Like It,* which in date almost certainly followed *Much Ado,* the date of the latter must be 1598-99.[2] That the play as we have it was completed in 1598-99 there is at present general agreement among scholars, including the editors of the New Cambridge Shakespeare, who hold that late in 1598 or early in 1599 Shakespeare produced the received text by recasting an old play of his own.[3] The arguments advanced to support the theory are unconvincing, and they have been answered by a number of scholars.[4] But the theory of revision need not concern us here since that alleged revision is said to have occurred in 1598-99, the date assigned the play on other grounds. What concerns us is the text as we have it, that is, the comedy Shakespeare gave his audience in 1598-99. Whether revised or not, the play falls in date somewhere between the composition of *The Merchant of Venice* and *As You Like It*.

Happily the question of the play's sources offers no serious difficulty to the student, for the matter has been thoroughly studied by Professor Charles T. Prouty, whose conclusions concerning Shakespeare's materials are generally accepted.[5] And although it is important to know precisely what source or sources Shakespeare used in writing his play, what he did with his materials—how he reshaped them—is much more revealing. No matter which of the more than a dozen versions of the Claudio-Hero story Shakespeare employed—he most probably used more than one—he made changes in the motives of the chief persons as well as in their characterization. One of the most striking is that whereas in the sources the slanderer is both the lover's rival and friend, Shakespeare rejected the love-friendship theme and instead made Don John a character unrelated to either Claudio or Hero. But he gave him something of a motive for hating Claudio and for desiring to harm him and thwart his marriage. Claudio, says Don John, is "that young start-up" who "hath all the glory of my overthrow" (I, iii, 62). This is not as strong a motive as that of a rival in love, but it is at least sufficient to place Don John's intrigue within the limits of probability. Shakespeare had very recently delved into the depths of Shylock's motives with such penetration and power that Shylock seems to have usurped complete dominance over his play. Here, Don John's motives were not, as were Shylock's, so important to the action: what was important was the response from Claudio and Don Pedro and Benedick and Beatrice which Don John's intrigue elicited.

But why did Shakespeare reject the love-friendship theme

which appears in all three of his major presumed sources? In making changes and in reinterpreting his materials was he reacting to the ideas and characters of his sources, as Professor Prouty believes?[6] It is more likely that Shakespeare's changes were required by the overriding theme which he had chosen to express in the play. For instance, the reason why Shakespeare refused to make Hero's slanderer a friend to Claudio is not that the love-friendship theme had by 1598 become stale. The reason is that it had already been satisfactorily treated in *The Merchant of Venice*. Professor Prouty argues that though the "idea" appears in *The Merchant of Venice,* there is no conflict; "the bond is not forfeit because of Bassanio's love for Portia."[7] Though it is true that Bassanio's love for Portia is not the cause of Antonio's forfeiting the bond, it is the cause of his signing such a bond. In that play the conflict between love and friendship is resolved in mutual sacrifice on the part of Antonio and Portia; the claims of love and friendship are satisfied by the happy exchange of giving. And the ideal relationship of the two is nowhere in Shakespeare expressed as beautifully as in Portia's lines:

> for in companions
> That do converse and waste the time together,
> Whose souls do bear an egal yoke of love,
> There must be needs a like proportion
> Of lineaments, of manners, and of spirit;
> Which makes me think that this Antonio,
> Being the bosom lover of my lord,
> Must needs be like my lord. If it be so,
> How little is the cost I have bestow'd
> In purchasing the semblance of my soul
> From out the state of hellish cruelty!

(III, iv, 11-21)

After so clear a statement of the ideal relationship of love and friendship—and Shakespeare was ultimately concerned with presenting the achievable ideal in the comedies—he may have been unwilling to return to the treatment of a theme he had attempted in *The Two Gentlemen of Verona,* a treatment scarcely satisfactory to him.

Having achieved a happy resolution of the friendship-love theme in *The Merchant of Venice,* Shakespeare would thenceforth employ that theme as a minor motif in the comedies which followed. In *Much Ado About Nothing* that motif is inserted twice into the action, both instances involving Claudio, once in his relationship to Don Pedro and later in his relationship to Benedick. In both instances, it should be noted, the movement points initially in the direction of tragic resolution since love seems to win over friendship. But in comedy such resolution would be antagonistic to the main purpose of the play; and on the other hand the supremacy of friendship over love, though contributing to a happy dénouement, is equally inappropriate in a romantic comedy. Having successfully resolved that dilemma in *The Merchant of Venice,* Shakespeare employs the conflict in *Much Ado* in brief episodes not for its own sake but rather for the purpose of stressing details of action or character. Thus Claudio's complaint that

> Friendship is constant in all other things
> Save in the office and affairs of love

is a means of emphasizing his immaturity and readiness to believe without evidence Don John's charge that his brother is wooing Hero for himself. Later, Benedick's resolve to challenge Claudio in response to Beatrice's command serves not only to confirm their love but also to present Benedick in the self-dramatizing, seriocomic attitude of the would-be avenging hero who, the audience knows, has nothing to avenge.

Another significant change Shakespeare made in his sources is having Claudio accuse Hero publicly in the effective church scene. Such an episode differs widely from Shakespeare's sources: in Bandello the lover sends a messenger to break off the engagement; in Ariosto the lover departs in silence, the accusation being made by his brother; and in Spenser the enraged lover slays both the lady and the slanderer. Having chosen to place the dramatic emphasis upon Claudio's super-ficial relationship to Hero, a relationship which can hardly be called "the marriage of true minds," that is, an attraction based upon mere appearances, Shakespeare very properly presents Claudio in the church scene wherein he not only gives further evidence of his immaturity but also displays its near-fatal consequences. Furthermore, the accusation makes an extraor-dinary scene on the stage, an action eliciting a variety of re-sponses, some sequential, others simultaneous. But it must be observed that Claudio's part in the accusation is not as deeply damning as it is sometimes held to be. The evidence against Hero is strong, both the visual assignation of Margaret and Borachio, witnessed by both Claudio and Don Pedro, and the contributing circumstance that on the night before her wedding Hero had not shared her bed with Beatrice as had been her custom. These are mitigating details, necessary for justifying both Claudio's credulity (and, it may be added, Don Pedro's and Leonato's) and also his later reunion with Hero.

A further change, structurally the most significant of all, is the way in which the truth of Hero's slander is discovered. In both Ariosto and Spenser the source of the dénouement is the maid (Shakespeare's Margaret), who confesses her part in the intrigue.[8] Since Shakespeare rather awkwardly chose to keep Margaret innocent of Borachio's intrigue, he was forced to invent his own means of discovering the truth. The device he employed borrows in small part from his sources in that Borachio reveals his own role in the slander of Hero, but of course Shakespeare created Dogberry and his watch, who over-hear Borachio, apprehend him, and in their own deliberate fashion report their discovery too late. Again, as has been his custom, Shakespeare brings into an aristocratic plot creatures from his own immediate observation of life in the country, though these may in broad outline also reflect old literary conventions. Be this as it may, Dogberry is the last in a series of special comic types designed for William Kempe, who left Shakespeare's company shortly after the initial performance of the play.

In addition to the watch Shakespeare created also Benedick and Beatrice, whose story he blended into that of Claudio and Hero. No direct source for that story has been discovered, and it is most unlikely that one exists. Their creation is perhaps the most telling proof that in these plays the dramatist's choice of theme determines both the direction of the plot and the characterization. Here the theme is one Shakespeare has dealt with before, the rejection or pretended rejection of love which as we have noted above had become a staple in Shakespearean romantic comedy. In *Much Ado About Nothing*, where the theme is given its definitive treatment, it was proper that Shakespeare, unencumbered by borrowed materials, should create his own characters and fashion his own episodes. It is generally believed that Benedick and Beatrice are a maturer Berowne and Rosaline, but of course their relationship is different from that of the earlier pair. In *Love's Labour's Lost* it is the men, the king and his courtiers, who reject for a time love and the society of ladies, while the ladies at no time express a like attitude towards love and men. In addition, Berowne is not as firmly opposed to love as his associates and, on the contrary, both forecasts and justifies their eventual failure. In *Much Ado About Nothing* both Benedick and Beatrice oppose love and wedlock, and though they recall the earlier pair, they are quite different from them; they resemble Berowne and Rosaline in their wit-combats rather than in their temperaments and attitudes towards love. In the same way Benedick and Beatrice recall Castiglione's Caspare Pallavicino and Lady Emilia Pia, but the parallels between the two pairs are of a very general sort.[9] Pallavicino and Lady Emilia Pia engage in clever dialogue, but their quarrels are not personal: there is no pretended dislike of each other which later turns out to be an attraction. Nor is Lady Emilia Pia against love; she merely defends her sex against Pallavicino's calumnies.

Equally general are the alleged similarities between Beatrice and Spenser's Mirabella who, having through her "dispiteous pride" destroyed many lovers, has been condemned by Cupid's Court to wander through the world for two years seeking to expiate her crime by saving as many lovers as she had destroyed.[10] In her journey she rides

> With these two lewd companions, and no more,
> Disdaine and Scorne. . . .[11]

Disdain and Scorn are the attributes Hero stresses in her description of her cousin:

> Disdain and scorn ride sparkling in her eyes,
> Misprising what they look on, and her wit
> Values itself so highly that to her
> All matter else seems weak.
>
> (III, i, 51-54)

Beatrice is "Lady Disdain," who mocks suitors out of their love-suit, "too curst" as she is called by Antonio. But although these and other points seem to connect her with Spenser's Mirabella, Beatrice is neither an imitation of Spenser's character nor yet simply the conventional "Disdainful Woman."[12] She is primarily a character who derives her being from her special relationship to a particular man she pretends to dislike but in fact falls in love with. That relationship is made to appear unique in its subtle complexity, a complexity rendering her characterization infinitely richer than that of any of her alleged models. And thus while Spenser's lines may have suggested a phrase or two to Shakespeare, the latter's conception of Beatrice owes nothing directly to any of the characters in *The Faerie Queene*.

Whatever the connections between Shakespeare's pair of reluctant lovers and their alleged models or sources, what is of special significance is the way in which their characterization is adjusted to the demands of the dramatist's overriding theme and therefore to the Claudio-Hero plot. For although Benedick and Beatrice are the most absorbing and most diverting characters of the comedy, their story is secondary in the design of the play. That design proposes to dramatize the fortunes in the love affair of Claudio and Hero, their union, separation, and reunion. Counterpointing that movement in the relationship of Claudio and Hero, and perfectly adjusted to it, is the slow, deliberate, and reluctant union of Benedick and Beatrice. In the technical sense the blending of the two stories, their dovetailing, is in E. K. Chambers' word, "faultless," so successful that there seems to be one story. But although the structure of the play achieves this high degree of perfection through episodic causality, does it also achieve a unity of mood or atmosphere? The most frequent answer given to this query is negative. E. K. Chambers' view of the matter represents the general dissatisfaction with the play. Though he admits the play's technical perfection, Chambers complains that its "harmony of atmosphere" suffers from the fact that the Claudio-Hero story moves in a melodramatic plane while the story of Benedick and Beatrice moves in a comic plane.[13] To answer this charge as well as others it is necessary to examine in detail not only the structural but also the thematic and "atmospheric" relationship of the two stories, including the role of Dogberry and his watch. Such an analysis will be given below, but first we must set down general remarks concerning the play's action, remarks we must keep in mind during our detailed examination of it.

III

First we should note that the play deals with the fortunes of two love affairs, and though the two pairs of lovers differ significantly—they are deliberately contrasted—their stories run a rough and slow course: one leads to quick union, then separation, and then reunion; the other is slow and deliberate from beginning to end. Both stories are obstructed, prevented from swift and happy conclusion, by the errors of mere seeming, by the deception of appearance. And this circumstantiality of seeming threads the two stories together in both action and thematic significance. We shall note also that as visual and more significantly "oral" appearance is the means of obstructing love in the play, its technical or stage agency for advancing the action is overhearing, accurate or inaccurate, and eavesdropping. We shall see that appearances are either put on by characters themselves, as Benedick and Beatrice do, or are created by others, as those practiced by Don John and Don Pedro. What results from this is an action made up of a series of deceptions.[14] For a short while Don Pedro's initial intrigue to woo Hero for Claudio deceives nearly everybody, including Antonio, Leonato, and Benedick. And Don John, likewise misled, convinces Claudio, whom he pretends to take for Benedick, that Don Pedro is wooing Hero for himself. But the two brothers, incorrigible intriguers that they are, attempt further deceptions, again the one aiming to unite lovers, the other to sever them. Don Pedro directs his intrigue against Benedick and Beatrice, whereas Don John mounts his against Claudio and Hero. It should be noted here that both intrigues depend upon the deception of appearances. In the scene witnessed by Don Pedro and Claudio it seemed that Hero received a lover at her window; in the other, Benedick and Beatrice are informed that though they seem to dislike each other, they are in truth in love. In the church scene after the accusation Hero seems dead, which leads to the Friar's intrigue aimed to deceive Claudio and Don Pedro; and in the final scene Leonato introduces his own little deception by presenting a masked Hero as a cousin.

In addition to this series of deceptions which bind the two stories and advance their action, we should note two points not sufficiently stressed by critics. First, we must remember that in both plots circumstantial appearances, false or otherwise, have to do with love; and second, Benedick's reason for eschewing marriage is his pretended belief that no wife is faithful, that every husband is a cuckold.[15] But this, it turns out, is what Don John seems to believe also and attempts to demonstrate in his intrigue against Hero.[16]

IV

The play opens with Leonato receiving news through a messenger that he will soon be visited by Don Pedro of Arragon, accompanied by his brother Don John and two Italian lords, who, we are told, have done "good service" during a recent military campaign. Of the two Italian lords Claudio, the Florentine, is seriously described as having "borne himself beyond the promise of his age, doing in the figure of a lamb the feats of a lion." This report of Claudio's achievement, besides indicating his youth and valor, associates him with tears of joy, tears shed by his uncle in Messina upon learning of his nephew's military accomplishments. In addition Claudio's description contrasts him with Benedick, his friend and companion, to whom the earliest allusion, made by Beatrice, is as disparaging as the messenger's reference to Claudio is laudatory. Beatrice calls Benedick "Signior Mountanto," that is, "Signior Duellist," and adds that he is anything but heroic: in truth "a very valiant trencherman," a braggart and a coward. "I pray you," she asks the messenger, "how many hath he killed and eaten in these wars? But how many hath he killed, for indeed I promised to eat all of his killing" (I, i, 42-5). As is appropriate to the content of her speeches, Beatrice's tone is mocking, but without bitterness, indeed gay, and that tone, together with Leonato's comment thereon, precludes overhasty judgment on our part. Claudio and Benedick are thus contrasted in the earliest allusions to them: the one is brave, heroic, associated with tears, honored by Don Pedro; the other is said to be a braggart, unheroic, with scarcely "wit enough to keep himself warm." The one portrait is romantic, the other satiric. The episode shows, furthermore, Beatrice's interest in Benedick, though ostensibly her reason is to heap ridicule upon him.

After the indirect introduction, through the messenger and Beatrice, of Claudio and Benedick, the play brings these two on the stage, together with Don Pedro and Don John the Bastard. During this episode Claudio is not given a single

speech, and the actor must of course indicate his interest in
Hero, who likewise remains silent in the course of the episode.
Their silence is emphasized by the clever and witty dialogue
of Benedick and Beatrice, who now take the stage, resuming
their unfinished skirmishes of old, and protesting a "dear
happiness" that they are not in love with each other. Before
leaving the episode we should note two important details.
First, the irony in Leonato's protestation to Don Pedro: "Never
came trouble to my house in the likeness of your Grace, for
trouble being gone, comfort should remain; but when you de-
part from me, sorrow abides and happiness takes his leave"
(I, i, 99-102). Second and far more important, Shakespeare introduces through Benedick the important theme of conjugal
infidelity in this early episode. To Don Pedro's question if
Hero is his daughter, Leonato replies: "Her mother hath many
times told me so." Benedick, unable to resist the opening, asks:
"Were you in doubt, sir, that you asked her?" This is, of course,
a brief reference to the theme, but though brief it is the first in a
long series of allusions to it by Benedick, for, as noted earlier, he
gives his fear of wifely infidelity as the reason for his pretended
aversion to the opposite sex, love, and wedlock. This then is
the first note, struck early in the play, to be followed by Benedick's comic elaboration, which in turn leads to Don John's
making infidelity the basis of his intrigue against Hero. For
Don John seems to believe what Benedick pretends to believe
about the woes of marriage. What is of note here is that
Benedick and Don John are concerned with the same idea,
though their attitudes toward it differ. But their concern
with the same motif contributes its share towards the play's
thematic as well as structural unity.

The third movement of the long opening scene extends
and establishes more firmly the contrast between the romantic
and satiric attitudes towards love and wedlock as represented
by Claudio and Benedick. Having seen Hero twice, Claudio has
fallen in love with her though he has evidently exchanged no
words with her. He has chosen "by the view," and on her appearance alone he has begun to idealize her. What might have

been a more passionate expression of his love for her is held down to hesitant acknowledgment by Benedick's strictures on such matters. It should be noted here that Benedick makes the revealing admission that though he can speak with "simple true judgment" about women, his custom is to be "a professed tyrant to their sex." In the face of this, Claudio is content to call Hero first a "modest young lady," then a "jewel," the "sweetest lady" that he ever looked on. Hero, says Benedick, may be handsome, but Beatrice "exceeds her as much in beauty as the first of May doth the last of December." But this is not the reason he tries to dissuade Claudio from marriage. The reason is that a husband is surely a woeful, a pitiful thing. "Is't come to this? In faith, hath not the world one man but he will wear his cap with suspicion? Shall I never see a bachelor of threescore again? Go to, i' faith, an thou wilt needs thrust thy neck into a yoke, wear the print of it, and sigh away Sundays" (I, i, 199-204).

Even when Don Pedro returns to the stage a moment later, Claudio retains his timidity and guarded expression of his love for Hero, for he is not certain of Don Pedro's attitude. Later on when, left alone with him, he is assured of the latter's more sympathetic response, Claudio breaks out into a much freer account of his feelings and does so in blank verse, the first in the play. But while the three are together on the stage, he is an easy target for the aroused Benedick, who with an assumed tolerance for his friend's infirmity accuses Claudio of being in love. And on his side, Benedick vows, he "will live a bachelor," for although a woman conceived him, none will deceive him: ". . . that I will have a recheat winded in my forehead, or hang my bugle in an invisible baldrick, all women shall pardon me. Because I will not do them the wrong to mistrust any, I will do myself the right to trust none" (ll. 242-46). It is his strongest protest against wedlock, what we may call his comic error anticipating his later capitulation which is likewise forecast by Don Pedro's conviction:

I shall see thee, ere I die, look pale with love.

And a line or two later he adds:

> In time the savage bull both bear the yoke.

But Benedick insists on his choice and the reasons for it: "The savage bull may; but if ever the sensible Benedick bear it, pluck off the bull's horns and set them in my forehead." Even Claudio adds his own allusion to horns in saying that, if after all this Benedick should take a wife, he would be "horn-mad."

The episode deals in the main with Benedick's overprotesting both his own heresy towards love and his disapproval of Claudio's surrender to it. For this double offense against Cupid he will pay dearly, and all this is ironically anticipated. But of great significance is Benedick's persistence upon the theme of cuckoldry, an idea made part of the general atmosphere of the play. For in accusing all womanhood of infidelity he is introducing the very basis of Hero's later undoing, though ironically Benedick is one of only three characters who are convinced of her innocence. Not only this, but we should note that in the concluding episode of the play Claudio fears Benedick himself would be a "double dealer" if Beatrice "do not look exceedingly narrowly" to him.

As we noted above, when he is left alone with Don Pedro on the stage in the concluding movement of this scene, Claudio leaves no doubt of his love for Hero. This is indicated by the use of verse but more clearly by Claudio's avowal that upon his return

> war-thoughts
> Have left their places vacant, in their rooms
> Come thronging soft and delicate desires,
> All prompting me how fair young Hero is. . . .
>
> (ll. 303-6)

Don Pedro, fearing that Claudio will be like a lover and "tire the hearer with a book of words," offers to help, to which

Claudio responds in the accents of the lover indeed:

> How sweetly you do minister to love,
> That know love's grief by his complexion!

Having presented a timid Claudio as the romantic lover in love with one he knows little about, Shakespeare introduces in the space of a half dozen lines the first instance of deception, the stage device which will propel and control the action of both stories in the play. Don Pedro will assume Claudio's part, will woo and win Hero for him. With this, the long opening scene comes to a close.

Don Pedro's plan to woo Hero for Claudio yields at least two by-products, both ultimately ineffectual, or rather rendered so by the discovery of the error of appearances. The first unforeseen result of Don Pedro's deception is recorded in the brief second scene with Antonio's report to Leonato that a man of his had overheard Don Pedro's plan to woo Hero for himself. The second outcome of Don Pedro's plan to woo Hero in Claudio's name occurs a little later in Act II, scene i, where Don John, pretending to take the masked Claudio for Benedick, tells him that Don Pedro woos for himself. Both of these episodes are brief and their effects are checked later in the same scene when Don Pedro, having won Hero, gives her to Claudio. But these two instances of the errors in seeming serve significant ends; they show how easy it is to be deceived by appearances, visual or oral. Antonio and Leonato are convinced that Don Pedro is wooing Hero for himself, and later so is Benedick. But what is far more important, Claudio, who knows Don Pedro's plan, likewise believes the report of the latter's betrayal of him. Now the fact that three other characters are deceived along with him is intended to mitigate but lightly Claudio's error, for unlike the others he is in on Don Pedro's secret. More significantly the episode lays emphasis on the general ease with which appearances can deceive and anticipates the later and much graver deception of Claudio and Don Pedro by Don John.

v

The opening scene of Act II, besides Don John's abortive
plan to vex Claudio, which occurs at the end of the masked
ball, includes Beatrice's own comic hamartia which parallels
Benedick's, the masked ball, the union of Claudio and Hero,
and Don Pedro's announcement of a second plan in Cupid's
behalf: "to bring Signior Benedick and the Lady Beatrice into
a mountain of affection the one with the other." And he plans
to do it through deception.

The scene opens with Beatrice recording her instinctive distrust of Don John and commenting upon his tart looks and excessive reticence. And she adds that a combination of Benedick, who tattles evermore, and Don John, who is "like an
image and says nothing," would result in a handsome husband.
And when she is told that if she remains shrewish and "too
curst," she will never get a husband, she replies:

> I shall lessen God's sending that way; for it is
> said, "God sends a curst cow short horns;" but to
> a cow too curst he sends none.
> *Leonato.* So, by being too curst, God will send you no horns.
> *Beatrice.* Just, if he send me no husband; for the which
> blessing I am at him upon my knees every morning
> and evening. Lord, I could not endure a husband
> with a beard on his face! I had rather lie in the
> woolen!
>
> (II, i, 23-32)

Her protestation, aside from ironically anticipating her later
conversion and thus paralleling Benedick's, resumes and maintains before us his insistence upon cuckoldry. Presently the
revellers enter, all masked, and soon they move in sequent pairs
within hearing of the audience. In each pair there is pretense
of hidden identity, and Benedick and Beatrice, taking advantage
of that pretense, ridicule each other without mercy: he by
saying that she has had her "good wit out of the 'Hundred
Merry Tales' "; and she by calling him the prince's jester,

whose gift is in devising "impossible slanders." As with the
theme of cuckoldry so the idea of slander is introduced early,
to be repeated again and again by different characters until the
very air of the play is filled with it. It is after this that Don
John tries his initial and briefly successful assault upon Claudio,
to be followed by Benedick's concurrence, both to be put aside
shortly by Don Pedro's explanation.

Before concluding, the scene records two brief episodes of
interest concerning the reluctant lovers. In the midst of his
complaints to Don Pedro against Beatrice's ridicule of him during the ball, Benedick suddenly exclaims: "I would not marry
her, though she were endowed with all that Adam had left
him before he transgress'd." Equally revealing is Beatrice's
own surprising allusion, a moment after Hero and Claudio
are united, to her own single state, hitherto by her own description a state of "dear happiness": "Good Lord, for al-
liance! Thus goes every one to the world but I, and I am sun-
burnt. I may sit in a corner and cry "Heigh-ho for a husband!" (ll. 330-32) Having heard both, Don Pedro concludes
the scene by proposing his second scheme, to undertake one of
"Hercules' Labours," to "practice" on Benedick and Beatrice
so that they shall fall in love.

In the following scene Don John under Borachio's prompt-
ing initiates the parallel intrigue aimed at separating Claudio
and Hero even as Don Pedro's aims at uniting Benedick and
Beatrice. Both intrigues are to employ appearances, visual and
oral, and in both the victims are gulled by being made to believe they have the advantage over those on whom they are
eavesdropping.

Don Pedro's intrigue aiming to unite Benedick and Beatrice
commences in Act II, scene iii, opening and closing with long
and important soliloquies by Benedick, who is the subject of the
episode. In his opening soliloquy he states in somewhat formal
fashion his comic hamartia, and in attacking love and Claudio's
romantic metamorphosis he anticipates a similar attack upon
his own later change; at the end of the scene he will be another
Claudio. Aside from this structural function the passage is of

the greatest significance in that it defines Claudio's change through his love for Hero, a subject upon which much has been written. It is true that Benedick cites no long list of conventional lovers' maladies visited upon Claudio, but he nevertheless isolates pointedly certain details in Claudio's deportment which leave no doubt as to his change and the reasons for it. So far as Benedick is concerned, Claudio's falling in love is both incredible and intolerable: "I do much wonder that one man, seeing how much another man is a fool when he dedicates his behaviours to love, will, after he hath laugh'd at such shallow follies in others, become the argument of his own scorn by falling in love; and such a man is Claudio." (II, iii, 7-12) What Benedick stresses here is not merely that Claudio has fallen in love but that, like himself, he had earlier scorned and laughed at the folly of it in others. Claudio had been quite different, then, before seeing Hero. "I have known when there was no music with him but the drum and the fife; and now had he rather hear the tabor and the pipe. I have known when he would have walk'd ten mile a-foot to see a good armour; and now will he lie ten nights awake, carving the fashion of a new doublet. He was wont to speak plain and to the purpose, like an honest man and a soldier; and now is he turn'd orthography; his words are a very fantastical banquet, just so many strange dishes." (ll. 12-22) Unless we accept these lines as expressing the facts in Claudio's behavior, the speech can possess no significance. Professor Prouty has argued that "such tirades are a part of Benedick's humor as an enemy of love and are not necessarily true."[17] But if these things are not true, why is Benedick so deeply concerned with them and why does he rehearse them in a soliloquy? As we have noted above, the point to bear in mind is that Claudio is here presented as another Benedick, laughing at lovers and scorning love: and now look at him, Benedick says. He has become "Monsieur Love"! (l. 37) But what really convinces us that Claudio has indeed suffered a lover's changes is Benedick's question: "May I be so converted, and see with these eyes?" It is inconceivable that Benedick should ask if he could "be so converted," that is, as Claudio has been, if he knew all the time that Claudio had not been converted at all. The point is that, in spite of his protestations, Benedick is not certain that he can long resist love, for he answers his own question thus: "I cannot tell; I think not. I will not be sworn but love may transform me to an oyster; but I'll take my oath on it, till he have made an oyster of me, he shall never make me such a fool." (ll. 23-28) It is true that thus far he has resisted love, yet the possibility of his submission is clearly implied in his conclusion: ". . . till all graces be in one woman, one woman shall not come in my grace. Rich shall she be . . . , virtuous . . . mild . . . , noble . . . , of good discourse, an excellent musician, and her hair shall be of what colour it please God." (ll. 30-37) Thus in addition to pointing to his own imminent change in his censure of Claudio, Benedick's soliloquy announces his readiness for such change. For it would not do for Shakespeare to show Benedick suddenly and unexpectedly admitting his love for Beatrice. The soliloquy suggests a psychological state in him which is appropriately receptive to the revelations soon to be made of Beatrice's love of him.

At this point Benedick sees "Monsieur Love" approaching, accompanied by Don Pedro and Leonato, and Balthasar with a lute. And of course Benedick, in hiding in the arbor, does precisely what they want him to do. In the episode which follows, the introduction of music is of the greatest significance, not simply thematic but psychological as well. And yet Balthasar's song has been curiously misunderstood by critics, some of whom make scant allusion to it.[18] As is his habit Shakespeare associates music with love and wooing, and music has become an indispensable symbol of harmony in the plays. And in addition the introduction of music here enables Shakespeare to write a light dialogue between Balthasar and Don Pedro, with much talk of wooing and wooers and noting-nothing, which critics have tended to overinterpret. In passing, it may be noted also that the "atmospheric" term "slander" drops casually from Balthasar's lips (l. 47), doubtless intended for our subconscious. Furthermore Balthasar's lute music elicits Benedick's appropriately anti-romantic, irony-laden response: "Is it not strange that sheeps' guts should hale souls out of men's bodies? Well, a horn for my money, when all's done."

But what of the song itself? Although its lines are addressed to "ladies," the words are really meant for Benedick, but its general meaning reaches beyond him and touches the others on the stage, particularly Claudio and Don Pedro:

> Sigh no more, ladies, sigh no more,
> Men were deceivers ever. . . .

Not only Benedick, then, but others as well have deceived or are about to deceive their loving ladies, for men "were deceivers ever," to "one thing constant never." How fittingly ironic that Benedick, who has hitherto made it his duty to question ladies' fidelity, should be addressed with such lines! And presently those on the stage will hint that his hard heart has brought Beatrice close to acts of self-violence! Such men are unworthy, the refrain sings, of ladies' tears.

> Then sigh not so, but let them go. . . .

The second stanza, more clearly than the first, not only alludes to men's deception generally and to the one aimed at Benedick in particular, but also pointedly anticipates Don John's fraud aimed at Hero:

> Sing no more ditties, sing no moe,
> Of dumps so dull and heavy;
> The fraud of men was ever so,
> Since summer first was leafy.

It cannot be maintained that Balthasar's song converts Benedick, but on the other hand it is clear that it creates a distinct impression, if not directly upon Benedick, certainly upon his subconscious, and indeed our own as well. Its content, then, is relevant both in its allusions to episodes, past and future, and also in creating the right psychological context which puts Benedick on the defensive, so to speak. Furthermore its refrain, with its strongly anticipatory "sounds of woe," forecasts also a comic resolution by asking ladies to convert such sounds into "Hey, nonny, nonny." Finally, the two stanzas with their refrain contribute to the play's over-all unity of tone and atmosphere by placing the two stories in the same thematic and psychological context.

The song having in a sense helped prepare Benedick for the deception, Don Pedro, in an anticipatory note, requests Balthasar to prepare "some excellent music" to be sung "tomorrow night . . . at the Lady Hero's chamber-window." And then Don Pedro and his two associates turn to the attack. The general tone they create is a master-stroke of psychology which convinces Benedick that Beatrice is indeed enamored of him. Benedick's first response is that "this is a gull," but he then dismisses the thought since so old and grave a "reverence" as Leonato could scarcely practice such "knavery." But Benedick's dismissal of any suspicion has already been determined, so to speak, by the three practicers. Two of them pretend that Beatrice may merely "counterfeit" her passion for Benedick, but Leonato's answer is proof enough: "O God, counterfeit! There was never counterfeit of passion came so near the life of passion as she discovers it." (II, iii, 109-11) Benedick is satisfied. Furthermore, their allusions to him, alternating between censure and praise, between his "contemptible spirit," and his "good outward happiness," have such an air of casual and incontestable truth about them that he is put completely at his ease, and disarmed thus he believes all he "overhears."

Benedick's soliloquy which follows the deception balances his opening speech by answering some of its questions. He may, indeed, be "so converted" and by a lady fair and virtuous, two of the attributes he had stipulated in the earlier passage. In the face of Beatrice's imaginary tears, Benedick capitulates, and he records his response to her love in an exquisitely jesting, half-hearted effort at self-deception: "I may chance to have some odd quirks and remnants of wit broken on me, because I have rail'd so long against marriage; but doth not the appetite alter? A man loves the meat in his youth that he cannot endure in his age . . . . No, the world must be peopled. When

I said I would die a bachelor, I did not think I should live till I were married." (ll. 244-52) The passage is one of the most significant in the entire play, for it records with Benedick's individual humor the recognition of his comic error.[19] What must be borne in mind when treating the matter of the play's unity is that Benedick's comic error is precisely what Claudio's had been, for he too, we have seen, had scorned love and its cares in favor of the more becoming occupation of the soldier. Benedick's submission to love follows Claudio's and is in turn followed by Beatrice's. The long scene comes to a close with the entry of Beatrice upon the stage to bid Benedick come to dinner. And suddenly Benedick can "spy some marks of love in her," and can also detect "a double meaning" in what she says. This is so and not so. Beatrice may be enamored of him but there are no marks of love in her, nor does he interpret accurately her double meaning, though her speech may not always reveal her feelings towards him. Certainly she "seems" and "sounds" different to him, but he is deceived!

VI

The opening scene of Act III spreads the same net for Beatrice that has caught Benedick, with Hero leading the hunt. In place of the song with its emotional and psychological contribution, the present scene is written entirely in verse, and it includes the first instance of Beatrice's speech in that medium.[20] Like Benedick, she is made to think that she is eavesdropping whereas she is merely intended to overhear what Hero and Ursula are saying. Their talk is of Benedick's love for her, and they praise his worth while censuring her pride, her wit and scorn. And as they pretend to believe that Beatrice would doubtless flout Benedick if she knew of his love, Hero resolves not to tell her of it.

> No; rather I will go to Benedick
> And counsel him to fight against his passion;
> And, truly, I'll devise some honest slanders
> To stain my cousin with.
>
> (III, i, 82-85)

The passage parallels much of the earlier scene with Benedick, and Hero's pretense at "slander" not only repeats Balthasar's earlier use of the term before his song, but also intensifies the irony of her own imminent calumny. In brief, Beatrice, who was not unprepared for the change, forswears pride and scorn, and vows to requite Benedick's passion, adding the significant "To bind our loves up in a holy band." Don Pedro's practice upon the reluctant lovers has succeeded in revealing to them their love for each other, and in this there is a fine sense of irony since the trick played upon them had little to do with causing them to fall in love. In other words, there is a kind of self-deception in Don Pedro's notion that bringing Benedick and Beatrice "into a mountain of affection" would be one of "Hercules' labours."

In the following scene of Act III Benedick's conversion into a lover is presented as identical with Claudio's and this of course confirms the parallel between the two men which we noted above. Claudio's strange metamorphosis, so stoutly ridiculed by Benedick earlier in the play, is precisely the change Don Pedro, Leonato, and Claudio now ridicule in him. He is sadder than he was wont to be, though Don Pedro explains the cause thereof as want of money. But there are other symptoms: he has a "fancy . . . to strange disguises," affecting a variety of costumes. He "brushes his hat o' mornings," "the old ornament of his cheek hath already stuffed tennis-balls," "he rubs himself with civet," he washes his face, and paints himself. He must be in love, they conclude, and "the greatest note of it is his melancholy." For "his jesting spirit . . . is new-crept into a lute-string and now governed with stops." Are not these the very changes Benedick had bewailed and ridiculed in Claudio? The notion that Benedick's tirades against Claudio are not true finds no support here, for the very changes Benedick attacks in Claudio are visible symptoms in himself.[21] His dress, the loss of his beard, his assumed gravity, his reticence—all these we see on the stage, and they are all attributes of the lover. It was certainly necessary for Shakespeare to show these matters in only one of them, and of the two Benedick is the right choice, for he is conceived in a comic vein whereas Claudio is not. And the mocking of the mocker is part of the comic idea of the play. Thus Benedick, who earlier in the play had heaped scornful mockery upon Claudio's love, in the present episode loses his perspective completely. And it is surely the height of comedy to hear his affectedly laconic speech to Leonato: "Old signior, walk aside with me. I have studied eight or nine wise words to speak with you. . . ." Alas, Benedick the lover has no idea how ridiculously serious he looks and sounds!

Benedick and Leonato having retired to consider Benedick's "eight or nine wise words," Don John enters the stage and accuses Hero of infidelity and offers Don Pedro and Claudio proof "tonight." Since Benedick, in spite of his earlier thrusts at wifely infidelity, would probably reject the accusation—and he does when he hears it in the church scene—he is kept ignorant of the charge against Hero, Don John's "proof," and Claudio's plan to disgrace her at the altar. Furthermore, his exclusion makes it easy for Benedick to align himself with Beatrice in Hero's behalf. And he not only agrees with her and the Friar that there "is some strange misprision in the princes," but divines the cause. "The practice of it," he says, "lives in John the Bastard."

But conviction that Hero is innocent cannot clear her good name. That is done by Dogberry and his fellows created by Shakespeare for that purpose, perhaps with hints from Lyly's *Endymion.* And what should be noted is that they overhear Borachio describe his slander of Hero. That the watch should accidentally penetrate to the truth while some of the clever ones are duped carries its own simple ironies. But what is far more important is that the watch fails to reveal their discovery before the wedding scene. Thus our suspense and anticipation are maintained, albeit on a lower pitch now since we are most certain that Dogberry will come out with the truth. The scene reveals to us both Borachio's success and Claudio's vow to shame Hero "before the whole congregation," as well as Borachio's apprehension by the watch.

While these matters are thus proceeding, Hero, aided by

her maids, makes ready for the wedding. Scene four of Act III is in two parts: the first half deals with Hero's preparation, suddenly clouded by a strange premonition which is soon relieved by Margaret's bawdry; and the second half takes up the teasing of the love-melancholy Beatrice by Hero and her maids, an episode intended to balance the earlier taunting of Benedick by his friends. The final scene of Act III, one of the most ironic in the play, brings Dogberry and Verges to Leonato's house, but though they are possessed of the truth they fail to communicate it to Leonato, for they are tediously deliberate and he is preoccupied and inattentive, and he is shortly called away from them by a messenger who reports the wedding is at hand. That the watch are at least attempting to reveal the truth reduces our anxiety and keeps it on a manageable level, both here and in the wedding scene which follows. Though the emphasis here is upon the comic incongruousness between the inherent ridiculousness of the watch and their assumed dignity, the scene nevertheless anticipates the ultimate righting of Hero's wrong in Leonato's request that Dogberry take the examination of the culprits himself and bring it to him later. Whereupon Dogberry commands his associate to get him "to Francis Seacoal, bid him bring his pen and inkhorn to the gaol. . . ."

VII

The wedding scene is the most difficult in the play and it has caused much controversy among the critics. Some defend Claudio's role while others find it utterly inexcusable. And more serious than that, most students of the play discover here the division in tone and atmosphere to which E. K. Chambers alludes in his essay on the play.[22] Is it true that the play's "harmony of atmosphere," as he puts it, suffers from the fact that the Claudio-Hero story moves in a melodramatic plane while the story of Benedick and Beatrice moves in a comic plane? Is this distinction between the two stories valid? An examination of the scene refutes Chambers' contention. And although in the foregoing analysis of the play thus far we have seen a blending of the two stories in terms of both theme and structure, the wedding scene is a crucial test of the notion that the play does indeed possess "unity of atmosphere." By way of introduction to our analysis, let us note that the scene presents episodes in the two stories dealing with the same melodramatic motive: Claudio is said to have killed Hero with his accusation, and Benedick, commanded by Beatrice, vows to kill Claudio. And Benedick will come no closer to killing Claudio than the latter comes to killing Hero. That this melodramatic theme is common to both stories is incontestable; yet the fact seems to have escaped those critics who see a fatal division in the atmosphere of the play.

The initial episode of the scene presents Claudio, in a somewhat self-dramatizing attitude, rejecting Hero before the altar, asserting that she is "but the sign and semblance of her honour." For Claudio, having himself engaged in an action wherein things were not what they seemed—the deception of Benedick —fails to consider that the scene at Hero's window may have been another instance of that same "truth." Aside from the irony inherent in this lapse on his part as well as Don Pedro's, what is of great significance here is the fact that Claudio, though he has fallen in love with Hero, knows nothing about her. There had been no courtship, and he had chosen "by the view" alone: "by the view" he chose Hero and "by the view" he rejects her. No doubt Claudio deserves censure for both choosing and rejecting Hero merely on the basis of externals. And as we noted earlier, this motif relates the play with *The Merchant of Venice,* wherein Bassanio, as well as Nerissa's song, had insisted upon an understanding of inner worth as the basis of a happy union. For love based on show alone is but fancy "which alters / When it alteration finds." But the injunction not to "choose by the view" does not imply that appearances *need* be deceptive, and certainly Hero is as true and loyal and innocent as she appears.

Claudio is no doubt an easy mark for Don John's aim, yet Shakespeare provides that our censure of him must not be too severe, for he must not appear utterly undeserving of Hero.

To that end Shakespeare makes the evidence against Hero of such strength that not only is Claudio convinced but Don Pedro also and for a while even Leonato. And this last, though it does not completely justify Claudio's conduct at the altar, surely explains much of it. Furthermore, the fact that the cause of the conflict is the work of Don John takes much from whatever force there may be in the charge that Claudio is irresponsible, callous, and cruel. For it must be kept in mind that he is the target of Don John's devilish scheme. Claudio, though not quite the "slandered groom," is nevertheless the one whose happiness is undermined by the slander of Hero.

What Shakespeare is clearly pursuing here is a complex emotional response by the audience. Though we are made unhappy by the rejection of Hero we know that the whole matter will be made right soon, and though we feel that Claudio is somewhat hasty and an easy gull, yet we see two others being gulled with him, and one of them, Leonato, should know—he should certainly *feel*—that Hero cannot be guilty. The point, then, is a simultaneous experience of conflicting, though not mutually cancelling, emotions on our part. The very same conflict of emotions makes up our response to Beatrice's instant rejection of the accusation and particularly her command to Benedick to kill Claudio. We approve of her vehemence against Hero's accusers and especially Claudio, but we do so knowing all along that the truth is even now being taken down by the officious Dogberry. We know that although Hero has been struck a fearful blow by the rejection, she is not dead; we respond to Beatrice's spirit and her flaming words in defense of Hero; yet we at no time subscribe to her call for Claudio's death. In her command "Kill Claudio!" there is the same melodramatic note which characterizes the rejection of Hero at the altar. And surely Claudio's "sad invention" and Balthasar's song sung over a tomb which the audience knows is empty are no more melodramatic than Benedick's challenge to Claudio in order to avenge Hero's death. In both there is a strong undercurrent of the comic beneath the seeming gravity of appearances.

This complexity of our emotional response to the scene is maintained to the end and particularly in Benedick's deliberate acceptance of Beatrice's command. Though the audience wishes Benedick to challenge Claudio, the knowledge that Hero is alive and that she will soon be vindicated modifies our feelings so that instead of grave apprehension we experience the double pleasure of first having Benedick do what we want him to do—that is to challenge Claudio—and also of knowing that all will be well.

Our controlled anxieties are further relieved by the action of the second and final scene of Act IV, for here the imperious Dogberry, in the company of Verges and appareled in the robes of office, examines Conrade and Borachio, and their deposition reassures us that Hero was indeed wrongfully accused, and adds the very important note that Don John "is this morning secretly stol'n away."

VIII

The opening scene of Act V is in three parts, the first two presenting challenges issued to Claudio and the third cancelling these by its revelation of the truth concerning Hero. Nevertheless the first two episodes maintain the complexity of our emotions, for they present first Antonio and Leonato and then Benedick challenging Claudio to a duel. Our response to the challenges is maintained at the level of immediate stage interest rather than of serious apprehension, and there is in both episodes an element of comedy. This is particularly true of Benedick's challenge, wherein he resumes, or rather maintains, his highly self-conscious gravity and laconic speech, both of which present an amusing contrast to his customary ways. To those earlier ways of his, allusion is made in the taunts of Don Pedro and Claudio, who insist that love has "transshaped him" and who threaten to "set the savage bull's horns on the sensible Benedick's head." Their speech, in content and form, contrasts sharply with Benedick's and throws into sharp relief the change love has wrought in him. In all this the intention is to create a comic impression which overlays the apparent gravity of the challenge, and to that impression is added again the casual note that Don John has fled from Messina. The result is that the two episodes elicit the same complexity of emotions to which we alluded earlier, and then with the entry of Dogberry and the watch with their two prisoners our chief anxiety is at long last completely dissipated. But while this is the effect of Borachio's confession upon our feelings, the effect upon Don Pedro's and Claudio's is quite the reverse, for they are now deeply shocked by the knowledge that Hero died innocent. Although there has been an important change in the emotions of both characters and audience, Shakespeare maintains a balance between the apparently serious and the comic. Leonato with apparent gravity requests of Claudio two acts of expiation, the singing of an epitaph over Hero's tomb and the promise to marry Antonio's daughter in lieu of Hero. To Leonato's assumed gravity Claudio adds his own, but of course the scene is kept from becoming maudlin by Dogberry's presence and also by the fact that the audience as well as most of the characters on the stage know that Hero is alive.

Scene iii of Act V extends the favorable turn of events in the preceding scene and points to the happy resolution of the plot. It opens with a colloquy between the irrepressible Margaret and Benedick, who sounds almost like his old self again in the bawdy exchange with her. Their brief episode is followed by a halting song and comment thereupon by Benedick. And here we should notice that Shakespeare is presenting us a somewhat different Benedick. He is in love, he cannot compose or sing love songs, he suffers much more pain than ever Leander did. But Benedick is a lover with a difference, and of course so is Beatrice. Here in his soliloquy he reveals something of Shakespeare's intention, namely to present Benedick as one in love who like Berowne before him is capable of seeing more than the romantic side of love. In other words Benedick is the sort of lover in whom the romantic attitude does not replace what had earlier seemed like an anti-romantic point of view. Instead, the two attitudes are juxtaposed in him. Surely

only such a lover would rehearse his ill success in writing sonnets as Benedick does: "I can find out no rhyme to 'lady' but
'baby,' an innocent rhyme; for 'scorn,' 'horn,' a hard rhyme;
for 'school,' 'fool,' a babbling rhyme; very ominous endings." (V, ii, 36-39) We should note that Benedick is in love,
that he wants and tries to compose a love sonnet but finds it
beyond his poetic capabilities. The notion that Benedick yields
to the convention only on the surface since he is unable to
write a sonnet cannot be accepted.[23] Although he finds the
writing of love poems difficult, he persists, and in the closing
scene there is reported a

> . . . halting sonnet of his own pure brain,
> Fashion'd to Beatrice.

In this he is not very different from other lovers, who, though
possessing greater facility, produce less than perfect love poems.
Certainly such are Orlando's ditties to Rosalind, and Hamlet
himself is by no means happy with his "numbers." What
matters is not the merits of these lovers as love poets but the
fact that they attempt love poetry, and the attempt is an incontestable attribute of the romantic lover. The comic tone
of the episode is briefly interrupted by the entry of Beatrice
and Benedick's report to her concerning his challenge of
Claudio, but it is resumed by Ursula's intelligence that "my
lady Hero hath been falsely accused . . . and that Don John
is the author of all. . . ." And the scene closes appropriately
with Benedick's bawdy reply to Beatrice's request that he
accompany her to hear further of "this news": "I will live in
thy heart, die in thy lap, and be buried in thy eyes; and moreover I will go with thee to thy uncle's."

The play's penultimate scene takes us to the churchyard and
Leonato's monument for Claudio's mourning rites over Hero.
The episode, as we said above, bears some analogy to the challenges offered Claudio earlier in the play particularly in a sense
of emptiness occasioned, in both cases, by the fact that Hero
has only *seemed* dead. Furthermore the brief scene in the

churchyard, while ostensibly concerned with Hero's memory, is actually a prelude to the happy conclusion now at hand. And this is suggested by Balthasar's song and later by Don Pedro's description of daybreak:

> The wolves have prey'd; and look, the gentle day,
> Before the wheels of Phoebus, round about
> Dapples the drowsy east with spots of grey.
>
> (V, iii, 25-27)

The concluding scene of the play begins with Leonato and Benedick expressing their relief at Hero's vindication, and when presently Claudio and Don Pedro enter the stage, Benedick and Claudio extend the feeling of ease and merriment by their bawdy exchange, which, be it noted, reverts for its humor to the cuckold's horn. The ladies are led on stage masked, Claudio takes his bride's hand who then unmasks and shows herself as the real Hero. To their union is then added that of Benedick and Beatrice, both of whom pretend to take each other for pity. But their assumed reluctance is defeated by the evidence of verses which they have composed for each other. Indeed Benedick proves a most philosophic lover when he contemplates his earlier apostasy, alluded to by Don Pedro: "In brief, since I do purpose to marry, I will think nothing to any purpose that the world can say against it; and therefore never flout at me for what I have said against it, for man is a giddy thing, and this is my conclusion." (V, iv, 104-9) Benedick's "conclusion" is one of the great utterances in Shakespearean comedy. But lest that moment of gravity should linger overlong, Shakespeare mixes it with the lighter satiric note in Claudio's charge that Benedick may prove a double-dealing husband. And Benedick on his side insists on merry-making, music, and dance before the marriage ceremony. Finally upon spying Don Pedro alone he offers him words of wisdom. "Prince, thou art sad; get thee a wife, get thee a wife. There is no staff more reverend than one tipp'd with horn." Much comfort in that staff, yet Benedick is in love and about to be married. The ironic juxtaposition of attitudes is maintained to the very end.[24]

IX

The foregoing analysis of *Much Ado About Nothing* shows that its two stories are closely related in structure as well as theme and tone, particularly the last, since this aspect of the play has been seriously questioned. Not only are the two stories concerned with the same idea, that is, the effect of appearances on the fortunes of lovers, but also the working out of the several episodes in the two plots is so managed that our responses to them are the same. For instance, we have noted that our general attitude toward certain scenes, and indeed to the play as a whole, is a complex one. And this is particularly true of the way we respond to the deportment of the chief characters. We may approve of Beatrice's defense of Hero but of course we are never at ease with her command that Benedick kill Claudio. Similarly, we are relieved to hear Benedick accuse Don John of responsibility for Hero's abuse, and we are happy to see him align himself with Beatrice; yet we are not quite at ease with his melodramatic resolve to challenge Claudio, especially since he appears convinced that someone else is to blame. Our feelings are complicated further by another matter: though on the moral side we disapprove of Benedick's challenge, our disapproval is greatly dissipated by two details. First, we are never in doubt that all will be well, and second we enjoy Benedick's comic metamorphosis through love, for it is most amusing that this "professed tyrant" to the female sex should now take arms against Claudio, and all for love.

This complexity of response to the story of Benedick and Beatrice is the same as our response to the story of Claudio and Hero, and particularly to the actions and words of Claudio and Leonato. The characters in both plots exhibit ambiguous attitudes and through them elicit complex responses on our part. Claudio is duped by Don John into believing what seems true, yet the way in which he accuses Hero is such that he seems her slanderer. And both the manner and the simple fact of his accusation justify in part Beatrice's vituperation. The same complexity appears in Leonato's response. His attitude towards Hero is mixed, combining easy credulity, despair, and vengefulness. He grieves over Hero's alleged misconduct, yet he is angered by it into wishing her dead indeed; and at the same time he longs to avenge her disgrace.

Whether revealed through direct speech or action or both or obliquely through the incongruity of style in a particular passage, ambiguity or complexity of effect is certainly an incontestable feature of *Much Ado About Nothing.* In the broadest terms, this complexity of effect, present in both stories and identified as a mixture of the comic and melodramatic, is responsible for a single pervasive tone, the most effective and most subtle means of achieving far greater unity than most critics are willing to admit.

The question of the play's unity of atmosphere is by far the most serious one, but there are other problems concerning *Much Ado About Nothing* which have a just claim upon our interest. One of these is Professor Prouty's interpretation of the Claudio-Hero story and its relationship to the Benedick-Beatrice plot. The foregoing analysis of the play has, either through direct allusion or by implication, dealt in part with Professor Prouty's view that the Claudio-Hero union is a marriage of convenience, that is, a realistic, non-romantic affair,[25] and that Benedick and Beatrice, another pair of realistic lovers, "are not really enemies of love: they are enemies of the dreary conventions."[26] According to Professor Prouty, we have here "two couples completely opposed to the romantic tradition and these two couples are, in turn, representatives of opposite ideas: for the one, love is a real emotion, for the other, a business arrangement."[27]

Although Claudio early in the play inquires of Don Pedro if Hero is Leonato's only heir, he makes no other reference to the matter, and in the remainder of the play no episode can be cited which supports the view that Claudio is seeking a marriage of convenience. It is true that Claudio does not woo

Hero in person, but this is a necessary detail showing that he is in love with Hero without really knowing her. Furthermore, we should note that although Claudio does not woo Hero himself, she is wooed in his person by Don Pedro. But wooed Hero is, and Don Pedro promises Claudio that he will do it in the romantic manner:

> I know we shall have revelling to-night.
> I will assume thy part in some disguise
> And tell fair Hero I am Claudio.
> And in her bosom I'll unclasp my heart
> And take her hearing prisoner with the force
> And strong encounter of my amorous tale.
>
> (I, i, 322-27)

And in the next line Don Pedro makes clear that the union will not be one of convenience, for he will broach the subject to Leonato *after* the wooing, after Hero has been wooed and won:

> Then after to her father will I break. . . .

In addition to this, it is clear from a number of passages that Claudio's feelings are indeed engaged. Certainly the lines describing Hero's attraction have nothing to do with a "business arrangement":

> But now I am return'd and that war-thoughts
> Have left their places vacant, in their rooms
> Come thronging soft and delicate desires,
> All prompting me how fair young Hero is. . . .

And when Don Pedro shows the sort of compassion Benedick had refused Claudio, the latter adds:

> How sweetly you do minister to love,
> That knows love's grief by his complexion!

Furthermore that Claudio is indeed in love is shown by the strange changes in him, for according to Benedick he has become a different man: his speech, his dress, his taste in music —all these have changed. And this cannot be one of Benedick's tirades against love and therefore false. If what he says were not true, Benedick would have no reason to rehearse Claudio's changes in a soliloquy, and, more important, he would never ask if he, too, might so change. And of course Benedick does change, and in that particular he repeats Claudio's experience. What both do is first scorn love and lovers, then become lovers themselves, and precisely the same is true of Beatrice. Neither she nor the other two ever attack the conventions of romantic love; they attack love and the opposite sex. And although Claudio's reasons for scorning love are not given in detail, they are said to be those of Benedick, and these are certainly underscored. For the latter, the chief deterrent to marriage is the fear of being cuckolded, which is made as explicit as Shakespeare can make it, and it is one of the themes connecting the two plots. Nor is Beatrice really concerned with the dreary conventions. She makes no allusion to them, and she insists that she is grateful to God for sparing her, not from the conventions, but from a husband.

It is true, of course, that Benedick and Beatrice maintain to the end their negative attitude towards the fashionable code of love-making; in this they do not change. But that attitude is not dramatically exciting, and it is not shown in conflict with any action within the play itself. For instance, such an attitude would be dramatically effective and meaningful if it were contrasted with the attitude represented by Claudio and Hero. But these two are nowhere in the play given the extravagant hyperboles of such lovers as the sonneteering lords of *Love's Labour's Lost*. The reason is that Shakespeare's concern here is with something else about their love and its contrast with that of Benedick and Beatrice. What is central to the thought of the play is the approach or attitude toward love of the two pairs and the way that attitude changes in the course of the play. For Claudio and Hero love, first swift and superficial, and based entirely on "the view," is slowly and after much pain matured into something of inner worth and permanence.

In contrast, Benedick and Beatrice begin by scorning love and each other and they end by falling in love. Thus both pairs of lovers are shown developing, though differently: Claudio and Hero grow towards understanding each other, while Benedick and Beatrice grow towards understanding themselves.

The chief event in the play, then, is the achievement by the lovers of self-awareness and a mature attitude towards love and each other. And the emphasis on this change is yet another step in the evolution of Shakespearean romantic comedy. For here the inner development of the lovers, especially Benedick and Beatrice, is made much more explicit than in both earlier as well as later romantic comedies. In *Love's Labour's Lost,* for instance, the change in the king and his lords is merely projected rather than achieved at the conclusion of the play. On the other hand, having fully dealt with the theme in *Much Ado About Nothing,* Shakespeare allows it far less scope in Phoebe's conversion in *As You Like It* and Olivia's in *Twelfth Night.* But in these plays he creates Rosalind and Viola who are already possessed of the self-awareness and mature view of love which Beatrice achieves at the conclusion of her play. The psychological exploration of Beatrice's character leads to the conception of the other two heroines, a conception presupposing and transcending her own.

As You Like It

Chapter VIII

*W*ith *As You Like It* Shakespeare reached a significant milestone in his career as comic dramatist, and here his mode of romantic comedy achieved so successful a form that further development of it seemed impossible. In *As You Like It* a number of experiments and trials carried out in earlier comedies find their full fruition. This is particularly true of Shakespeare's unceasing search for a harmonious relationship of idea or theme and the story or metaphor with which to give it expression. He had already attempted this metaphorical dramatization of his theme in such plays as *The Two Gentlemen of Verona, Love's Labour's Lost,* and most especially in *A Midsummer Night's Dream* and *The Merchant of Venice.* But in none of these earlier plays had he achieved the perfect agreement of idea and symbol that we find in *As You Like It.*

In addition to achieving this just relationship of story and theme, *As You Like It* is the first comedy in which the chief idea in the play is enshrined in the temperament and attitudes of the heroine. And this is no small matter, seeing that the dramatist had travailed long to bring into agreement the psychological realism necessary to the creation of character and that character's expression in word and deed of Shakespeare's long-standing theme of romantic comedy. Rosalind surpasses Shakespeare's earlier romantic heroines precisely in this very point. The story of her flight to Arden and her adventures there may not be of the most absorbing interest; the story may be, as some students of the play believe, of minor importance.[1] But Rosalind is realized on the stage as a living character, one possessed of so much that is verifiable by experience that we never question the genuineness of her being. But she is more than that. Her temperament, as we shall see, is of a special sort, like that of no other heroine before or after in Shakespearean comedy. And what makes her unique is the special but true-to-character combination in her of certain attitudes towards love and life, towards herself and her fellow human beings.

II

In our present study of *As You Like It* it is necessary to investigate briefly the matter of date since from some quarters doubts have been raised concerning the general agreement that the play was written some time between 1598 and 1600.[2] Although he accepts 1598-1600 as the date of the play as we have it in the Folio text, John Dover Wilson has argued that that text represents a substantial revision of an earlier version which he believes Shakespeare had composed in the summer months of 1593.[3] His evidence is of two kinds. First, textual inconsistencies in such matters as the relative statures of Rosalind and Celia, the names of the two Dukes, and the length of time Duke Senior spends in the Forest of Arden. Such inconsistencies, not uncommon in Shakespeare, can be explained as oversights or misprints, errors due to carelessness,

not changes due to revision. Second, the presence of alleged
verse-fossils in the text, that is, scannable lines of prose which,
the argument goes, originally had been written in verse. This
sort of revision is not easy to demonstrate, for scannable lines
of prose occur in the work of many writers and in many other
Shakespearean plays. E. K. Chambers believes that in Shakespeare such lines come thickest at about the time of *As You
Like It* and *Twelfth Night*.[4] In *As You Like It*, for instance,
there are many more such prose passages than Professor Wilson cites, and by way of illustration E. K. Chambers prints
as verse a prose passage (ll. 133-40) from the same scene (I, ii)
in which Professor Wilson finds verse-fossils only in ll. 158-233.[5]

The theory of revision, in addition to questioning the generally accepted date of the play, raises a further problem,
namely the extent to which Shakespeare may have revised
the structure of his play and the conception of his chief characters. This is a matter of great seriousness, since the characterization of Rosalind, for instance, was presumably changed
very little in the allegedly revised text. At least this is the
inference one draws from the arguments presented in the New
Cambridge Shakespeare. Is the Rosalind of the 1623 text the
same as the Rosalind of the alleged 1593 version of the play?
Furthermore, is the happy and most effective association of
idea and symbol in the play, to which reference was made
earlier, part of the original version or of the revised text?
In other terms, was the revision merely a matter of style, a
change of a few verse lines into prose and of some minor matters such as the relative statures of Celia and Rosalind? If so,
then we must conclude that in 1593 Shakespeare composed
As You Like It substantially as it has come down in the Folio
text. And this is quite difficult to accept, for the play's structure, its conception of character, and the harmony and perfect
adjustment of these two to its theme are achievements no student of Shakespeare will grant him in 1593. There is a further
difficulty. Professor Wilson is among those who believe that the
part of Touchstone was created by Shakespeare for Robert
Armin, who had replaced Will Kempe in 1598 or 1599.[6] But

if the play was first composed in 1593, unless the role of Touchstone was either added or transformed in the allegedly revised version of 1598-1600, Shakespeare must have created a new comic character in 1593, that is, he must have conceived Touchstone long before Armin became a member of the Chamberlain's Company. The contradiction can be eliminated only by the assumption that Touchstone was added to the original in the revised version. And for this there is no evidence whatever.

This is not to say that the original version of *As You Like It* was precisely the same as the text of the Folio. Some revision may have taken place, but if so it must have occurred either shortly before the play was first acted or some time between 1600, when it was entered in the *Stationers' Register,* and 1623. In the light of the available evidence we can do no more than speculate as to the precise time, nature, and extent of a revision; indeed we cannot be certain that *any* revision took place. What *is* certain is that the play as we have it is the work of Shakespeare's mature years, the years in which he produced his most successful romantic comedies, not the years in which he was experimenting with materials and forms and searching for a comic mode which would accommodate certain themes he wished to dramatize. *As You Like It* is not an experimental play; it is as far from it as any play could be. That this is so a cursory glance at the play makes clear, but I hope it may be even clearer after an analysis of the play's achievement.

III

Our examination of *As You Like It* may begin with the simple questions we have raised in the study of earlier comedies. What sort of play is *As You Like It*? What is its theme or main idea and by what means is it expressed? What is the play's connection with earlier comedies as well as with those which follow? What are its special qualities, the chief points of its success?

As we have noted earlier in this study, certain of Shakespeare's comedies emphasize one set of motifs while other comedies lay stress on different motifs or ideas. The rejection of love, for instance, the mockery of lovers, implied or expressed, is a common motif in Shakespearean romantic comedy, although in some plays it receives only minor treatment. For instance, it appears briefly in *The Two Gentlemen of Verona* and *The Taming of The Shrew*. In *As You Like It* the motif of the reluctant or disdainful lover is appropriately the story of the pastoral lovers Silvius and Phoebe, and though given limited scope, it is made a relevant part of the action and it contributes significantly to the statement of the play's larger theme.

Now this motif of the disdainful lover, which *Much Ado About Nothing* treats at great length, is not the chief idea of Shakespearean romantic comedy; it is only an aspect of it. The chief idea of that comedy is the discovery and expression of an ideal attitude towards love and life. This, I believe, is the serious purpose of Shakespeare's romantic comedies, although of course they deal with other matters as well. In order to arrive at this ideal attitude, and by "ideal" is meant the best possible in our world as we know it, at least three other distinct attitudes or points of view are presented in significant juxtapositions: the rejection of love by a proud and disdainful lover; the realistic or anti-romantic attitude which lays stress on physical attraction; and the extravagantly romantic attitude. In the plays we have examined, these attitudes are dramatized with varying emphases with the aim of arriving at what was earlier called the ideal attitude. But that ideal attitude has been merely hinted at in the earlier plays; or where it was clearly pointed to, this was achieved by the juxtaposition of characters who expressed extreme attitudes which were made to point to a golden mean. It is true that in *A Midsummer Night's Dream* Theseus and Hippolyta represent the ideal point of view which is presumably what the two pairs of lovers will attain through their union. But very little is made of Theseus and Hippolyta's point of view, and rightly so, since the chief interest of the action resides in the adventures of the four lovers. In *Much Ado About Nothing* what is implied at the conclusion of the play is that Benedick and Beatrice have attained an attitude which is midway between their earlier disdain and the romantic idealizing of love. But again it must be noted that these characters are presented in the play not as *possessing* such an attitude but rather as attaining it at the play's conclusion. The first heroine of Shakespearean comedy who may be said to have achieved what we have called the middle or ideal point of view is Portia in *The Merchant of Venice,* but here, as we noted in an earlier chapter, it must be kept in mind that Portia has a double role, as a lover in Belmont and as a judge in the court of Venice. Her attitudes toward love are implied rather than expressed. Rosalind of *As You Like It* is the first Shakespearean heroine who not only possesses those attitudes but who is also most charmingly articulate about them. While in earlier comedies Shakespeare had juxtaposed characters representing different—sometimes opposed—attitudes and by such a device pointed to an ideal view, in *As You Like It* he presents that point of view in the temperament of his comic heroine.

Shakespeare's comic point of view, instead of merely rejecting extremes, juxtaposes or combines them into a balanced doctrine; it qualifies both the Petrarchan hyperboles of romantic lovers like Orlando and the exclusively physical concerns of anti-romantic characters like Touchstone; it fuses the Platonic idealism expressed in the phrase *amor intellectualis dei* with the *amor vulgaris* of its opposite extreme. In love and in all life's processes, this comic point of view brings together idealism and realism, and in their juxtaposition points to an optimum, a best possible attitude that men may attain in the world of experience. Shakespeare's comic view sets as its aim the crystallization of this best possible attitude by gently mocking different extremes into mutual qualification.

How can a comic dramatist best represent this mutual qualification of attitudes which must point to an ideal or best possible concept of love? How best can he represent the opposite or extreme attitudes which, through juxtaposition and mutual qualification, may point to the ideal but an ideal consistent with the nature of the world we know? What, in other words, is the best metaphor or symbol by means of which the dramatist can simultaneously achieve the mockery of extremes and their resolution into an optimum point of view? Some such question we must consider in looking at Shakespeare's romantic comedies, and most especially at those employing what we have called a symbolic structure. For by symbolic structure we mean a story offering far more than its overt action and the immediate relationship of its characters in the course of that action. For instance it is clear that the structure of *A Midsummer Night's Dream* differs significantly from that of *Much Ado About Nothing*. The difference lies mainly in the nature of the story or rather stories Shakespeare combined into the plot of the former. Those stories deal with places and characters whose significance goes far beyond their objective relationship. In *A Midsummer Night's Dream* the court and the enchanted wood beyond Athens differ very significantly in their symbolic representation. And the same is true of the lovers and the fairies and Bottom's mechanicals. The same quality we find in the plot of *The Merchant of Venice,* where again the places of action as well as certain episodes transcend the objective context of the story.

In *A Midsummer Night's Dream* both the wood and the action occurring in it during the night are given a frame of special reference by the presence of the fairies. These are spirits outside the human ken, and their chief contribution is to create and sustain an otherworldliness, a region or state of being above that of objective experience. Through them the wood attains an extra-human quality, a context we would justly associate with a romantic attitude. The atmosphere created by the world of the fairies one would naturally relate to the dreams of romantic lovers, to the hyperboles of Petrarchism. Surely the land inhabited by such spirits is the proper scene of the capricious and unpredictable events of romance. The division between the court with its human characters in daytime and the wood with its fairies by night is so clear-cut that it threatens to reach awkward formality. For that reason the symbolic quality of that contrast is quite obvious; and for the same reason the fusion of the two is extraordinarily difficult.

In *A Midsummer Night's Dream,* then, we have a formal division between the two *loci* with their worlds, but the two are connected by the dramatist in a most important manner: the fairy-world is a metaphorical or symbolic representation of the world of romance, the world dreamed or imagined by romantic lovers. Romantic love is thus presented in analogy with the world of spirits and fairies, the world we, as well as the lovers, conceive in imagination. And here, in this special relationship of the two themes, we come upon one of the most brilliant devices of Shakespearean romantic comedy, a unique conception of structure. In a good many of Shakespeare's romantic comedies, the selection of materials and the relationship imposed upon them by the dramatist aim at creating an analogy between a story of romantic love and another story whose romanticism is simultaneously exposed to the searchings of the comic spirit. Here the romanticism inherent in our concept of the fairy world is subjected to the same and concurrent correction as romantic love and the excess of Petrarchan extravagance. As we noted in an earlier section on *A Midsummer Night's Dream,* the world of the fairies is beset with limitations, the very shortcomings of married lovers which the romanticism of the human characters completely ignores. Oberon and Titania are at this very point divided, separated, and their conflict tends to qualify significantly our heretofore romantic attitude towards the ethereal, extra-human world we imagine them to inhabit. Here, then, are fairy lovers who are not happy "for ever and a day," as the romantic Orlando would have lovers in *As You Like It.* And our gently qualified attitude towards the fairy lovers carries over into the romantic story of the two Athenian couples. The process operating here is, then, the reduction of the romantic or Petrarchan approach by means of analogy. And the device is a Shakespearean contribution to the structure of romantic comedy.

But the success of this device in *A Midsummer Night's Dream* followed long experimentation and search. The search, perhaps unconscious in the beginning, may be seen in the earliest of the comedies. For the visitors to Ephesus, the city smacks of the supernatural, its reputation having placed it apart as a city of magic and the occult. In the end it is shown that there is nothing supernatural either in the city or in the identity of two apparent strangers who look alike. In *Love's Labour's Lost,* as was pointed out in an earlier section, the analogy is between romantic love and language, particularly the language of romantic love itself. In *The Merchant of Venice* the analogy is between romantic love and pure justice, the romantic insistence on the abstract letter of the law, both in the bond story and in the ring episode. Even Bassanio and Gratiano, happy wooers in romantic Belmont, must violate their promises and part with the rings in Venice. And Portia's acceptance of the limitation and her forgiveness is a precondition of her happy union with Bassanio.

In none of these plays, however, is the choice and analogical adjustment of themes as successful as in *A Midsummer Night's Dream.* For here the analogy possesses a point of correspondence which is of great significance: both stories or plots are love stories, or at least they both deal with lovers, although Oberon and Titania are husband and wife. The world of Oberon and Titania should be precisely the sort of world romantic lovers dream of, but it is not. And what is more startling is that Titania, alienated from Oberon, is made to dote on Bottom with his ass's head. In the romantic context of the wood and the fairy world which temporarily inhabits it, the episode of Titania and Bottom is utterly anti-romantic. And this anti-romanticism is one of the chief aims of the play's symbolic structure. But of course that anti-romanticism is not the ultimate aim and purpose of the play; it is but a means to a more nearly even and balanced view of love. Precisely the same is true of the structure and dramatic effects of *As You Like It,* with this difference: here the effects are achieved in a superior fashion since they proceed exclusively from the actions of human characters.

If it is true that in his search for an effective comic mode Shakespeare created the sort of analogical structure we saw in these early plays, then we should expect him to employ it again, especially if that structure had proved successful, or, if merely promising, for the purpose of exploring it further. The pattern might be improved by means of more effective characterization or by the use of stories dealing with exclusively human characters, or both. Or better still by the choice of themes that could be made to reflect more readily and meaningfully upon each other. These may have been among Shakespeare's reasons for employing an analogical structure in the composition of *As You Like It*. And the analogy he chose here is between romantic love and pastoralism.

The choice of pastoralism as the theme to dramatize in analogical relationship to romantic love was surely inevitable, especially as literary pastoralism was enjoying a wide currency in England at the time.[7] Yet Shakespeare showed no eagerness to reproduce for its own sake the sort of pastoral story which since Theocritus had inspired poets to extol the beauty and contentment of Arcadian life. As we shall see presently, Shakespeare's treatment of the pastoral theme is quite different from that of Sidney and Spenser and Lodge. And the most important difference is that his concern is not for the pastoral theme itself but for what it can be made to express concerning a larger doctrine.[8]

To the pastoral theme Shakespeare came rather slowly, in widely spaced and most carefully taken steps. He first employed the scene proper to a pastoral story, though not the story itself, in *The Two Gentlemen of Verona* and *Love's Labour's Lost*.[9] In both plays lovers are transferred from the court to an Arcadian scene, where love and general harmony ultimately triumph. But in these plays the scene carries no symbolic significance, and it is only tentatively related to the theme of romantic love. Nevertheless, it appears that Shakespeare kept it near the center of his thought, at least in the period of experimenting with comic structure. Years later he was to employ it again, though for different purposes, in *The Winter's Tale* and *Cymbeline*. In *A Midsummer Night's Dream* the

world of Athens is contrasted with the enchanted wood with
its fairies, and in *The Merchant of Venice* the world of the
Rialto is opposed to the world of Belmont. But in none of
these plays did Shakespeare employ an explicitly pastoral scene
or story. It is in *As You Like It* that for the first time he chose
a pastoral story as the basis of his plot. But again it must be
observed that the pastoral story was chosen not for itself but
rather for what it could be made to do. In *As You Like It*
Shakespeare placed within a dramatic structure the conflict
between literary pastoralism, as well as the pastoralism of
fashionable Elizabethan conversation, and the real world of
the country, but that conflict, though of interest in itself, is
here made to reflect on the larger theme of romantic love.
For the conflict between pastoral convention and reality includes
the motif of pastoral love and its literary conventions, its sighs
and tears, its imagined and exaggerated sufferings, as well as
the true and actual loves of real shepherds and country yokels
who struggle hard to earn a bare living from the unyielding
earth. Romantic love had been associated with pastoralism
for centuries and indeed had formed its principal motive.
The young shepherd of conventional literary pastoralism is
inevitably the lover of a disdainful shepherdess, or, himself
disdainful, rejects the love of a fair shepherdess and thinks only
of the chase; in the end all such lovers are united.[10] Thus in
addition to presenting an idealized view of country life the
pastoral dealt with the all-important theme of unrequited
love which ultimately triumphs. Shakespeare could not long
overlook the splendid possibilities of such a subject for his
romantic comedy. And when he chose to treat it in *As You
Like It* he was most fortunate to find ready at hand Lodge's
little book which dealt with the very subject Shakespeare was
bound to dramatize sooner or later, a story of romantic love in
a pastoral setting. In this and in most details of the tale Shakespeare and Lodge are at one, but they have few other points of
contact in dealing with the story of Rosalynde.

A love story in a pastoral setting is, then, the first and most significant point of identity between *Rosalynde* and *As You Like It*; and it is the most significant feature of Lodge's novel so far as Shakespeare's choice of it is concerned. It is precisely the sort of tale Shakespeare would have had to invent, had not Lodge most conveniently accommodated him. Although in earlier plays Shakespeare had placed the wooing of lovers in the country or the wood, he had not made the scene explicitly pastoral, nor had he introduced pastoral characters in characteristic action. What he still had to do, and Lodge did it for him, was to present the wooing of shepherds and shepherdesses on the stage. There are outlaws in *The Two Gentlemen of Verona*, fairies in *A Midsummer Night's Dream*, but no shepherds. Even Jaquenetta, the country wench in *Love's Labour's Lost*, though she prefigures Touchstone's Audrey, is not a shepherdess, and she is in no way identified with a pastoral setting. Shepherds and shepherdesses appear in Shakespeare for the first time in *As You Like It*. Rosalind and Celia and their wooing are placed in a pastoral scene; they even play at being shepherds themselves. But the scene in which the play is laid contains also its own lovers, Silvius and Phoebe and William and Audrey. And Lodge's *Rosalynde* had provided both the scene for the transferred loves of the aristocratic couples as well as its own love stories. In doing so the novel offered Shakespeare a pastoral story which could be made to comment not only upon the romantic loves of the princely exiles but also on its own pastoral wooing. And this is what Shakespeare must have found most attractive in Lodge's *Rosalynde*.[11]

To Lodge's pastoral novel Shakespeare went for the chief characters and action of *As You Like It*. Whether he knew Lodge's own source, *The Tale of Gamelyn*, a fourteenth-century lay printed for the first time in 1721, cannot be determined, although some scholars are convinced that he did.[12] If he saw the poem, as Lodge had done, in manuscript, his indebtedness to it must be of the slightest sort, so slight as to be negligible. But we must again stress the features in Lodge's novel which attracted Shakespeare. It was not the dramatist's

aim to create a pastoral play in imitation of the type known
as Renaissance pastoral drama. A student of the play's relation
to its sources has commented that "as a subsummation of
Renaissance types of pastoral the play fails singularly in that
the most important strain, that represented by the *Arcadia,*
the *Pastor Fido* and *Aminta* with their background of a pastoral state with its laws, rites and observances, is lacking."[13]
This is certainly true, but it is in no way a blemish since
Shakespeare's aim was not the reproduction of the conventional pastoral but rather the use of certain of its features for
dramatic purposes of his own. Nor was his chief purpose to
satirize the literary pastoral, as some of his students have maintained. This is not to say that Shakespeare does not mock some
of the postures of pastoral poetry and pastoral drama, but his
doing so has a larger and far more serious purpose.[14]

From Lodge's *Rosalynde* Shakespeare took his main story
which, it has been suggested, belongs to "the world of fairy-
tale or folk-lore"; it is indeed a romantic tale of love which is
first frustrated by circumstances, then consummated in the adventures of the lovers in the Forest of Arden. Lodge supplied
also the subsidiary action of a strictly pastoral kind which we
may designate as the subplot, the chief characters, and even
suggested individual passages and at least one song.[15] Indeed
one may say that Lodge supplied Shakespeare with everything
he needed in composing *As You Like It*.[16] For that very reason
the difference between the two works is all the more striking,
and it is due to the profound difference in the two authors'
attitudes towards the same material and the use they made of
it. For Lodge the chief aim was to compose a graceful love
story laid in a pastoral setting and written in fashionable
euphuistic style. In the novel both the romantic love stories
and the pastoral theme are presented with a minimum of what
we may call the comic attitude or point of view. For in general
Lodge seems to accept without serious comic reservations the
conventions of both romantic love and literary pastoral. In
this he differs most significantly from Shakespeare, whose attitude to both themes is not only unlike Lodge's but truly

unique. And this special and individual attitude is responsible for both the general treatment of Lodge's story in *As You Like It* and also the changes, omissions, and additions made by the dramatist.

In fashioning his play out of Lodge's novel, Shakespeare shortened the story and at the same time gave it a larger scope. He cut off years from the novel and also invented characters and episodes whereby he was able to represent a larger sweep of human experience. But in shortening Lodge's story Shakespeare did not intend merely to make his own plot more manageable; he discarded episodes for more important reasons. For instance he eliminated a great deal from both the beginning and the end of Lodge's novel. He reduced both the violence and number of the quarrels (from three to one) between Orlando and Oliver, and he discarded altogether the revolt at the end and the ensuing battle in which the usurping Duke is slain. By thus softening the action Shakespeare was able to maintain throughout a unity of atmosphere consistent with the idea of reconciliation which invariably concludes the action of his romantic comedy.

Among other significant changes made by Shakespeare which contribute to a unity of both structure and mood are the following: he omitted the extravagant blusterings of Rosader (Orlando); he made the two dukes brothers; he made Celia choose to accompany Rosalind into exile, instead of being exiled by her father, as Lodge has it; he made Orlando offer to fight the wrestler instead of being urged to do so by his brother, as in Lodge; he made Orlando's father a friend of the banished Duke and an enemy of the usurper; he made Orlando carve verses on trees instead of Montanus (Silvius) as in Lodge; his Orlando is wounded by the lioness while he attempts to rescue Oliver, and not by outlaws as in Lodge; his Orlando's momentary hesitation to save his sleeping brother menaced by the lioness is due to vengeful impulse rather than the thought of material profit, as in Lodge;[17] Shakespeare's usurping Duke is not slain, as in Lodge, but converted.

These are significant alterations and yet in the novel and

the play the general movement of the story is very nearly the same, and this in spite of other differences between the two, for instance the invention of new characters, like Jaques, and Touchstone. Neither these nor any other changes or additions, then, affect momentously the story itself. They are necessitated by Shakespeare's artistic purpose, which was not to reproduce a romantic tale laid in a pastoral scene with its conventional attributes but rather to express a significant relationship between romantic love and the pastoral convention and to dramatize certain attitudes towards them.

By the mid-1590's Shakespeare, it seems, was no longer content to deal singly with the isolated theme of romantic love; and it is likewise clear that he had shown no enthusiasm for pastoral poetry. But of course he was throughout profoundly concerned with expressing a certain comment upon romantic love and its conventions, and in the play before us he resolved to do so both directly and also by means of an analogical dramatization of the pastoral theme. Thus what in *As You Like It* is truly different from *Rosalynde* is the way romantic love and the pastoral are related in the play, the way in which attitudes towards the one are employed to reflect and comment upon attitudes towards the other. It is true, as Professor Prouty insists, that the major themes of the play are "the Arcadian existence and love, both of which had been well worked over in Elizabethan literature and . . . in fashionable conversation."[18] But these are also Lodge's themes in *Rosalynde*; what makes the difference, and it is a very great one, is the way in which these two themes are combined in the play. Unable or unwilling to view the pastoral convention and romantic love in perspective, Lodge presents them in sequence, flatly and independently. He makes no significant comment upon them or upon what might prove a significant relationship between them. In a sense Lodge fails to connect the two themes.

Thus one of the differences between Lodge's treatment of the pastoral and Shakespeare's is Lodge's singleness of attitude as opposed to Shakespeare's complex point of view. Lodge is content to see the idyllic aspect of the pastoral theme and he reproduces it faithfully and without ironic or comic qualification. This single and unqualified attitude toward the convention which informs Lodge's novel appears in *As You Like It* only in the conception of Silvius and Phoebe, and even here their pastoralism is somewhat more complex than that of *Rosalynde*. For instance, Shakespeare's Silvius, though Rosalind charges him as well as Phoebe with lack of common sense, is yet conscious that some of his actions are "most ridiculous" and thus shows a slight variation from the conventional lover of pastoral story.[19] And Phoebe, too, though clearly modelled after the type of scornful shepherdess, includes in her conception the awareness that Silvius' wooing is somewhat ridiculous because removed from strict fact.

> O, for shame, for shame,
> Lie not, to say mine eyes are murderers!
> Now show the wound mine eye hath made in thee.
>
> (III, v, 18-20)

This is not to say that Phoebe rejects love in the manner of Beatrice, and yet in one small particular the two have something in common. In Lodge, Phoebe's conventional rejection of Montanus' suit is vaguely motivated. In opposing his courtship she says: "Yet *Montanus* I speake not this in pride, but in disdaine; not that I scorne thee, but that I hate Love: for I count it as great honour to triumph over Fancie, as over Fortune."[20] In *As You Like It* Phoebe's reason for rejecting Silvius is relevant to Shakespeare's over-all treatment of romantic love. Both Silvius and Phoebe, then, though the products of a literary tradition which goes back to Theocritus, are by Shakespeare endowed with sufficient awareness to modify that tradition.

But of course their criticism of that convention is limited and it is certainly obscured by the far more forceful comment of other characters and episodes. For Shakespeare presents a variety of attitudes toward pastoralism, not all of them connected with the wooing of shepherds and shepherdesses, although the criticism of pastoralism at large is intended to reflect upon the larger theme of romantic love. The conventional pastoralism of Silvius and Phoebe, gently mocking itself, as we have seen, is contrasted at the other extreme by William and Audrey, whose rusticity supplies what has become an indispensable realism in Shakespearean romantic comedy. To the idealized existence of literary Arcadian pastoralism Audrey and William oppose the crude actualities of a shepherd's life. But such realism, negating the bucolic ideal, is itself an extreme and therefore by no means the final statement on the theme. That final comment is introduced by another shepherd in whose attitudes the opposed sentimentality of Silvius and the realism of William are reconciled. Silvius may be the unrequited lover sighing "upon a midnight pillow," and William on his side may be the uncouth bumpkin whose interest in Audrey is utterly devoid of sentiment, but their opposition is balanced not by the critical mockery of Touchstone or even Rosalind but rather by Corin's temperament and point of view. He is a very different shepherd from both Silvius and William. Real shepherds need not be like either of them, and in the play Corin, himself a product of the literary pastoral, represents a middle ground, that balanced view of life and love which we have come to expect in Shakespearean comedy.

In his first appearance on the stage Corin engages Silvius in an eclogue-like passage which stamps them both as natives of the pastoral convention. Corin, however, modifies that convention by means of concrete reference. He is a working shepherd who earns his living by serving another man whom he describes as of "churlish disposition." Both here and later with Touchstone, Corin establishes his identity by means of concrete detail relating to the sort of work he does as well as by his attitude towards that work and the world at large. But he makes a further contribution to the themes of the play by his attitude towards the love of Silvius for Phoebe, for Corin is a shepherd who is aware of both the pangs of unrequited love and also the amusing postures of romantic lovers. He has been a lover himself, and now in his more settled years he is able to tutor his young colleague in the ways of it. He rejects the sentimental self-abandonment of the posing Silvius and in its place offers practical means whereby to win Phoebe. In all this—in his attitude towards a shepherd's life and towards love, in his exchanges with Silvius, Touchstone, Rosalind, and Celia—Corin exhibits a near ideal, a temperament and a point of view in which sentiment and common sense are reconciled into an agreeable balance, an equilibrium matched in the play only by Rosalind.

What is common in both characters is a stability and incisiveness of view, a clarity absent in the rest of the *dramatis personae,* including Touchstone. The latter's attitude towards both a shepherd's life and his own courtly existence, or rather his way of expressing that attitude, admits sufficient variation to blur the total effect. This is particularly true in his colloquy with Corin, where the two engage in a kind of contest such as is to be found in pastoral literary tradition. In contrast with Corin's straightforward declarations concerning his shepherd's ways and convictions, Touchstone offers now a direct, now an ironic commentary. Although he pretends to pity Corin's simplicity and his lack of courtly manners and refinement, he simultaneously implies a criticism of these. To Corin's inquiry as to how he likes "this shepherd's life" Touchstone replies with ironic ambiguities. "Truly, shepherd, in respect of itself, it is a good life; but in respect that it is a shepherd's life, it is naught." Again in contrasting Corin's pastoral existence with life at court Touchstone employs simple irony in his warning that because he has never been in court, Corin is damned and in "parlous state." Because Touchstone's irony escapes him— and this is not to his discredit—Corin avers that courtly manners would "be as ridiculous in the country, as the behaviour of the country is most mockable at the court." And this is one of the chief points of their colloquy, that is, to bring about Corin's forthright and sensible comment that each place has its own manners and that such manners, when transplanted, appear "most mockable." The pastoral life, if seen from the city, appears somewhat different from what it actually is, and the same can be said of court life. But Touchstone is not done, and his irony persists in his inquiry into the propriety of manners even in their proper place. Corin believes that the courtly fashion of kissing one's hands in salutation would be "uncleanly" in the country, for shepherds' hands would be greasy from handling their ewes. "And they are often tarred over with the surgery of our sheep; and would you have us kiss tar? The courtier's hands are perfumed with civet." But all these are shallow instances, and Touchstone proceeds to show that the kissing of hands in the country would be no more disagreeable than it is in the court. "Why, do not your courtier's hands sweat? And is not the grease of a mutton as wholesome as the sweat of a man?" And he further declares that "civet is of a baser birth than tar, the very uncleanly flux of a cat."

In this exchange between them Shakespeare reveals the difference in the roles of Corin and Touchstone. Corin represents a stable and positive point of view, and his attitudes, clear and uncomplicated, are expressed directly. Touchstone, on the other hand, instead of representing or expressing a forthright point of view, is intended to expose and mock, in straightforward statement or by means of irony, the attitudes of other people. In mockingly warning Corin that he is "in a parlous state" because he is ignorant of courtly manners, Touchstone's aim is to satirize those manners, although his irony escapes the simple shepherd. "You have too courtly a wit for me," he says, and his complaint is itself a gentle mockery of Touchstone's own exhibition of an aspect of those courtly manners he is himself satirizing. Corin's position is clear and his attitude towards the country and the court never changes. It is an attitude Shakespeare stresses as the most reasonable when seen from the point of view of the country. It is a compromise between Silvius' sentimentalism and William's extreme realism.[21] And that attitude towards pastoral life and the world at large parallels and sustains Corin's view of love which he in vain communicates to Silvius.

Unlike Corin's, Touchstone's estimate of pastoral life appears inconclusive, and it is not true, as some have argued, that he "judiciously evaluates pastoralism as represented in literature. . . ."[22] What he considers and comments upon is the very

life before him, the life he has been forced to live in the Forest
of Arden in the company of Rosalind and Celia. Corin's initial
question when they meet is "And how like you this shepherd's
life, Master Touchstone?" The latter is indifferently impressed
by it, and his comments have to do with the here and now: he
likes and does not like it; he says Corin is damned for being
innocent of courtly manners, and yet Touchstone shows that
those very manners are ridiculous. Thus his comments on
the conflict between pastoral life and life at court cannot be
taken in a strict biographical and psychologically consistent
sense. They are instead comments made at strategic moments
in the play, comments necessary for their specific and thus
limited effect in particular episodes. They do not represent a
man's stable point of view nor do they serve as the dramatist's
own—or the play's—final statement on the theme concerned.
This is also true of Touchstone's commentary on Silvius' romantic love. While Corin views the younger shepherd's posturings good-humoredly and advises how Silvius might win the
love of the disdainful Phoebe, Touchstone's attitude or
rather comment is exclusively satirical. Silvius' love reminds
Touchstone of his own affair with Jane Smile, and his recall
of specific details is intended to ridicule the pastoral wooing
of literary convention and through it the wooing of all romantic
lovers. This is the purpose of his choice of particular details
such as his "kissing of her batler and the cow's dugs that her
pretty chopt hands had milk'd," and the punning reference to
the peascod. While it is clear that such comment is intended
to reduce Silvius' pastoralism and particularly his playing the
romantic lover by the book, the effect of Touchstone's contribution is inconclusive. What his parody succeeds in doing is
simply to bring into play certain unromantic and even violently realistic details in the life and wooing of shepherds.
The implicit presence later on of realistic comment in the persons of Audrey and William is not sufficient for Shakespeare's
purposes. To that implicit comment he adds Touchstone's
parody as well Rosalind's more sympathetic and ultimately
more significant comment. While Touchstone merely attempts

to bring down with a crash Silvius' pastoral wooing, Rosalind admits it as cognate in part with her own love experience. But her doing so does not prevent her from later censuring Silvius' sentimentality and perverse submission to the tyrannical Phoebe. It is true, as some have argued, that Touchstone's bathos is not destructive merely and that its effect is "to open the way to a more soundly based attitude to life."[23] But his parodic effect is primarily to refer to that other side of life— at the opposite extreme—and thus to provide a temporary comic shock. But that contribution is slight and it merely points to Rosalind's later definitive reconciliation of the extremes presented in the episode. Touchstone's role, then, in so far as he comments upon the pastoral theme and the related theme of romantic love is partial: it has a functional and somewhat static significance. In the present episode and elsewhere in the play Touchstone has a function rather than a life, and that is to record the reservations of the comic spirit concerning both idealized pastoral life and romantic love.

Certainly no clearer index of Touchstone's contribution can be found in the play than his first comment upon reaching the Forest of Arden. To Rosalind's complaint that her spirits are weary Touchstone replies: "I care not for my spirits, if my legs were not weary." Shakespeare will not have his audience conceive of Arden as an idyllic scene although early in the play he makes the unlikely wrestler compare it to the "golden world" and relate it also to the "old Robin Hood of England." Shakespeare's Arden is neither the ideal here hinted at in Charles's words nor yet the utterly commonplace suggested in the drab world of William and Audrey. Touchstone is not impressed by the Forest of Arden, and his two mistresses had expressed fears concerning their safety in it. What Touchstone finds in Arden is fatigue and hunger as well as Audrey, and in addition shepherds like Corin, who get their living "by the copulation of cattle." And he ironically pretends to be shocked by Corin's betrayal of "a she-lamb of a twelvemonth to a crooked-pated, old, cuckoldly ram, out of all reasonable match." Moreover it is Touchstone who in the concluding scene of the

play tells the Duke that with Audrey he presses "amongst the
rest of the country copulatives, to swear and forswear, according
as marriage binds and blood breaks." To call the romantic
lovers "country copulatives" and to suggest that those whom
marriage—or romantic love—binds blood can break is very
startling indeed. The speech has, then, its temporary shock
effect, as so much else of Touchstone's utterance, but in addition it supplies the indispensable element of realism which contributes to the creation of the proper attitude toward pastoralism, love, and life generally.

In Touchstone Shakespeare presents the ironic satirist of
both idealized pastoralism and romantic love. In that role
the jester mocks the ideal by placing by its side aspects of
reality which that ideal overlooks. In his exchange with Corin,
Touchstone merely pretends to find fault with a real shepherd's life.[24] But he refuses to idealize life in Arden or the
ways of pastoral wooing. On the contrary he knows all too
well the physical discomfort of such life, and he knows also
that in general shepherdesses are not won by means of love
poetry. His own wooing of Audrey is in contrast with Silvius'
and Orlando's, yet Touchstone too has written verses to his
lady although Audrey fails to respond to them, for alas she is
not "poetical." Nor does she know the meaning of the word.
"I do not know what 'poetical' is; is it honest in deed and
word? is it a true thing?" In his reply to her, Touchstone re-
moves the subject from the immediate scene where it scarcely
belongs and in a few lines not only touches the larger meanings of poetry but also relates it, as Theseus had done, to the
theme of love. "No, truly; for the truest poetry is the most
feigning; and lovers are given to poetry, and what they swear
in poetry may be said as lovers they do feign." Again it must
be noted that Touchstone's comment on poetry and lovers is
equivocal just as his opinions on pastoral and court life had
been in his colloquy with Corin; and thus what he says here,
though consistent with his attitudes throughout the play, must
be taken not so much as revelation of character as something
needed to be said. It is material to be synthesized into an

optimum comment and point of view, but that synthesis is not Touchstone's concern but Rosalind's. Touchstone's contribution is indispensable to Shakespeare's conception of the theme of the play: he added Touchstone to Lodge's *dramatis personae* for the purpose of recording, through him, certain aspects of that theme.[25]

IV

The same reason explains the presence and conduct of the other characters added by Shakespeare to the story he found in his sources. This is certainly true of William and Audrey, who represent an aspect of pastoral life—and love—which the Arcadian convention often leaves out of account. Not their own character but what they contribute to the theme, then, is what is significant in this pair of shepherds. Nor can they be truly called realistic conceptions of pastoral life. They are somewhat below it, providing not a standard of life in contrast to that of Silvius and Phoebe but an opposite extreme to theirs. And they are contrasted with Silvius and Phoebe as well as with Corin, who stands somewhere between the two pairs.

Jaques, the fourth and last of Shakespeare's significant additions to the *dramatis personae,* likewise functions more as an agent than as an individual life with his own psychological integrity. Like the other three, his role is primarily to say certain things, to record particular attitudes which need to be brought upon the stage.[26] And like the others his attitudes towards pastoralism and love and everything else are extreme, and they serve as component parts of a larger synthesis, a broader vision to be expressed by the heroine. But because his view of the world is that of the self-appointed satirist stressing the less attractive aspects of life, some of the play's critics have tended to dismiss him as an alien force not in keeping with the play's mood. Such a view of Jaques misconceives the dramatist's intention in including that character among his *dramatis personae.* For it can be maintained that Jaques' views are indispensable to the working out of a balanced but comprehensive outlook. It is true, as has been pointed out, that a "certain sour distaste for life is voided through him, something most of us feel at some time or other," and that if "he were not there to give expression to it, we might be tempted to find the picture of life in the forest too sweet."[27] But Jaques' main concern is not with the country and the vaunted sweetness of pastoral life. His constant target is man, whether in city, court, or forest, and his chief aim is to press upon us his own misguided conviction that man's life is altogether evil and detestable. It is this extreme statement of the deliberate satirist that seems to jar against the spirit of the play. But although Jaques' point of view is extreme, the play offers at least partial illustration of human evil. For instance the conflict between the two pairs of brothers in the play tends to support the notion of human strife and pain. But though the play begins with the record of such strife and pain, its action works out a conversion of the two evil brothers. And it offers in addition overwhelming evidence of goodness, of love and loyalty and sacrifice. There can be little doubt that Shakespeare's intention in creating Jaques was not only to introduce into the scheme of the play allusions to the less attractive features of human life but also to satirize a particular type as well as the general attitude of the new satiric school at the turn of the century.[28]

But to return to what Jaques has to do with the pastoral theme of the play. Although his chief concern is larger than the pastoral theme, it should be stressed that pastoralism offers him the means of illustrating human depravity. For Arcadian life with its simplicity and innocence, he believes, has been destroyed by man's intrusion. Nature has been debauched by human influence to the degree that Jaques finds it convenient and proper to speak of the forest and its animals, now fallen, in human terms. For instance he sees a clear correspondence between human action and the wounded stag's needlessly augmenting the stream with its tears. The First Lord reports one or two of Jaques' "thousand similes."

> "Poor deer," quoth he, "thou mak'st a testament
> As worldlings do, giving thy sum of more
> To that which had too much."
>
> (II, i, 47-49)

And then when the herd had failed to stop by the wounded stag, Jaques had this to say:

> "Ay," quoth Jaques,
> "Sweep on, you fat and greasy citizens.
> 'Tis just the fashion. Wherefore do you look
> Upon that poor and broken bankrupt there?"
>
> (ll. 54-57)

And in his concluding lines the First Lord summarizes the scope of Jaques' satiric preoccupation:

> Thus most invectively he pierceth through
> The body of the country, city, court,
> Yea, and of this our life; swearing that we
> Are mere usurpers, tyrants, and what's worse,
> To fright the animals and to kill them up
> In their assign'd and native dwelling-place.
>
> (ll. 58-63)

The self-satire implicit in Jaques' comments on man's intrusion into the world of nature, that is, the pastoral world, is intended, I believe, to reflect on his equally self-satirical remarks on man's activity in city and court. Both views are equally extreme and thus they are included in the play's world for that reason: they represent a comic deviation from what we should consider the middle or sensible position, the view expressed by the very juxtaposition and mutual qualification of opposite extremes. All this is of course very clear, but what needs to be stressed is the means whereby Jaques describes the enormity of man's evil. That means is the pastoral scene as it is both invaded or rather intruded upon by man, and also as it is changed by that intrusion. For man's ultimate, and to Jaques the most horrible, influence upon the innocence of nature is that the normal movement of life in the country is debauched by man's depravity. Somehow, to Jaques it appears that the unfeeling disregard of the herd of deer for the wounded stag is to be charged to man's own inhumanity to man.

It is precisely the preposterousness of such a view which Touchstone recognizes and in his first meeting with Jaques employs to ridicule him. For Touchstone's tongue-in-cheek pseudo-philosophy takes prisoner Jaques' ear, and the most brilliant aspect of the scene is that the motley fool proceeds to "moral on the time" in Jaques' own idiom. It is this which causes the latter's "lungs . . . to crow like Chanticleer" when Touchstone, in lines reported by Jaques, pronounces the ponderous fact that, as it was ten o'clock,

> 'Tis but an hour ago since it was nine;
> And after one hour more 'twill be eleven;
> And so, from hour to hour, we ripe and ripe,
> And then, from hour to hour, we rot and rot. . . .
>
> (II, vii, 24-27)

This is precisely the way Jaques would have phrased it and indeed does since he is here repeating Touchstone's words to him. Particularly dear to Jaques' heart is the concluding line in the passage, a line which, though attributed to Touchstone, is really Jaques' own. For the dramatist makes a clear distinction between the views and therefore the roles of these two. While Jaques is obsessed with the evil of things as they are, that is with real life and its shortcomings, Touchstone's concern is to burlesque idealized life. While Jaques satirizes real life, Touchstone mocks the idealized expressions of pastoralism and romantic love. And here we must note that Jaques is included among the objects of Touchstone's mockery since he is the most vulnerable pseudo-idealist in the play.[29]

From all this it follows that although both Touchstone and Jaques comment upon the themes of pastoralism and romantic love, the ways they go about it are quite different. For instance Jaques' attitude towards the pastoral is not directly

satirical, as many critics have argued. Nowhere in the play does he ridicule directly the concept of conventional pastoral life. The mocking of the convention is made *through* Jaques rather than *by* him. For Jaques believes in an extreme form of pastoralism which he opposes not only to the sophistication of court and city life but also to the life led in Arden by the exiled Duke and his followers. To Jaques the Duke's presence in Arden impinges upon the harmony of pure pastoralism and destroys the innocence of a prelapsarian existence in nature. Thus he sees the banished Duke and his men as "mere usurpers, tyrants."

The same distinction between Touchstone and Jaques is to be seen in their attitudes towards romantic love. As we have noted, Touchstone brings within our view the concrete or physical aspects of love, and his concern for the sensual is the means whereby Shakespeare gently mocks the excessive sentiment of such romantic lovers as Silvius and Orlando. Jaques, on the other hand, is opposed to romantic love altogether, and he finds fault not only with Orlando's carving songs on the barks of trees but also with the very name of Rosalind. Furthermore, forgetting that in earlier scenes he has himself spoken very little prose, Jaques leaves in affected disgust when Orlando greets Rosalind in verse.

> Nay then, God buy you, an you talk in blank verse.

In his artificial bitterness towards life Jaques is opposed and mocked, as we have seen, by Touchstone, but also and more significantly by the principal pair of lovers. Shakespeare presents Jaques in colloquy, first with Orlando and later with Rosalind. And in both instances his exchange with the lovers significantly precedes the two most delightful wooing scenes in the play. When Orlando refuses Jaques' request to "sit down . . . and . . . rail against our mistress the world," the latter leaves the stage with these words:

> I'll tarry no longer with you. Farewell, good Signior Love.

To this Orlando replies:

> I am glad of your departure. Adieu, good Monsieur Melancholy.

In his exchange with Rosalind, though he is allowed, as elsewhere, to mock himself, Jaques is put down even more decidedly by the far more incisive comment of the heroine:

> *Rosalind.* They say you are a melancholy fellow.
> *Jaques.* I am so; I do love it better than laughing.
> *Rosalind.* Those that are in extremity of either are abominable
> fellows, and betray themselves to every modern
> censure worse than drunkards.

But Rosalind heaps more direct ridicule than this on the departing pseudo-cynic. When Jaques explains that his melancholy is "of mine own, compounded of many simples, extracted from many objects, and indeed the sundry contemplation of my travels. . . ," she hurls the following on his turned back: "Farewell, Monsieur Traveller. Look you lisp and wear strange suits, disable all the benefits of your own country, be out of love with your nativity, and almost chide God for making you that countenance you are. . . ." (IV, i, 33-37) Finally Jaques' cynicism is rejected in two further episodes. In the first instance the Duke attacks his constant and undiscriminating pessimism in what must surely be the most damaging lines concerning Jaques:

> Most mischievous foul sin, in chiding sin.
> For thou thyself hast been a libertine,
> As sensual as the brutish sting itself;
> And all th'embossed sores and headed evils
> That thou with license of free foot hast caught,
> Wouldst thou disgorge into the general world.
>
> (II, vii, 64-69)

The second instance, far less direct than the Duke's heated outburst, occurs a short time later in the same scene. Just as Jaques completes his famous speech on the seven ages of man with its stress on the less noble features of each age, "Orlando returns with Adam in his arms." The stage direction or rather the silent action it describes is an oblique but forceful negation of what Jaques has been saying. As elsewhere his abstract and theoretical cynicism is undercut by some one else's word or action on the stage. But it must be noted that Jaques' artificial pessimism leaves a substantial residue, enough to contribute to the final synthesis. The point to be stressed is that Jaques' view of the human condition is extreme and for that reason unacceptable. Its role in the play is to provide a reminder, so to speak, in the final formulation of the thought of the play.

Although Jaques is roundly reprimanded by the Duke, he remains a member of the ducal group in Arden, and his factitious melancholy is approximately echoed, at least in part, in the first two of the songs sung by Amiens. The songs are identical in tone although the carefully controlled pessimism of the second seems a bit stronger. In brief they complain of "man's ingratitude" in city life and in its place offer a happier pastoral existence, although this latter involves physical discomforts. It should be noted that the first song, "Under the greenwood tree," is sung for Jaques, although there are others present, for at the end of the first stanza Jaques requests "another stanzo."

Jaques. More, more, I prithee, more.
Amiens. It will make you melancholy, Monsieur Jaques.
Jaques. I thank it. More, I prithee, more. I can suck
melancholy out of a song, as a weasel sucks eggs.
More, I prithee, more.

(II, v, 10-14)

From his insistence that Amiens should sing more lines we should conclude that Jaques approves the song and its invitation to all those who "ambition shun" to come and "live i' th' sun." But if this is so, what shall we make of Jaques' own "verse to this note," which he recites to Amiens?

> If it do come to pass
> That any man turn ass,
> Leaving his wealth and ease
> A stubborn will to please,
> Ducdame, ducdame, ducdame!
>   Here shall he see
>   Gross fools as he,
> An if he will come to me.

(ll. 52-59)

Are these lines merely a mockery of pastoral contentment, as some critics have suggested?[30] It may be so. And such an effect would be consistent with Shakespeare's care to maintain a balanced view of pastoralism; Jaques' "verse" would thus keep within bounds the suggestion in Amiens' song that pastoral life is truly ideal. It is also possible that in addition to seconding the notion in Amiens' song that pastoral life is not altogether pleasant, Jaques' lines offer a second comment, a corollary to the first. And this is to mock the idea expressed in the second stanza of the song that there *could* be one who "doth ambition shun," who could "come hither, come hither." In brief, Jaques' verse may be taken as an ironic reply to the song's invitation. Certainly the Duke and his group, though they have adjusted to life in Arden, and though their songs insist that such a life is superior to that of the court, nevertheless hasten to return to the latter at the conclusion of the play. And this is justly so, for in spite of their enforced sojourn in Arden the Duke and his followers belong in the court and their life there need be no less felicitous than pastoral life. For after all, the play suggests, only those who can be happy in one place can be happy in any other.

The second song is sung by Amiens at the invitation of the Duke a moment after Orlando has returned with Adam in his arms. And thus Orlando's return and the stage direction describing it form a silent yet forceful comment upon Jaques' speech on the seven ages. But Orlando's devotion serves as an even more powerful opposite to the chief idea of Amiens' song which follows. For though it may be true that man's ingratitude is more unkind than the winter wind, Orlando's tender care of Adam shows that it is far from true that "most friendship is feigning, most loving mere folly." Nor does the very loyalty of the Duke's friends offer any support to the theme of Amiens' song. In the present scene, then, Jaques' speech on the seven ages of man and Amiens' song on man's ingratitude are opposed not only by Orlando's devotion to Adam but also by the Duke's reception of them, and by the action of the very persons who complain of man's inhumanity to man. Furthermore, the very fact that the complaint is sung helps to soften its impact. As elsewhere, Shakespeare manages to include, both in the statement of the two songs as well as in their contexts, an element of self-criticism, a device by which he limits the force of an extreme view in the very act of stating it. Thus the chief effect of the two songs is a note of laxness and artificiality in their complaint. The cynicism of the verses, distant and theoretical at best, is not only qualified by the tone but also negated by concurrent comment or action on the stage. And out of all this emerges the conclusion, hinted at rather than stated, that even as man's inhumanity to man is exaggerated, so is the notion that the country is the only place where happiness can be achieved. The forest possesses no exclusive path to contentment, and only those who can be content in court can find contentment in Arden.[31]

v

Before taking up Rosalind's role in the play we must consider briefly that of Duke Senior and his contribution to the play's concept of pastoral and court life. It is not difficult to see that although the Duke, like his "co-mates and brothers in exile," finds life in Arden

> more sweet
> Than that of painted pomp,

that sweetness and harmony are qualities he has imported into the forest rather than found there. We should make allowances for his overstatement that he finds

> books in the running brooks,
> sermons in stones. . . .

Like Amiens' songs the Duke's lines overstress the inherent
nobility of Arden, and that exaggeration is again a means for
securing balance. Nevertheless, if the Duke does indeed find
particular books and sermons in nature, he has brought with
him the temperament and disposition necessary for such discovery. He has carried into Arden the impulse towards generosity and sympathy, which, we may infer, he had shown in court
and which may have been in part responsible for his removal.
For it is clear that the lessons he finds in (or rather brings to) the
forest are very different from those discovered (or brought
in) by Jaques.[32] In any case, one need not go to Arden to feel
"the penalty of Adam" and "the season's difference." Nor is
it possible only in the country to conclude that the "icy fang"
and "churlish chiding of the winter's wind" is no flattery. In
truth the Duke's pastoralism, though urbane, is by no means as
detached as we should wish it. On the contrary it is colored by
a sentimentality and conscious melancholy revealed by his insistence upon stressing his exile and upon finding socio-philo-
sophic lessons in Arden. If the Duke believes that the woods
are "more free from peril than the envious court," he comes
near to contradicting himself later in his exchange with Orlando when the latter breaks in upon the ducal group while
at dinner. It should be observed first that Orlando's appeal
for succor is couched in very significant terms:

> But whate'er you are
> That in this desert inaccessible
> Under the shade of melancholy boughs
> Lose and neglect the creeping hours of time. . . .
>
> (II, vii, 109-12)

There is a gentle and oblique reprimand in the reference to
"melancholy boughs" as well as to the loss and neglect of time.[33]
And this suggestion of languor and sentimentality is yet another means whereby the dramatist controls our response to

the concept of pastoralism expressed by the Duke and his lords. But as suggested above, the Duke's own words later in the scene qualify his earlier declarations concerning pastoral existence. In replying to Orlando's appeal, the Duke voices a different view of country and city life.

> True is it [he says] that we have seen better days,
> And have with holy bell been knoll'd to church,
> And sat at good men's feasts, and wip'd our eyes
> Of drops that sacred pity hath engend'red. . . .
>
> (II, vii, 120-23)

Whereas Jaques finds evil everywhere, the Duke finds good in the same places. For though he had earlier contended that life in Arden was superior to that of the "envious court," he now adds that he has known "better days" elsewhere. There is no inconsistency here, for those who enter the forest bring their own visions with them: the Duke finds good in everything, not merely in Arden but everywhere. And thus he can truly say of either city or country life that it is "better." This is also the inference to be drawn at the conclusion of Touchstone's colloquy with Corin, though there the idea is expressed in negative terms: Touchstone would say that neither place is "better."

This, then, is the Duke's role in the play's exposition of the pastoral theme. Shakespeare, as we have said, wishes certain things to be stated about the chief ideas in his comedies. In *As You Like It* one of these is the theme of pastoralism, and various episodes are designed chiefly for the purpose of providing comment upon that theme. And that comment is so directed as to reflect upon the greater theme of romantic love. Although the Duke's attitude towards pastoralism, although his own pastoralism, is not free of sentiment, that attitude is not thereby vitiated, for the same sentiment appears in his reminiscence of city life. The effect is to suggest a more balanced view of the matter than that of either Touchstone or Jaques. But the Duke's view is far from the final comment of *As You*

Like It, the reason being that his twin attitudes lack sufficient detachment, the sort of objectivity which places fact by the side of sentiment. In short, the Duke's comment upon the pastoral theme is vulnerable to the searchings of the comic spirit whose touchstone is reality. The simultaneous sense of the real and the ideal which Shakespeare has been pointing to in his earlier comedies is to be found only in Rosalind. In her conception Shakespeare is at last able to express at once engagement and detachment, the capacity to feel as well as to control emotion, the commingling in her temperament of feeling and judgment in perfect equilibrium. It is this which makes Rosalind the dramatist's climactic achievement in his search for a comic heroine who would express in word and act a particular comic vision.

What is truly different and even startling in her characterization is not only the simultaneous expression of these opposites but also its adjustment to the psychological realism necessary for the creation of a highly complex and individual personality. We may go even further. In Shakespearean drama it is extremely difficult as well as unwise to single out characters who allegedly act as the dramatist's spokesmen. Nevertheless, in so far as Rosalind is able to see and respond to the world with feeling as well as judgment, to partake of human illusion even as she acknowledges the fact and is amused by it, to adjust the real to the ideal—in so far as she is capable of doing this— she can be truly said to express Shakespeare's comic approach or attitude to the human situation. In earlier plays that approach is to be interpolated by the reader or audience by placing together different attitudes expressed by different characters or by the same characters at different stages of the play's action. In *As You Like It* these attitudes are given voice by Rosalind throughout the play.

This awareness or multiple vision which expresses itself most clearly in the comic valuation of her own feelings enables Rosalind to advance and direct the action of the play, particularly the part dealing with love. Having chosen to treat the pastoral theme through the attitudes of Corin, Touchstone,

Jaques, the Duke, William, and Audrey, and some of the songs, Shakespeare made the love theme Rosalind's special, though not exclusive, concern.[34] In particular her chief function in the play is, as it has been said, to bring about a synthesis of different and even conflicting attitudes to love as these are expressed in the love affairs of four pairs of lovers. This she does by means of her own love for Orlando, by the way she controls and directs their wooing, and also by her various comments on the other love affairs, particularly that of Silvius and Phoebe.

VI

In her first appearance onstage Rosalind exhibits briefly the sort of melancholy proper to the daughter of an exiled Duke, but such concession to simple realism is soon replaced by a hint of more characteristic complexities. For instance, the note of self-pity revealed in her initial speech disappears when Touchstone joins her and Celia a few lines later. A moment thereafter, upon Orlando's arrival, Rosalind is swept by love at first sight, and during the remainder of the scene behaves in the conventional way of romantic lovers. But the way of romantic lovers, though amusing even to Rosalind in the balance of the play, is here presented as something actual and true. What is recorded in the episode is that Orlando and Rosalind fall in love; what among other things will be recorded later, mostly through Rosalind's agency, is that the way of lovers, including these two, whether they follow literary convention or not, is amusing and not infrequently ridiculous. After establishing this most necessary fact that Rosalind and Orlando are in love and that both have behaved in the way of romantic lovers, Shakespeare may proceed to the far more entertaining and meaningful complexities of Rosalind's role in the play. By way of bridging the simplicity of the early episode with those complexities of later action, Shakespeare in Act I, scene 3, shows a Rosalind on her way to that self-awareness which is one of the most characteristic and most necessary features of her temperament. When the scene opens Rosalind is so sad that she has not a word "to throw at a dog."

> *Celia.*   But is all this for your father?
> *Rosalind.* No, some of it is for my child's father. Or, how
>   full of briers is this working-day world!
>
> (I, iii, 10-12)

The concluding line recalls the heroine's melancholy revealed upon her first appearance on the stage, but Shakespeare has already injected a note of self-awareness in her speech which gives it a lightness and flexibility and in addition a special quality of humor. Her reply that some of her sadness is "for [her] child's father" illustrates at this early stage the comic tone of her language, a very individual tone which distinguishes her not only from the rest of the *dramatis personae* but also from Shakespeare's earlier comic heroines as well. "Is it possible," Celia asks a moment later, "on such a sudden you should fall into so strong a liking with old Sir Roland's youngest son?" And Rosalind replies: "The Duke my father lov'd his father dearly." Although very brief, Rosalind's reply illustrates in this early episode both an attitude and a tone of speech which enable her to convey at once her deepest feeling and her comic valuation of it.[35]

When Rosalind and Celia, accompanied by Touchstone, reach Arden, they first encounter Silvius and Corin who are engaged in a sort of debate on the most likely pastoral theme, love. When a few moments later the tearful Silvius, acting the role of the pastoral unrequited lover, leaves the stage, Rosalind responds with the sympathy of one suffering like pain.

> Alas, poor shepherd! searching of thy wound,
> I have by hard adventure found mine own.
>
> (II, iv, 44-45)

The lines strike us as sentimental, and we may find it difficult to relate their tone to the Rosalind we know from the rest of the play. Furthermore, Shakespeare makes sure that the passage, as well as Silvius' complaint preceding it, are gently mocked by Touchstone's own reminiscence of his affair with Jane Smile. But although the sentimental passages are thus vulnerable, they nevertheless record the fact that lovers, including Rosalind, no matter how they express or exaggerate their feelings, do indeed suffer this pleasurable pain. Although she will never again reveal her emotions in this manner, and although she will later severely reprimand Silvius' sentimental self-abandonment, Rosalind here lends significant support to the romantic aspect of love. In the rest of the play she may comment upon her own love and that of others in a far richer, more complex tone, but Rosalind remains a romantic lover to the end, even though in the wooing scenes with Orlando she seems to mock everything we associate with romantic love. The outstanding thing about her is that she is capable of expressing both attitudes simultaneously and with equal conviction.

This complex attitude, already hinted at earlier, is revealed in full in the first of the wooing scenes between Orlando and Rosalind. The scene opens most appropriately with Orlando affixing upon the trunks of trees in Arden love poems addressed to the "fair, the chaste, and unexpressive she." It is this Petrarchism of Orlando's and his insistence upon wooing by the romantic book, so to speak, that Rosalind will deflate later in the scene, but she will do this without for a moment abandoning her own romantic sentiments. After the intervening debate between Corin and Touchstone to which detailed reference was made above, Rosalind enters reading one of Orlando's love poems. Her gentle mockery of the lines gives way to Touchstone's sexual realism in the poem he recites in answer to Orlando's. What is of interest in the clown's rhymes is that they bluntly qualify Orlando's blazon of the "chaste and unexpressive she."

> If a hart do lack a hind,
> Let him seek out Rosalind.
> If the cat will after kind,
> So be sure will Rosalind.

> (III, ii, 107-10)

These lines are in shocking contrast to Orlando's but Rosalind offers no defense. On the contrary, her allusion to grafting and medlars momentarily sustains the sexual context created by Touchstone. At that point Celia enters with more of Orlando's lines, and there follows her revelation that Orlando is the author and that he is in the forest. To this, Rosalind responds in the breathless manner of the romantic lover: "Alas the day! what shall I do with my doublet and hose? What did he when thou saw'st him? What said he? How look'd he? Wherein went he? What makes he here? Did he ask for me? Where remains he? How parted he with thee? And when shalt thou see him again? Answer me in one word." (ll. 231-37) And she maintains this romantic attitude throughout the episode. When Celia informs her that she found Orlando "under a tree, like a dropp'd acorn," Rosalind replies: "It may well be called Jove's tree, when it drops forth such fruit." When Celia tells her that "There lay he, stretch'd along, like a wounded knight," Rosalind says: "Though it be pity to see such a sight, it well becomes the ground." Finally, when Celia further informs her that Orlando "was furnish'd like a hunter," Rosalind replies: "O, ominous! he comes to kill my heart." Although her lines sustain the romantic approach to love, the tone Rosalind employs in speaking them lends a new complexity to her role. We may, of course, see these lines as "straight" and flat, but we would be nearer Shakespeare's intention, I believe, if we admit a hint of self-irony in Rosalind's tone. And this would fit well her deportment later in the scene when she accosts Orlando, for there her tone is nothing if not ironic.

After the interlude between Jaques and Orlando, and as soon as Jaques has left the stage, Rosalind, now in the simultaneous role of herself as well as Ganymede, opens her long conference with Orlando. Immediately she broaches the theme of love, and in her very first reference to it she voices that complexity of attitude already hinted at in earlier episodes. If there is no clock in the forest, she says, then "there is no true lover in the forest; else sighing every minute and groaning every hour would detect the lazy foot of Time as well as a clock." While she longs to know if Orlando is a true lover she simultaneously mocks the conventional lover's "sighing every minute and groaning every hour." She is at once Rosalind and Ganymede, or rather Rosalind and Rosalind as Ganymede, at once in love and insisting upon her lover's romantic posturing and also gently mocking both that very romantic posturing as well as her twin attitudes to it. As Ganymede she can recall her uncle's "many lectures" against love and also the "many giddy offenses" women are "touched with." When Orlando begs her to recount some of those offenses, she protests she will not "cast away . . . physic but on those that are sick," that is, men in love. And she adds that she would give "some good counsel" to the "fancy-monger" who has been abusing "our young plants with carving Rosalind on their barks" and hanging "odes upon hawthorns and elegies on brambles; all, forsooth, deifying the name of Rosalind." Here the complexity of simultaneous attitudes is at last expressed by both the dramatic situation and what might seem an arbitrary tone. But the tone, already emerging in earlier episodes, is here triumphantly united with the dramatic or stage contrivance in the meeting of Orlando and the disguised Rosalind. As noted earlier, her disguise enables Rosalind to include in her disquisition on love not only the alleged attitudes of Ganymede but also those of the Rosalind he is soon to impersonate. And all this gives extraordinary richness to the heroine's role and allows her to bring about that final synthesis of the play's chief ideas.

Orlando gladly admits that he is the guilty one "that is so love-shak'd," whereupon Rosalind announces, to his considerable distress, that he cannot be in love, for he exhibits none of her "uncle's marks" upon him. Those marks of the conventional lover, she tells him, are a lean cheek, a blue eye and sunken, an "unquestionable" spirit, a beard neglected, a hose ungartered, a bonnet unbanded, a sleeve unbuttoned, a shoe untied, and so on. But none of these are to be seen in Orlando, for he is, she tells him, "rather point-device in your accoutre-

ments, as loving yourself than seeming the lover of any other."
Though she is here gently mocking the convention, Rosalind
also aims at eliciting from Orlando the assurance he so eagerly
voices in his reply. "Fair youth, I would I could make thee
believe I love." And now, content with that for the moment,
she returns to her gentle censure of her sex in matters of love,
and as always she includes herself: "Me believe it! you may
as soon make her that you love believe it; which, I warrant,
she is apter to do than to confess she does . . . ." (III, ii, 406-8)
In sharp contrast to Rosalind's awareness, Orlando keeps in
the beaten path of the conventional lover. When she inquires
again if he is the author of the verses hanging on the trees, he
replies in predictable language:

> I swear to thee, youth, by the white hand of
> Rosalind, I am that he, that unfortunate he.
> *Rosalind.* But are you so much in love as your rhymes speak?
> *Orlando.* Neither rhyme nor reason can express how much.
>
> (ll. 414-17)

It is this flatly conventional language and the attitude it expresses that Rosalind essays to change when she offers to "cure"
Orlando of his love sickness. That cure consists simply in
exposing her sex's tyranny of their lovers and offering it in
corrective contrast to the Petrarchan blazon to which Orlando
is totally dedicated. Again her gentle ridicule of her sex,
herself included, is made obliquely through a double impersonation which softens its effect. She has cured a lover in
this fashion: "He was to imagine me his love, his mistress,
and I set him every day to woo me; at which time would I,
being but a moonish youth, grieve, be effeminate, changeable,
longing and liking, proud, fantastical, apish, shallow, inconstant,
full of tears, full of smiles; for every passion something and
for no passion truly any thing, as boys and women are for
the most part cattle of this colour. . . . (ll. 427-35) But all
this is lost upon Orlando, who when they meet again, as promised, in IV, i, returns to his romantic ways. And Rosalind on
her part resumes the lesson or cure, but not without first

revealing her own deepest longing for reassurance that Orlando loves her.

> *Orlando.* My fair Rosalind, I come within an hour of my
> promise.
> *Rosalind.* Break an hour's promise in love! He that will
> divide a minute into a thousand parts, and break
> but a part of the thousandth part of a minute in
> the affairs of love, it may be said of him that
> Cupid hath clapp'd him o' th' shoulder but I'll
> warrant him heartwhole.
>
> (IV, i, 42-49)

In a moment she will turn to a stronger and more direct satire of romantic conventions but always with an immediate reference to something Orlando has said and especially the manner of his saying it. After her passing allusion to the snail's horns and Orlando's avowal that his "Rosalind is virtuous," she asks him to woo her. And when she says she will not have him, he replies "Then in mine own person I die." To this she offers her strongest "cure," a brief anatomy of two classical archetypes of romantic love.

> No, faith, die by attorney. The poor world is almost six
> thousand years old, and in all this time there was not any
> man died in his own person, *videlicet,* in a love-cause. Troilus
> had his brains dash'd out with a Grecian club; yet he did
> what he could to die before, and he is one of the patterns
> of love. Leander, he would have liv'd many a fair year
> though Hero had turn'd nun, if it had not been for a hot
> mid-summer night; for, good youth, he went but forth to
> wash him in the Hellespont and being taken with the cramp
> was drown'd; and the foolish chroniclers of that age found it
> was—Hero of Sestos. But these are all lies. Men have died
> from time to time and worms have eaten them, but not
> for love.
>
> (ll. 93-108)

This, too, is lost upon Orlando, who continues his wooing by the book, insisting that Rosalind's frown would kill him, that

"all thoughts . . . are winged," that he would love and have
Rosalind for "ever and a day." To this last, Rosalind offers
yet another anti-romantic lecture, this one half-mockingly warning him against the wifely tyranny which she places by the
side of his own romantic illusions about her, though she cherishes those illusions even as she mocks them: "Say 'a day,' without the 'ever.' No, no, Orlando. Men are April when they woo,
December when they wed; maids are May when they are maids,
but the sky changes when they are wives. I will be more jealous
of thee than a Barbary cock-pigeon over his hen, more clamorous than a parrot against rain, more new-fangled than an
ape, more giddy in my desires than a monkey." (ll. 146-53)
And she follows this with allusions to wayward wives, concluding that "that woman that cannot make her fault her husband's occasion, let her never nurse her child herself, for she
will breed it like a fool." No wonder Celia complains a
moment later that Rosalind has "simply misused our sex in
your love-prate." But it is all to a purpose, though it comes
short of immediate fulfillment, for Orlando will not be "cured."
Nor should we take Rosalind's "misuse" of her sex at its face
value. It is but a half-serious, half-mocking, anti-romantic
lecture, delivered by one who a moment after Orlando's departure admits herself hopelessly in love: "O coz, coz, coz, my
pretty little coz, that thou didst know how many fathom deep
I am in love!" (ll. 209-11) And just as her grave matter turns
out to be half-jesting, so her jest and double jest is in the end
all too serious. When Orlando bids her farewell, saying for
"these two hours, Rosalind, I will leave thee," she replies:
"Alas, dear love, I cannot lack thee two hours!" It is, as E. E.
Stoll remarks, "a jest between them, and another jest for herself
and Celia, and underneath no jest at all."[36]

VII

Orlando is not the only character in the play whose romantic approach to love engages Rosalind. As we noted earlier,
she has a great deal to say about Silvius' sentimental self-abandonment to Phoebe's disdain. On the one hand, Rosalind re-

sponds to his plaints in the manner of one also in love and in like pain, but this is only one side of her attitude towards his love affair. Because neither Silvius nor Phoebe can see themselves or each other in any sort of perspective, Rosalind essays to qualify their single-minded attachment to the convention. Just as in her wooing scenes with Orlando she refuses to be what he and convention say she is, so in her counsel to Silvius and Phoebe Rosalind insists that they abandon their self-deception and look at themselves and each other as persons living in this "working-day world." In order to shock them into such a change of outlook she employs strong language, some of the most harshly anti-romantic lines in the play.

> You foolish shepherd, wherefore do you follow her,
> Like foggy south, puffing with wind and rain?
> You are a thousand times a properer man
> Than she a woman. 'Tis such fools as you
> That makes the world full of ill-favour'd children.
> 'Tis not her glass, but you, that flatters her;
> And out of you she sees herself more proper
> Than any of her lineaments can show her.
> But, mistress, know yourself. Down on your knees,
> And thank heaven, fasting, for a good man's love;
> For I must tell you friendly in your ear,
> Sell when you can; you are not for all markets.
>
> (III, v, 49-60)

This may or may not be a "lesson in economics," as one critic has phrased it, but it is clear that the anti-romanticism of the lines is deliberately gross for effect.[37] More significant than her disdain of Silvius is Phoebe's rejection of love, for although that rejection inheres in her role of the disdainful shepherdess, it is one of the chief themes in Shakespearean comedy. It is true that Phoebe's falling in love with Ganymede recalls yet another feature of the pastoral convention, which is described in the title of a poem attributed to Surrey by the first edition of *England's Helicon*: "Harpalus complaynt on Phillidaes love bestowed on *Corin*, who loved her not, and denyed him that loved her.''[38] But what is more relevant to Shakespeare's theme is that Phoebe not only falls in love at first sight with another shepherd but that she becomes enamored of Ganymede. This particular detail has point in providing the shock needed for Phoebe's conversion. It recalls a related motif in *Much Ado,* where those who mock and disdain love and each other suddenly discover that they are in love. And it anticipates the same circumstance in *Twelfth Night,* where the disdainful Olivia falls in love with the disguised Viola.

Even in this passive way Rosalind is made to affect and even control not only changes in a character's attitude but also the movement and direction of the play's action. Her remarks to Jaques reject extremes in whatever context; her own love affair illustrates most clearly her adjustment of the ideal with the real; her comment upon the pastoral convention, direct and oblique, points to the same adjustment. In all her words and actions Rosalind reveals in herself, and recommends to others, a combination of sentiment and good sense, the ideal and the actual, yielding to neither sentimentality nor cynicism. How superbly she is able to control sentiment is shown, for instance, in her report to Celia of a meeting with her father, the exiled Duke, in the forest: "I met the Duke yesterday and had much question with him. He asked me of what parentage I was. I told him of as good as he; so he laugh'd and let me go." (III, iv, 38-41) Whether in the wooing scenes with Orlando or in her colloquies with Celia, Jaques, or the Duke, or in the episodes with Silvius and Phoebe, whether deeply moved or amused, Rosalind maintains unclouded good judgment, a clarity of vision which, as many readers of the play have observed, is the chief value of the play.

In order to stress Rosalind's role Shakespeare comes very near to raising her speech and act to the level of symbol, and this is particularly true of the episode in which she promises the lovers that she will bring them together. She will join Orlando and Rosalind, Oliver and Celia, Silvius and Phoebe. "Believe then, if you please, that I can do strange things. I have, since I was three years old, convers'd with a magician,

most profound in his art, and yet not damnable." (V, ii, 64-67)
And of course in the concluding scene she does as she here
promises, "make all this matter even." There is no claim here
that Rosalind is a symbolic character. She is far too recog-
nizably human for that. But the concluding scene of the play
forces us to admit that a symbolic element is surely present in
the appearance, and particularly the words, of Hymen. This
final scene concludes happily the two strands of the play's
action: the conflict of the two pairs of brothers and the love
affairs of the four couples. Both actions end in union and
reconciliation, and as in all non-satiric comedy the wedding
ceremony symbolizes the union not only of the lovers but of
nearly all persons in the play. And here that union is dignified
by Hymen himself as he sings:

> Then is there mirth in heaven,
> When earthly things made even
> Atone together.

Surely here the dramatist, as other poets of his age and in particular Spenser, brings together Neoplatonist and Christian
notions concerning the meaning and power of love. And in
doing so he touches the very soul of romance. But we should
remember that Shakespeare places romance in a comic context
instead of merely reproducing it. To the cynic as well as the
satiric poet or dramatist the theme of romance is at variance
with reality and therefore unacceptable. To Shakespeare that
same theme is not only acceptable but the chief subject for
comic treatment. And what makes that theme eminently
attractive is the very fact that certain aspects of it are different
from or opposed to what is called the actual. In Shakespearean
comedy the heart of the action is this conflict or opposition
of the idealism of romance and the facts of the real world.
Touchstone is at great pains to bring together these two and
the same is true of Rosalind. Moreover, Shakespeare, in *As You
Like It* as in all his comedies, takes pains to juxtapose in different or in the same characters at different stages of the plot

the two contrasted themes. In Rosalind, as we have noted, the two appear together throughout the play. The soul of romance, its chief idea, is man's longing to achieve the beatitude which Hymen expresses in the lines quoted above. Of this something was said in earlier sections of this study, particularly those dealing with *The Merchant of Venice*. In fusing Platonic doctrine with Christian ideas, romance proposes that beatitude can be achieved only through love. But this is precisely the chief, the all-embracing, theme of Renaissance poetry; hence romance becomes its logical subject matter. But there are different ways of treating romance in literature. In Shakespearean romantic comedy, though romance is its subject, the dramatist refuses to reproduce, merely to dramatize, romance. Instead, he chooses to present it in a comic mode, to place its longing for the ideal against the fact of human limitation. This is what Shakespearean romantic comedy is about, and failure to see this has often led critics astray. One often comes upon the comment, from Jonson to our own day, that romantic love, being at variance with the truth, is unfit for comic treatment. Such a notion overlooks the fact that in Shakespearean romantic comedy the truth, the actual, is as indispensable as romance itself. As we have been saying throughout this study, the fusion or balance of these two is Shakespeare's chief concern in his comedies. And it is precisely because Rosalind is able to express this perfect equilibrium that she may be said to represent a culmination of Shakespeare's quest for the ideal comic heroine. For *As You Like It,* in its action generally, in its structure, in its variety of characters and their relationship, but most especially in the temperament of its heroine, expresses better than any other comedy the balance between the idealism of romance and the realism of the working-day world. The longing for ideal forms is qualified and balanced by the knowledge that full realization is impossible.

In *As You Like It* the pastoral theme is employed for the purpose of both stressing and qualifying the theme of romance and romantic love. And just as the attitudes of Silvius and Phoebe reach the limit of illusion, so the deportment of Wil-

liam and Audrey, and especially of Touchstone, goes to the
other extreme of naturalistic fact. As noted earlier, the play's
comment upon the pastoral theme—and that comment is made
by the juxtaposition of extremes—is intended by the dramatist
to carry over into the larger theme of romantic love. That
comment crystallizes the wisdom which can be achieved only
by the simultaneous experience of yielding to and controlling
emotion, of combining feeling with clarity of judgment. This
is the wisdom which underlies the thought of all Shakespearean
drama.

Twelfth Night

Chapter IX

I

*T*welfth *Night* has been called a masterpiece not of invention but recapitulation, a summing-up of the admirable features of the "joyous" comedies. It is certainly that and much more. Its connections with earlier Shakespearean comedies are many and they have to do with large elements of the plot, although of course we should bear in mind that some of these elements are present also in the sources of the play. In any case, it is clear that the confusion of twins goes back to *The Comedy of Errors*. The theme of a disguised lady serving the man she loves in his courtship of another woman, though present in the sources of *Twelfth Night*, had been employed in *The Two Gentlemen of Verona*. And here it may be worth mentioning that the disguised Julia in *The Two Gentlemen of Verona* calls herself Sebastian. Sebastian's devoted Antonio in *Twelfth Night* recalls Bassanio's equally devoted friend of the same name in *The Merchant of Venice*. With *Much Ado About Nothing*, as with other comedies, *Twelfth Night* has in common the motif of the disdainful lover, a motif it develops rather in the way of *As You Like It*, where Phoebe in some ways anticipates Olivia's fruitless love for a disguised lady. Another connection with *As You Like It* is an analogy in the roles of Viola and Silvius, both of whom undertake to advance rival love affairs of those they love themselves. Furthermore, and far more significant, is the fact that Feste, though of course a fresh, independent character, is a creation in the new manner of Touchstone, and he is intended to supply something like the latter's point of view and commentary.[1] These and other features of earlier comedies *Twelfth Night* employs in fresh combinations, in an action that, in spite of these borrowings, produces the impression of complete novelty. But although the story is fresh and although Shakespeare invents episodes and characters, the total effect of the play, its chief thematic concern, repeats the large meaning we have discovered in the earlier plays and particularly in the other two joyous comedies. If we accept as the play's chief theme the education in the ways of love of the disdainful as well as the romantic lover then it is clear that in this it repeats the central ideas of *As You Like It* and *Much Ado About Nothing*. And if in addition we accept Rosalind as the representative of the ideally balanced temperament and exemplar of the proper attitude toward love, then we shall conclude that Shakespeare intends something very like that in his conception of Viola. This is not to say that the two heroines have the same temperament but rather that through them, in somewhat different ways, the dramatist defines the proper point of view towards life's processes. Through their intelligent, levelheaded, and generous approach to the challenges of this "working-day world," they demonstrate the sure way to maximum happiness for themselves and those around them. Of this more presently.

In chronology *Twelfth Night* appears to have followed the other two joyous comedies, and its date can be fixed with fair accuracy. To begin with, the limits of that date are 1598, the year of Meres' *Palladis Tamia*, which fails to mention the play, and the first allusion to it on February 2, 1601/2 (Candlemas), in John Manningham's *Diary*, where he records that at "our feast wee had a play called 'Twelue Night or What you Will.' "[2] But before this performance of February, 1601/2, the play must have been acted in a private or public theatre or both. The title strongly suggests that it was first acted on Twelfth Night, and this would defeat Dover Wilson's view that it was originally drafted for the performance at the Inns of Court on February 2, 1601/2, to which Manningham alludes in his diary.[3] Two contemporary facts, though seeming to raise difficulties, ultimately contribute to a precise dating of the play. Shakespeare's company acted a play at court on Twelfth Night, January 6, 1600/1, and on that same day the Queen entertained Don Virginio Orsino, Duke of Bracciano, who was visiting her court. And what is even more tantalizing is his report in a letter to his Duchess that the Queen's entertainment had included *una commedia mescolata, con musiche e balli*, "a mingled comedy with bits of music and dances."[4] Unfortunately Don Virginio gives no further details but promises his Duchess to tell her more by word of mouth. From this and other contributory records Leslie Hotson has concluded that *Twelfth Night* was the play in question, that Shakespeare's Orsino is a graceful compliment to the visiting Duke, that Olivia is intended to suggest the Queen, and that Malvolio is indeed, as other critics had supposed, an audacious though by no means impudent satiric portrait of Sir William Knollys, the Queen's controller.[5] Some connection between the name of Shakespeare's Orsino and the Queen's royal visitor there must be, but it is scarcely possible that Shakespeare wrote the play especially for the Duke's entertainment. One reason is that he would have had scant time—just eleven days—to compose the comedy since firm news of the Duke's journey and of the probable date of his arrival reached Whitehall on Christmas Day, 1600.[6] It was thus on Christmas Day or shortly thereafter that the Queen gave detailed directions to her Lord Chamberlain which he was to follow in planning the grand entertainment. Among these directions occur the following: "To Confer with my Lord Admirall and the Master of the Revells for takeing order generally with the players to make choyse of [?the] play that shalbe best furnished with rich apparell, have greate variety and change of Musicke and daunces, and of a Subiect that may be most pleasing to her Majestie."[7] The probability is strong that "to make choyse" here means select a play in existence, not commission a new one, a play with music and dance and a theme pleasing to the Queen. The care and minuteness of detail in the royal directions suggest that the Queen was unwilling to allow chance and improvisation to detract from the splendor of the royal celebration, and it seems logical to conclude that she wished to present to her visitor a play known to possess the qualities she specified. Furthermore, it is not certain that Shakespeare's Orsino and Olivia would have been sufficiently flattering to Don Virginio and his imperial hostess. In all probability the play was written later in the year 1601, when the name Orsino could be employed with greater propriety and the character could be presented with greater freedom than would have been possible in 1600. Other evidence points to a date after 1600. The new map alluded to in III, ii, 66, is that in Hakluyt's *Voyages* which was printed in 1600. In addition, 1600 is the date of Robert Jones's *First Booke of Songs and Ayres* from which Shakespeare borrowed the song "Farewell, dear heart," which is sung alternately by Feste and Sir Toby Belch.[8] What all this does is to narrow the probable date of the play by placing it in or after 1600 and before Manningham's allusion on February 2, 1601/2. Since, as we have seen, 1600 will not do, the only Twelfth Night available was that of 1601, and this means that the play, the last of Shakespeare's romantic comedies, must have been acted for the first time a few weeks before Manningham's reference to it on February 2, 1601/2.

For the love story of the four chief characters in the play
Shakespeare may have turned to a variety of sources, dramatic
and non-dramatic. The chief of these seems to have been the
story of Apolonius and Silla in Barnaby Riche's *Farewell to
Militarie Profession,* first printed in 1581. Here Shakespeare
found the story of twins of different sexes, which would admit
a romantic treatment of the sort of confusion of identity which
in a different context had formed the central theme of *The
Comedy of Errors.* In addition he found a shipwreck on a
strange coast which forces the heroine to take the sex and name
of her brother. Thus disguised, Silla (Viola) seeks employment
with Apolonius (Orsino), the man she loves, who sends her to
court Juliana (Olivia) for him. The latter, rejecting Apolonius' suit, falls in love with the disguised Silla, who is later
replaced by her long-absent twin brother, Silvio (Sebastian).
Silvio's acceptance of Juliana's invitation, Juliana's revelation
of her betrothal, her criticism of the page's refusal to acknowl-
edge it, and the Duke's anger with his page—these matters are
so close to the corresponding episodes in *Twelfth Night* that
Shakespeare must have known Riche's version of the tale.[9]

The alleged topicality of the conflict between Sir Toby and
Malvolio has been the subject of much speculation. In addition
to Leslie Hotson's theory alluded to above, it has been observed
that another contemporary quarrel may have given Shakespeare
the impetus and even details for the attack upon Malvolio.
The quarrel was that between Sir Posthumus Hoby and
two or three gentlemen, including Sir Richard Cholmley and
William Eure, who, after a day's hunting in the country, in-
vited themselves to spend the night in Hoby's house and
proceeded to disturb that household with their boisterous
drinking. The matter was brought to trial and seems to have
been the talk of London during the years 1600-02.[10] Still another source for the Malvolio episodes has been found in
Sidney's *Arcadia,* in the broad comedy dealing with Dametas
and his family.[11] A more likely influence upon the episodes

with Malvolio and his tormentors may have been the severe onslaught upon humour characters in Jonsonian comedy. Such influence may have been particularly strong in Shakespeare's conception of Malvolio and Sir Andrew Aguecheek. The latter may be seen in part as a composite of Matthew and Stephen, Jonson's city and country gulls in his *Every Man in His Humour*.[12]

III

The materials available to Shakespeare were, then, extensive; and it is possible that he was indebted to a good many of them. But what is of great interest is that the two chief actions in the play, the mistaking of twins and the service by a disguised lady of the man she loves in his courtship of another woman, had each been dramatized in different plays by Shakespeare at the very outset of his career. In *Twelfth Night,* where he combines these two actions, he seems to complete the circle. But the way the two themes are combined and the conception of the characters, especially the heroines, clearly give proof of the distance Shakespeare had measured since the composition of *The Comedy of Errors* and *The Two Gentlemen of Verona.* And thus the structure of *Twelfth Night,* the way its episodes are conceived and related, the re-creation of characters found in the sources, the invention of new episodes and characters, the function of music and song, and in general the mutual qualification of the play's several parts—these matters derive in great part from earlier comedies written in the long interval of nearly ten years. Whether Shakespeare was indebted to a contemporary quarrel or Sidney's *Arcadia* for a few details in the Malvolio episodes it is impossible to say.[13] What is clear is that those episodes owe their presence to Shakespeare's concern with different attitudes toward love. And it is equally clear that those episodes are presented in close relationship to the chief events in the comedy. Malvolio is not simply the butt of the inebriated Sir Toby and Andrew Aguecheek. He is conceived in terms which bear close relevance to the love theme of the play.[14] Malvolio is first and last one of Olivia's *malvolio.*

suitors, and his chief contribution to the play is in representing a particular attitude toward love as well as toward himself and his world. In this he recalls Jaques of *As You Like It,* and it is his peculiar response to love and his rigid objection to all indulgence which exclude him for a time from the happy and harmonious conclusion of the play. Malvolio's opposition to indulgence, in itself an important theme of the play, is the immediate cause of his undoing, but that undoing has to do with him as Olivia's suitor, one who represents a particular conception of love. Malvolio has clearly evolved out of Shakespeare's preoccupation, in his romantic comedies, with different and often conflicting conceptions of man's ideal relationship to woman.[15]

Malvolio's love for Olivia, or what he takes to be love, is limited or rather vitiated by his extreme and humorless self-love. But there is another side in Shakespeare's conception of the pompous steward. The complete absence of humor and self-awareness in him is coupled with a fierce indictment of all liberality and pleasure.[16] In this he stands for an extreme view which, by juxtaposition with its opposite, is intended to point to an ideal attitude. But the theme of indulgence is not a gratuitous adjunct to the main concern of *Twelfth Night.* It is instead a theme dramatized in analogical relationship to the theme of love. Thus Malvolio, involved in both themes, must be seen as a central character, and the dramatist's conception of him is clearly dictated by thematic considerations. He evolves in great part out of Shakespeare's choice to dramatize the analogy between romantic love and self-indulgence.[17]

Other features in the action of *Twelfth Night* which derive from earlier plays may be cited. The scene in which Orsino declares his love for Olivia in the hearing of the disguised Viola repeats in the main the action of a similar episode in *The Two Gentlemen of Verona.* There is of course an important difference, namely the fact that, unlike Proteus, Orsino is not violating any love vows made earlier to the disguised woman who loves him. And this difference is dictated by the dramatist's choice to stress different motifs in the two scenes. In the scene

in *The Two Gentlemen of Verona* the emphasis is upon
Proteus' violation of his vows and the effect of his action upon
the disguised Julia. In *Twelfth Night* the stress is upon the
Duke's manner of expressing his infatuation with Olivia, his
hyperbolic romanticism, as well as upon its painful effect on
the disguised Viola. Here there is no immediate question of
fickleness on the part of Orsino in the sense of the episode in
The Two Gentlemen of Verona.[18] Orsino's outpouring of what
he considers his great passion for Olivia is of course undermined by his rhetoric, but it is also thrown into comic relief
in retrospect later on in the play by his all too sudden transference of that passion from Olivia to Viola.

Among the many links connecting the comedy with *Much
Ado About Nothing* is the ruse employed in the intrigues aimed
at the pair of reluctant lovers in the earlier play and at Malvolio
in *Twelfth Night*. The ironic effect of the conversations which
are intended to be overheard by Benedick and Beatrice is here
repeated through the letter which Maria drops in Malvolio's
path. Maria's letter is but a variation of Don Pedro's plan to
bring Beatrice and Benedick together. There are of course
the obvious differences in the circumstances of the ruse and
its ultimate effects upon its "victims." But there are also
certain striking correspondences of detail. Before he overhears
talk of Beatrice's love for him, Benedick, it will be recalled,
is shown in a long soliloquy attacking Claudio's recent transformation from soldier to lover. But at the conclusion of that
passage Benedick asks if he, himself, could be changed by love
in the same manner. The question and Benedick's uncertain
answer reveal that he is vulnerable, indeed ready to receive
the impact of Don Pedro's plan. In like manner Malvolio is
shown in the act of revealing his own readiness to be duped
by Maria's letter and its "revelations." He is presented in
soliloquy imagining himself worthy of Olivia's love. Indeed he
imagines himself married to her and in the act of making ready
to deal rather severely with Sir Toby. And at that very moment
his eye falls upon the letter. The episode is furthermore given
a refinement which likewise recalls and surpasses something

similar in the earlier play. Benedick is convinced that what he overhears is not counterfeited: the very thought that someone is trying to gull somebody is instantly rejected. And this is brought about by having that suspicion utterly demolished by the grave witness of the elderly Leonato. The words onstage merge into Benedick's own thoughts so imperceptibly that he would have thought "this a gull but that the white-bearded fellow speaks it." And later he concludes that "This can be no trick." In *Twelfth Night* Shakespeare in like manner provided a device by which Malvolio is tricked into the conviction that Maria's letter is genuine. What Malvolio reads in the letter are of course his own thoughts and most devout wishes, but there is more. When we consider the letter's style, particularly in the last long passage—"Let thy tongue tang arguments of state; put thyself into the trick of singularity"—we can see clearly that this is neither Olivia's style nor Maria's but Malvolio's own. It is a brilliant stroke. Both the thoughts and words in the letter are so expressive of Malvolio's being that they produce instant conviction.[19]

IV

Shakespeare's dependence on earlier comedies for certain elements of *Twelfth Night* ranged beyond his use in fresh combinations of certain episodes. As we have already noted, he repeats certain characters, though of course he recreates them in a fashion to fit the structural and thematic necessities of the story he is dramatizing. This is true in the creation or recreation of minor as well as major characters. Though lacking the brilliant virtuosity of Rosalind and her superior comic awareness, Viola is nevertheless meant to represent the same balance of sentiment with common sense, the same steady and level view of the world around her. In this she repeats Rosalind's function in the earlier play, a function made indispensable by the dramatist's chief concern in these plays. But of course the dramatic terms of her existence require individual features in Viola which are quite different from Rosalind's. Rosalind could not be repeated. Certainly in Viola's position Rosalind would never allow Orsino to maintain even a semblance of an initiative. But her general attitude towards love is repeated in Viola, though more profoundly, albeit more obliquely expressed in the latter. Rosalind's direct attempts to "cure" both Orlando and Phoebe, the one of his bookish Petrarchism and the other of disdain, are repeated by Viola in the later play. But a glance at her scenes with Orsino and Olivia will show how tentative Viola's approach is. She seldom opposes Orsino's whims, and when she differs with him, her comments are gentle and indirect. When she confronts Olivia in their initial meeting, her comment on the latter's disinterest in love is gentler than Rosalind's similar criticism of Phoebe. But Viola's words to Olivia carry greater significance, a maturer vision as befits her own temperament and also the character and position of Olivia. To Viola's inquiry if she is "the lady of the house," Olivia replies: "If I do not usurp myself, I am." Viola's comment on this expresses one of Shakespeare's favorite themes: "Most certain, if you are she, you do usurp yourself; for what is yours to bestow is not yours to reserve." The import of such a speech would have been beyond Phoebe, and perhaps it is beyond Olivia as well. But what is far more significant is that the speech could not have come from Rosalind, for the words proceed from the sort of stillness and reflection we would not associate with her temperament. The attitude expressed in the passage, though repeating Rosalind's general point of view concerning the rejection of love, is enriched by evidence of serious thought. It is an attitude presupposing Rosalind's and transcending it. Although rationality and incisive intellect combine to produce that most attractive quality in Rosalind which we identified with the comic spirit, it is also true that she is not innocent of emotion and the romantic attitude towards love and her lover. But with all this, it must be admitted that Rosalind is master of her emotions; she is in complete control of these as she is of her destiny. Though exiled and forced to disguise herself for safety, she is never in any danger. Rosalind is never in pain, and this is one of the chief points in which she differs from Viola. While Rosalind has "convers'd with a magician" and can do "strange things"—she promises to unite all the lovers on the morrow—Viola is bewildered by her dilemma.[20]

> O time! thou must untangle this, not I.
> It is too hard a knot for me t' untie!
>
> (II, ii, 41-42)

It may be said of Rosalind that she controls not only her emotions and her destiny but also the action of the whole play. The same cannot be said of Viola, whose role is somewhat passive by comparison.

This general difference in the conception of Rosalind and Viola is to be found also in other characters. Feste, for instance, though he repeats in part Touchstone's function, achieves his ends by more oblique means. Like Touchstone, his chief role is to comment upon and thereby deflate the sentimental pretensions of such characters as Orsino and Olivia. But his comment upon Orsino's love-melancholy and Olivia's capriciously excessive mourning is both more oblique in manner and more serious in tone than Touchstone's had been in the earlier play. In both cases Feste addresses his reducing commentary in part through songs of time's passing and lovers' deaths and thereby implies at once a subtler attitude towards the aberrations of Orsino and Olivia as well as a measure of sympathy.[21] These features of Feste's character and function suggest greater reflection, perhaps we should say greater maturity, than is revealed in Touchstone.

This reflectiveness implied in the character of Viola and Feste accords with—and indeed generates—a sense of melancholy characteristic of the general mood of the play. In spite of much revelry in its action, *Twelfth Night* impresses one with a certain air of gravity which is quite different from the high spirits of *As You Like It*. The world of *Twelfth Night* appears a little more complex and thus more puzzling than that of the earlier comedies. And this complexity anticipates the greater seriousness not only of the tragedies which are soon to follow but also of the problem plays and the romances.

V

Another significant relationship between *Twelfth Night* and *As You Like It* has to do with an aspect of their structure, for here again Shakespeare presents the theme of love in analogical relationship with a secondary theme, the theme of indulgence. In an earlier section the point was made that Malvolio's role has to do with both love and the theme of indulgence which is presented in a special relationship to it. Malvolio is both a lover, one of Olivia's suitors, and also the exponent of opposition to all pleasure. His interest in Olivia, which he calls love, is vitiated by his self-love, and in this he is the antithesis of Viola, whose generous and self-sacrificing love of Orsino may be said to represent the opposite extreme. In his attitude toward indulgence, Malvolio is contrasted with Sir Toby Belch and Sir Andrew Aguecheek, whose overindulgence clearly throws into relief the steward's austerity. But although Malvolio rejects the kind of indulgence practiced by the other two, he overindulges in self-love, so surfeiting that in Olivia's words he becomes "sick of self-love." What is to be noted here is that Shakespeare presents extravagant attitudes toward the themes of love and indulgence, extremes which by juxtaposition tend toward mutual qualification. Malvolio is but one of the characters whose attitudes form the main action of the comedy. But he is central to that action in his double role of being both a lover, or would-be lover, and an exponent of a particular attitude toward indulgence.

The theme of indulgence, as we have said, is here presented in such a way that attitudes toward it are made to reflect upon analogous attitudes toward love. The relationship of the two themes can be seen as it affects other characters besides Malvolio. Orsino and Olivia are both gluttons in their way, both gorging themselves upon boundless sentiment: he upon extravagant passion (as he calls it) for Olivia, she upon equally excessive mourning for a dead brother. In effect he is overfond of love-melancholy, she of grief. Both, then, overindulge in certain emotions, and that extravagance, and especially the rhetoric of its expression, form yet another instance of comic reduction. And thus it may be said that Orsino, Olivia, Malvolio, Sir Toby, and Sir Andrew are presented in postures of overindulgence of one sort or another. Furthermore, that part of the plot which deals with Malvolio and his enemies dramatizes indulgence itself, that is, what in the main action is a metaphor here becomes a theme. And the comic reduction of excess in this part of the play, the comic comment upon extreme attitudes toward indulgence, reinforces the comic reduction of extreme attitudes toward love. And as we have seen, this last is accomplished in part by the metaphoric function of the term indulgence in the main action of the comedy. From the point of view of structure, this circumstance represents the highest point to which Shakespeare could raise the analogical relationship of the two themes.

The theme of indulgence, then, occupies an important position in the play, but we should remember that it is secondary to the theme of love, that it is employed in support of it. Because *Twelfth Night* is associated with revelry, it is quite possible to over-stress this element of the plot. Thus one critic has proposed that "*Twelfth Night* is a philosophical defence of a moderate indulgence in pleasure, in opposition on the one hand to an extreme hostility to pleasure and on the other hand to an extreme self-indulgence."[22] A related view finds that the play "develops an ethic of indulgence based on the notion that the personality of any individual is a function not of the static proportions of the humors within him, but of the dynamic appetites that may more purposefully, as well as more pragmatically, be said to govern his behavior."[23] This is relevant and just so long as we do not raise the theme of indulgence to a position above that assigned to it by the dramatist. In a second and equally provocative essay on *Twelfth Night*, Professor Hollander sees the play as "representing the killing off of excessive appetite through indulgence of it, leading to the rebirth of the unencumbered self."[24] Though an exciting notion of comic catharsis, such a view lays undue stress on what we have called the play's chief metaphor at the expense of its central idea.[25]

In addition to the primary metaphor of indulgence, and most significantly associated with it, is the subsidiary concept of musical order and due proportion. Even as order and proportion are indispensable to harmony, whether musical, celestial, or political, so they are to the well-being and inner unity of the individual. Here music, which fills *Twelfth Night,* achieves the status of motif in the thought of the play. "The general concern of *Twelfth Night,*" says Professor Hollander, "is *musica humana,* the Boethian application of abstract order and proportion to human behavior."[26] This is unquestionably so, and what is said here of *Twelfth Night* applies with equal force to Shakespearean drama generally. But again it should be noted that the play is concerned with a particular application, an application to a particular aspect of human behavior. That *Twelfth Night* dramatizes the concept of proportion and moderation there can be no question. We may go so far as to say that the play's chief theme has to do with proportion and moderation. But it is proportion and moderation neither in terms of general behavior nor of revelry, eating, and drinking, though these provide both metaphoric and thematic support. The play is primarily concerned with proportion and moderation in matters concerning romantic love, the general subject of all Shakespeare's romantic comedies.

VI

The chief idea of *Twelfth Night* has been variously identified. Some have argued that the leading note of the play is fun; others have held that the play's "lesson is . . . 'Sweet are the uses of adversity.' "[27] Unrequited love is another choice.[28] Still another is social security. According to this view *Twelfth Night* is not a story of love "but of the very realistic struggles and intrigues over the betrothal of a rich countess, whose selection of a mate determines the future of all the major and most of the minor characters."[29] Much closer to the mark than any of these is the view that *Twelfth Night* "exhibits in its action one of the fundamental motifs of comedy: the education of a man or woman.''[30] What needs to be added here is that the motif exhibited in the action of the play has to do with the education of characters in matters of love. As in the comedies we have so far considered, so here the main action presents in juxtaposition attitudes toward love, with the result that such attitudes by mutual qualification point to the best attitude possible in the world created by the play, a world ultimately not different from our own.

The initial episode introduces the two contrasting attitudes toward love which we have found at the center of Shakespeare's other romantic comedies. Orsino in his opening lines reveals and exposes to the censure of the comic spirit his immoderately sentimental conception of what he thinks is his passion for Olivia. His fancy is, in his own words, "high fantastical," and the pain it causes him is insupportable. For that reason he calls for music as a way to relieve his passion.

> If music be the food of love, play on!
> Give me excess of it, that, surfeiting,
> The appetite may sicken, and so die.
>
> (I, i, 1-3)

Notwithstanding its "capacity," love may be so surfeited with music, he hopes, that its force will abate for a short while. It is all in excess, all expressed in one comic hyperbole after another.

> O, when mine eyes did see Olivia first,
> Methought she purg'd the air of pestilence!
> That instant was I turn'd into a hart;
>
> (ll. 19-21)

With the entrance of Valentine at line 23 and his report to the Duke, Shakespeare matches Orsino's hyperboles with Olivia's own extreme sentimentality in rejecting his suit in order to abandon herself to excessive grief over her brother's death. The extravagance of Olivia's mourning, like Orsino's passion, is given a comic note by the language in which it is expressed.

Furthermore, Valentine's description tends to qualify the genuineness of the vow by the elaborate insistence on its austerity:

> The element itself, till seven years' heat,
> Shall not behold her face at ample view;
> But, like a cloistress, she will veiled walk,
> And water once a day her chamber round
> With eye-offending brine;
>
> (ll. 26-30)

The two attitudes toward love are here bound together more significantly than in earlier comedies. Orsino is the romantic lover who vaunts his alleged passion in hyperboles. And Olivia is the reluctant lover who rejects the Duke's addresses to her. But she is very different from such disdainful lovers as Phoebe of *As You Like It,* the king and his lords in *Love's Labour's Lost,* and Benedick and Beatrice. Like all these, Olivia rejects thoughts of love, but she does so in favor of something else, a passionate surrender to what seems to be her love of grief. In this, though she rejects Orsino, she acts very much like him. Both exhibit excessive sentimentality which shows as folly, though the object of that folly is different in the two characters. Their attitudes toward love and grief are extreme and they are best expressed by the thematic metaphor of indulgence, the very image the Duke employs in the opening lines of the play. Orsino and Olivia overindulge their passions or what they consider their passions. And so in the initial episode Shakespeare briefly but pointedly defines the comic errors of these two, errors to be recognized before the conclusion of the play. But he does much more in these early lines. He binds Orsino's and Olivia's contrasting attitudes towards love by means of an identical attitude towards their respective passions, love and grief. And furthermore he relates all this to the idea of indulgence, the theme of the secondary action.

The opening scene, then, presents Orsino and Olivia in contrasting attitudes towards love but in identical attitudes towards themselves. In the second scene the two are contrasted with

Viola, both in their attitudes towards themselves and towards
love. From the first lines she speaks Viola reveals the absence
in her of sentimentality and self-pity.

> Viola.   What country, friends, is this?
> Captain.   This is Illyria, lady.
> Viola.   And what should I do in Illyria?
>   My brother he is in Elysium.
>   Perchance he is not drown'd. What think you,
>   sailors?
>
>   (I, ii, 1-5)

The captain encourages her to hope, for he saw her brother,
"most provident in peril," "bind himself" to "a strong mast
that liv'd upon the sea." Whereupon she turns to the present
moment and demands to know who governs Illyria.

> Captain.   A noble duke, in nature as in name.
> Viola.   What is his name?
> Captain.   Orsino.
> Viola.   Orsino! I have heard my father name him.
>   He was a bachelor then.
>
>   (ll. 25-29)

Viola is as eager to know the Duke as she is unwilling to give
herself over to excessive grief over her brother's feared death.
Her feelings and the words expressing them are level and direct,
avoiding the extremes we have noted in the alleged passions of
Orsino and Olivia. In this she clearly presents a contrast to
these two, and her role in the rest of the play will be to aid
them in amending their ways. On the one hand, Viola essays
to persuade Olivia that falling in love—with Orsino or another
—is her unavoidable responsibility (else she usurps herself);
on the other, she tells the Duke that he is not the only one
who suffers from unrequited love. From the above we should
conclude that Viola is intended to represent the norm, an attitude we might call ideal. And we may add that her words
and acts are so aimed as to bring about comic recognition by
Orsino and Olivia. In due course he learns that he was never in

love with Olivia but someone else; and the latter soon discovers that far from being able to remain heart-whole she falls in love at first sight with Orsino's page, who she later finds is a lady in disguise. To such recognition and self-knowledge these two are led by the agency of Viola, by what she says and does, by what she is.

VII

But Viola is not the only character whose words and actions are employed to those ends. Feste, who as his name suggests occupies a significant position in the development of the theme of indulgence in the subplot, carries an equal responsibility in the conduct of the main action as well. In the subplot his chief purpose is to oppose Malvolio's austerity with the notion of revelry, though perhaps not in the extreme form practiced by Sir Andrew and Sir Toby.[31] When Sir Toby tells Malvolio that there shall be "cakes and ale" in spite of the steward's "virtuousness," Feste adds: "Yes, by Saint Anne, and ginger shall be hot i' th' mouth too." In addition, Feste helps bring about Malvolio's comic retribution. He defines both the steward's austerity and his presumption that Olivia could love him as a kind of madness and thus proves him a fool. In so doing Feste in his own way essays to lead Malvolio toward a recognition of his folly. This is especially clear in the scene wherein Feste, both in his own person and as Sir Topas, engages the steward in conversation while the latter is locked in the dark room.

Feste's allusion to Malvolio's folly in his notions about Olivia is made obliquely in the song he sings to him:

Clown.	"Hey, Robin, jolly Robin,
	Tell me how thy lady does."
Malvolio.	Fool!
Clown.	"My lady is unkind, perdy."
Malvolio.	Fool!
Clown.	"Alas, why is she so?"
Malvolio.	Fool, I say!
Clown.	"She loves another"—Who calls, ha?

(IV, ii, 78-85)

The steward's persistent calling of "Fool!" points ironically to the very term most properly applying to himself in the scene. And this is followed by an even clearer allusion to his folly in the following exchange with Feste a few lines later.

> *Clown.*   Alas, sir, how fell you besides your five wits?
> *Malvolio.* Fool, there was never man so notoriously abus'd.
>   I am as well in my wits, fool, as thou art.
> *Clown.*   But as well? Then you are mad indeed, if you be
>   no better in your wits than a fool.
>
> (ll. 92-97)

Precisely the same purpose as shown here is to be seen in Feste's role in the main plot, that is, in the words he addresses to Orsino and Olivia. Again his most pregnant comments on the self-deception of those two are made through songs, that is, in the same oblique manner he employs in part in his treatment of Malvolio, for Orsino and Olivia in what they say and do enact extreme attitudes identical with those exhibited by the steward. Professor Dover Wilson is partly right in suggesting that Malvolio "reflects in a kind of distorting mirror the emotional situation of the main plot. For Malvolio is a dreamer, after his kind; like Orsino he aspires for the hand of Olivia; and like both Orsino and Olivia he mistakes dreams for realities."[32] It is certainly true that there is something of the dreamer in a steward who is so self-endeared that he supposes himself the object of Olivia's love. Malvolio does not merely aspire for the hand of Olivia; he believes that she has chosen him for her husband. But it can scarcely be said that Orsino and Olivia are dreamers unless by the term we mean persons who by their extravagant posturings reveal utter failure to understand themselves and their relationships with others. Such posturing is perhaps more vulnerable to the comic spirit than dreaming can ever be. What is accurate in Professor Wilson's comment is the notion that Malvolio's comic shortcomings in the subplot are a reflex of Orsino's and Olivia's shortcomings in the main action. Hence Feste's analogous comment, in matter and form, upon the aberrations of those two.

When first confronted with Olivia, Feste proceeds to "cate-chise" her, to demonstrate in playful fashion that she, instead of himself, is the fool. Her calling him a fool is, he instructs her, "Misprision in the highest degree!" In contrast, he adds, his mistress has been acting foolishly in the excessive show of grief, especially since she believes her brother's soul in heaven: "The more fool, madonna, to mourn for your brother's soul being in heaven." (I, v, 76-77) This initial comment upon Olivia's folly is followed shortly by another, this one in the form of the clown's first song. Although "O Mistress Mine" is ostensibly sung for the delectation of Sir Toby and Sir An-drew, it really concerns Olivia, though of course she is not present while it is sung. But the content, from the first line, "O mistress mine, where are you roaming," to the concluding invitation to love since "Youth's a stuff will not endure," has exclusive application to her, gently reprimanding her careless wasting, in Viola's phrase usurping, her own youth and beauty. The lines are in a sense addressed to Olivia, pointing gently to her folly in refusing love in favor of immoderate sorrow. Furthermore, the song anticipates her eventual capitulation and hints at the strange conjunction into which she will be thrown. For it announces that her "true love's coming / That can sing both high and low." Olivia will fall in love with Cesario-Sebastian, but in the end all will be well.[33]

Likewise the song Feste addresses to the Duke in the follow-ing scene serves the purpose of gently mocking his exaggerated sense of his own grief in love, a grief that could find release only in death. Because it expresses his love-melancholy as well as the self-pity occasioned by it Orsino prefers that song over all others. And he calls upon Cesario to heed its lines, little knowing that his page is the one who truly suffers genuine love-grief. In the lines following the song, Feste leaves no doubt as to its comic intention. For he adds to its mockery of the Duke's love melancholy his own direct comment. "Now, the melancholy god protect thee, and the tailor make thy doublet of changeable taffeta, for thy mind is a very opal."

And he adds the further mocking note that he would have "men of such constancy put to sea, that their business might be everything and their intent everywhere." The gentle mockery of the Duke's inconstancy is resumed a few lines later when Orsino in conversation with Viola draws a distinction between the strength of his own passion for Olivia and a woman's love.

> There is no woman's sides
> Can bide the beating of so strong a passion
> As love doth give my heart; no woman's heart
> So big, to hold so much. They lack retention.
>
> (II, iv, 96-99)

His insistence on his own steadfast passion in contrast to a woman's incapacity for such love not only anticipates ironically his swift transference of that passion from Olivia to Viola at the conclusion of the play but also points with equal irony to the latter's constancy and devotion throughout. And this difference between Orsino's extravagant protestations and her own reticence is further stressed by Viola in her allusion to her father's fictional daughter who, because of unrequited love,

> sat, like Patience on a monument,
> Smiling at grief.
>
> (ll. 117-18)

To which she adds:

> Was not this love indeed?
> We men may say more, swear more; but indeed
> Our shows are more than will, for still we prove
> Much in our vows, but little in our love.
>
> (ll. 118-21)

Both in the image of Patience smiling at grief and in the presence of rhyme in the second passage Shakespeare introduces a faint tinge of self-consciousness, perhaps even of self-pity, just sufficient to enrich Viola's attitude toward her dilemma.

VIII

The comic process of *Twelfth Night,* then, presents episodes which are intended to expose and reduce extravagant attitudes on the part of Orsino and Olivia as well as Malvolio. And the function of this comic reduction is carried out in the main by Viola and Feste. But there is a further action dealing with Sebastian, Sir Toby, Sir Andrew Aguecheek, and Fabian. Just as Maria initiates the intrigue against Malvolio, so Sir Toby puts into practice a second intrigue aimed at Sir Andrew Aguecheek and the disguised Viola. But Aguecheek is the main target. Sir Toby's purpose in forcing a duel upon those two is the sheer comedy of exposing Sir Andrew's pretensions to bravery. For some moments there is also the additional effect of Viola's discomfiture, perhaps intended as a comment upon the liability of her disguise. Structurally, the most significant effect of the intrigue is the challenge of the newly arrived Sebastian by Sir Andrew and Sir Toby. And the severe beating they receive at his hands is a kind of censure upon their overindulgence and boisterousness. But far more important, their challenge of Sebastian brings him into the action of the love-triangle so that his reunion with Viola resolves the lovers' dilemma.

As noted above, the action of *Twelfth Night* presents episodes which expose and reduce attitudes toward love and the related theme of indulgence. That reduction is brought about by direct statement, by the juxtaposition of opposed attitudes, by song. And out of such action there emerges a simple conception of the way to happiness, namely through individual as well as communal integration. That level and sensible way is the way we reach through experience, leading to both self-understanding and a clear awareness of one's role as a social being. And this simple wisdom is precisely the meaning of the song Feste sings at the conclusion of the play.

Most critics have expressed doubts concerning the authenticity and dramatic appropriateness of the song.[34] Among the very few who have defended it was A. C. Bradley, who thought it most appropriate to the singer, and even conceded that Shakespeare may have written the concluding stanza.[35] Richmond Noble also defends the song as Shakespearean, a song of wise nonsense, fitting commentary on the events of the play.[36] And he alludes to the following lines by John Weiss which he considers the most sensible interpretation of Feste's concluding song: "Then he sings a song which conveys to us his feeling of the world's impartiality: all things proceed according to law; nobody is humored; people must abide the consequences of their actions, 'for the rain it raineth every day.' A 'little tiny boy' may have his toy; but a man must guard against knavery and thieving: marriage itself cannot be sweetened by swaggering; whoso drinks with 'toss-pots' will get a 'drunken head:' it is a very old world, and began so long ago that no change in its habits can be looked for."[37] This is indeed the general meaning of the song, a crystallization of that simple wisdom to which the comic spirit is always pointing. Such wisdom is a fitting epilogue not only to this particular play but to the series of comedies it brings to a conclusion. Whether in childhood, adulthood, or old age, we find that certain things are constant; they have not changed and we cannot change them. Such changes are really what Orsino and Olivia and others like them would bring about, but in the end they are made to shed their aberrations. The sovereignty of nature asserts itself in Olivia's precipitous falling in love, even as it does in the case of Benedick and Beatrice and the rest. Nor are other pretensions less vulnerable as Malvolio and Sir Toby and Sir Andrew discover. "A great while ago the world began" and its laws, which are but the laws of nature, cannot change to accommodate some strange caprice or posturing. The individual, in these plays the lover, whether romantic or disdainful, must become a part of society, must be integrated into it. But the lover must first achieve an individual fulfillment, an inner integration. How fitting, then, that in the closing song of this last of his romantic comedies Shakespeare should express through the wise fool's seeming nonsense, and in the simplest terms, the comic vision he had been dramatizing during the last decade of the century.

In form *Twelfth Night* represents the ultimate plane to which Shakespeare could raise the structure of his romantic comedy. For here Shakespeare at last achieved a completely independent and fully unified romantic plot, a plot from which he eliminated the kind of external obstacle to love's fruition represented by Don John's machinations in *Much Ado* and by the conflict of the two pairs of brothers in *As You Like It*. Instead, *Twelfth Night* unites the romantic concerns of the two earlier plays, that is, the two aspects of the *internal* conflict which for a time delays love's fulfillment. It combines the disdain of love, which forms the most absorbing theme of *Much Ado,* with the education of a romantic lover, which is at the center of *As You Like It*. Orlando and Silvius are here replaced by Orsino, while Benedick and Beatrice are replaced by Olivia. And, as was shown above, the two attitudes toward love are related metaphorically by the idea of indulgence which forms the theme of the secondary action. It is, then, in this perfect combination of the two master-themes that *Twelfth Night* may be said to represent the final and near-pure form of Shakespearean romantic comedy. But the play marks also another milestone in Shakespeare's dramatic career. It is the last of his romantic comedies. Having perfected a comic form through which he could reflect his responses to one aspect of human destiny, Shakespeare immediately turned away from romantic comedy and its theme of romantic love and proceeded to give dramatic expression to other responses by means of other modes.

This turn to other dramatic modes is anticipated perhaps in a special quality of *Twelfth Night*. Although it sums up and recapitulates the earlier comedies, the play differs from them in one particular. Its atmosphere, in spite of the play's revelry, is characterized by a reflectiveness which at moments tends towards gravity. This quality of the play is in great part associated with the temperament of Viola and Feste who, though deriving from earlier creations, prefigure later and greater studies to be placed in the graver air of the tragedies and the romances. Viola's character, though owing a good deal to

earlier conceptions, really points to the heroines of the romances, particularly Hermione and Imogen. And Feste, though not unlike Touchstone in his function, is by temperament quite different. His individuality is to be seen especially in a certain quality of apartness which gives him a special perspective and also contributes to a measure of pathos in his relationships with others. In this and in the irony which plays about his name and circumstances Feste anticipates Lear's fool. If Feste's concluding song is by Shakespeare, it may well be that the dramatist thought of him and Lear's fool together, since the latter sings a stanza of the same song in *King Lear*. Indeed it appears that what is needed to draw from Feste the kind of devotion we see in the fool of the later play is a worthy object of such devotion, a great and greatly suffering nature such as Lear's.

In these matters *Twelfth Night* may be said to reflect, albeit distantly, Shakespeare's growing concern with those other aspects of human motive and destiny which were soon to fill the world of the later plays. But *Twelfth Night* is a romantic comedy, bringing to a brilliant conclusion Shakespeare's search for a comic structure which could treat most divertingly and significantly man's relationship to woman. Like its predecessors, and especially the other two "joyous" comedies, it projects a vision of the lovers' ideal, the best possible way to achieve inner as well as outer fulfillment, a unity within and a harmony with the world in which we live. That vision expresses man's longing for a state of being which transcends human limitation, the limitation against which it is here dramatized. And it is precisely in responding to and gratifying that longing by presenting the ideal as achievable that romantic comedy is so deeply satisfying.

Notes and Index

$\mathcal{N}otes$

CHAPTER I

1. Line-references are to *The Complete Plays and Poems of William Shakespeare,* ed. William A. Neilson and Charles J. Hill (Cambridge, Mass., 1942).

2. At one extreme are 1584-89, proposed by Peter Alexander in his *Shakespeare's Life and Art* (London, 1939), pp. 67-69, and 1589, by T. W. Baldwin in his edition of *The Comedy of Errors* (New York, 1928), pp. x-xvi, as well as in his *William Shakespeare Adapts a Hanging* (Princeton, 1931); see also his *On the Compositional Genetics of The Comedy of Errors* (Urbana, 1965). At the other extreme is 1594, more accurately the night of December 28, 1594, spiritedly defended by Sidney Thomas in "The Date of *The Comedy of Errors,*" *SQ,* VII (1956), 376-84. For comment on his arguments see *The Comedy of Errors,* ed. R. A. Foakes, New Arden (Cambridge, Mass., 1962), pp. xxi-xxiii.

3. See Harold Brooks, "Themes and Structure in *The Comedy of Errors,* in *Early Shakespeare,* eds. John R. Brown and Bernard Harris (London, 1961), pp. 55-71.

4. *Gesta Grayorum,* ed. W. W. Greg, Malone Society Reprints (Oxford, 1914), p. 1.

5. It may be worth adding that the line "If this be not a dream, I see and hear," *The Comedy of Errors,* V, i, 376, reappears in *The Taming of the Shrew,* I, ii, 69-70, as "Or do I dream? Or have I dreamed till now? / I do not sleep; I see, I hear. . . ." In *The Two Gentlemen of Verona,* V, iv, 26, the line reads: "How like a dream is this! I see and hear." It is impossible to be certain as to which of these was written first, but the line in *The Two Gentlemen of Verona* is richer and maturer than the other two.

6. New Arden, p. xxiii.

7. Bertrand Evans, *Shakespeare's Comedies* (Oxford, 1960), p. 1.

8. Apollonius, separated from his daughter and his wife Lucina, is after many sea-journeys reunited with them. It is noteworthy that during the separation Lucina had become a priestess in the temple of Diana at Ephesus.

9. See Arden, pp. xxxii-xxxiv; also Geoffrey Bullough, *Narrative and Dramatic Sources of Shakespeare* (London, 1961), I, 10-11, 50-54.

10. Analogous elements to the story of Egeon are to be found in Plautus' *Rudens,* where there is a shipwreck, a daughter lost by her father but later reunited with him, and also a priestess at the temple of Venus who aids the daughter.

11. From this source is probably derived the name of Hermia's father Egeus in *A Midsummer Night's Dream.*

12. "It is not composed in the hackneyed style, is quite unlike other plays; nor does it contain filthy lines that one must not repeat. In this comedy you will meet no perjured pimp, or unprincipled courtesan, or braggart soldier" (ll. 55-58).

13. "Why, this is Tyndarus, your own son. . . ."

14. "I am miserable and happy both, if what you two say is true."

15. John Dover Wilson, *Shakespeare's Happy Comedies* (London, 1962), p. 40.

16. These lines and the puzzlement they reflect may or may not be taken in the gravest seriousness, but I believe Francis Fergusson errs in suggesting that they are laughable. "*The Comedy of Errors* and *Much Ado About Nothing*," *Sewanee Review*, LXII (1954), 28.

17. For an excellent commentary on this aspect of the play to which I am greatly indebted, see John R. Brown, *Shakespeare and His Comedies* (London, 1957), pp. 54-57.

18. C. R. Baskervill, "Bassanio as an Ideal Lover," *The Manly Anniversary Studies in Language and Literature* (Chicago, 1923), pp. 90-103.

CHAPTER II

1. Besides 1594, *A Shrew* was printed also in 1596, 1607, and 1631.

2. E. K. Chambers, *Elizabethan Stage* (Oxford, 1945), IV, 48.

3. Taking note of that state, Professor Hardin Craig expressed the hope that the long debate over the connection between the two plays had covered the ground so thoroughly that a solution satisfactory to all sides might be forthcoming. And he urged scholars to accept one of the three hypotheses explaining the relationship of the two plays, the so-called modern view that both comedies go back to a common original. He further suggested certain approaches which might support that hypothesis. "*The Shrew and A Shrew:* Possible Settlement of an Old Debate," *Elizabethan Studies and Other Essays in Honor of George F. Reynolds* (Boulder, Colorado, 1945), pp. 150-54. This view had been defended by H. D. Gray, in "*The Taming of a Shrew*," *PQ*, XX (1941), 325-33; by G. I. Duthie in "*The Taming of a Shrew* and *The Taming of the Shrew*," *RES*, XIX (1943), 337-56; by Raymond A. Houk in "The Evolution of *The Taming of the Shrew*," *PMLA*, LVII (1942), 1009-38. The view was also supported more recently by W. W. Greg in *The Shakespeare First Folio* (Oxford, 1955), pp. 210-12. Unfortunately Professor Craig's plea was being rejected at the moment of its inception, for in the same volume and in the pages next following, Professor Thomas Marc Parrott argued that *A Shrew* was the source of Shakespeare's play. "*The Taming of the Shrew*—A New Study of an Old Play," *Elizabethan Studies and Other Essays in Honor of George F. Reynolds* (Boulder, Colorado, 1945), pp. 155-65. For support of the reverse hypothesis, that *The Shrew* was the source of *A Shrew*, see Samuel Hickson, "Marlowe and the Old *Taming of a Shrew*," *N&Q*, I (1850), 194, 221-27; "*The Taming of the Shrew*," *ibid.*, 345-47; Peter Alexander, "*The Taming of a Shrew*," *TLS*, Sept. 16, 1926, p. 614; B. A. P. Van Dam, "*The Taming of a Shrew*," *English Studies*, X (1928), 97-106; and the New Cambridge edition. And lately, instead of closing the long debate, Professor John W. Shroeder pleads that it be kept "open and alive," and he helps to do so by returning to the "old" theory that *A Shrew* must after all be the source of Shakespeare's play. "*The Taming of a Shrew* and *The Taming of the Shrew*: A Case Reopened," *JEGP*, LVII (1958), 424-43.

4. See T. M. Parrott, *William Shakespeare, A Handbook* (New York, 1934), p. 144; E. K. Chambers, *William Shakespeare: A Study of Facts and Problems* (Oxford, 1931), I, 324.

5. Ernest P. Kuhl, "The Authorship of *The Taming of the Shrew*," *PMLA*, XL (1925), 551-618; K. Wentersdorf, "The Authenticity of *The Taming of the Shrew*," *SQ*, V (1954), 11-32. Other scholars who have accepted Shakespeare's unaided authorship are: F. S. Boas, *Shakespeare and his Predecessors*

(New York, 1896), pp. 173-75); Sir Arthur Quiller-Couch, New Cambridge Shakespeare (Cambridge, 1928), pp. vii-xii; Peter Alexander, *Shakespeare's Life and Art* (London, 1939), pp. 69-70.

6. A further connection between *The Comedy of Errors* and *The Taming of the Shrew* is the precise danger which allegedly awaits the Pedant upon his arrival at Padua. The danger and the reasons for it, as detailed by Tranio (IV, ii, 81-87), are precisely those Egeon meets upon his arrival in Ephesus (I, i, 3-25).

7. *Johnson on Shakespeare*, ed. Walter Raleigh (Oxford, 1940), p. 96.

8. See Wentersdorf, "The Authenticity of *The Taming of the Shrew*," pp. 29-31.

9. H. B. Charlton, *Shakespearian Comedy* (London, 1938), p. 45.

10. *Ibid.*, p. 44.

11. *Ibid.*

12. *Ibid.*, p. 45.

13. *Ibid.*, p. 47.

14. *Ibid.*

15. *Ibid.*, p. 19.

16. *Ibid.*, p. 99.

17. When he says that courtship in *The Shrew* "is transferred from moonlit pleasances to be set in lawyers' offices. . . ," and that it speaks, "not with flowers and songs and flageolets . . ." (*ibid.*, pp. 44-45), Professor Charlton is completely overlooking both Lucentio's affair with Bianca, and even an important portion of Petruchio's own wooing of Katherina.

18. Cf. "If this be not a dream, I see and hear," *The Comedy of Errors*, V, i, 376; and "How like a dream is this! I see and hear," *The Two Gentlemen of Verona*, V, iv, 26.

19. John Masefield, *William Shakespeare* (London, 1911), p. 108.

20. For a different interpretation of the scene see Cecil C. Seronsy, " 'Supposes' as the Unifying Theme in *The Taming of the Shrew*," *SQ*, XIV (1963), 15-30.

21. John R. Brown, *Shakespeare and His Comedies* (London, 1957), p. 99.

22. Geoffrey Bullough, *Narrative and Dramatic Sources of Shakespeare* (London, 1961), I, 65.

23. In Shakespeare this theme of enforced marriage is to be contrasted with a variant of it in *The Merchant of Venice*, where Portia's father decrees that she shall marry the man who chooses the right casket. But here the right choice, we are told many times, will be made by one who truly loves her. Nerissa tells her mistress that the casket will "never be chosen by any rightly but one you shall rightly love" (I, ii, 34-36). And Portia repeats the same idea to Bassanio:

> I am lock'd in one of them;
> If you do love me, you will find me out.
>
> (III, ii, 40-41)

24. Bullough, *Narrative and Dramatic Sources*, I, 112.

25. Other theories explaining Sly's disappearance after I, i, are summarized by Richard Hosley in "Was There a 'Dramatic Epilogue' to *The Taming of the Shrew*?" *Studies in English Literature*, I, No. 2 (1961), 17-34.

CHAPTER III

1. For critical comment on the play see E. K. Chambers, *Shakespeare: A Survey* (London, 1925), pp. 49-57; H. B. Charlton, *Shakespearian Comedy* (Lon-

don, 1938), pp. 23-43; T. M. Parrott, *Shakespearean Comedy* (New York, 1949), pp. 108-18; John R. Brown, *Shakespeare and His Comedies* (London, 1957), pp. 103-6; John Vyvyan, *Shakespeare and the Rose of Love* (New York, 1960), pp. 98-135; John Dover Wilson, *Shakespeare's Happy Comedies* (London, 1962), pp. 40-54.

2. Among recent critics, Stanley Wells finds "partial success" in the play. "The Failure of *The Two Gentlemen of Verona*," *Shakespeare Jahrbuch*, XCIX (1963), 161-73.

3. *A Chronicle History of the Life and Work of William Shakespeare* (New York, 1886), pp. 188-91. R. W. Bond adopts 1590 as the date of the original version and 1595 as that of the revised one. See Arden, p. xvi.

4. E. K. Chambers, *William Shakespeare: A Study of Facts and Problems* (Oxford, 1931), I, 324.

5. New Cambridge Shakespeare (Cambridge, 1921), p. vii.

6. George B. Parks, "The Development of *The Two Gentlemen of Verona*," *The Huntington Library Bulletin*, No. 11 (1937), 1-11.

7. See R. W. Bond, Arden, 1906, pp. xvi-xxxi.

8. Chambers, *William Shakespeare: A Study of Facts and Problems*, p. 331.

9. T. P. Harrison, Jr., makes a strong case against Shakespeare's indebtedness to the play and for his use, instead, of Montemayor's *Diana*. Among his arguments are the following: Shakespeare knew the story of Felix and Felismena in versions other than the lost play, as for example *Gl'Ingannati;* the lost play was the property of the Queen's Men and thus could not have come into Shakespeare's hands; the Queen's Men were in the provinces during 1593-94, the year in which Shakespeare wrote *The Two Gentlemen of Verona.* See Harrison's "Concerning *The Two Gentlemen of Verona* and Montemayor's *Diana*," *MLN*, XLI (1926), 251-52; and "Shakespeare and Montemayor's *Diana*," *University of Texas Studies in English*, VI (1926), 72-120.

10. For studies of the sources see *The Two Gentlemen of Verona*, ed. R. W. Bond, Arden (London, 1906); Paul Reyher, "*The Two Gentlemen of Verona* et *Twelfth Night*, leurs sources communes," *Revue de l'Enseignement des Langues Vivantes*, XLI (1924), 438-46; Mozelle Scaff Allen, "Brooke's *Romeus and Juliet* as a Source for the Valentine-Silvia Plot in *The Two Gentlemen of Verona*," *UTSE*, XVIII (1938), 25-46; Thomas H. Neal, "Who is Silvia—and Other Problems in the Greene-Shakespeare Relationship," *The Shakespeare Association Bulletin*, XIII (1938), 240-54; John A. Guinn, "The Letter Device in the First Act of *The Two Gentlemen of Verona*," *UTSE*, XX (1940), 72-81; Dorothy F. Atkinson, "The Source of *The Two Gentlemen of Verona*," *Studies in Philology*, XLI (1944), 223-34; Ralph M. Sargent, "Sir Thomas Elyot and the Integrity of *The Two Gentlemen of Verona*," *PMLA*, LXV (1950), 1166-80; René Pruvost, "*The Two Gentlemen of Verona, Twelfth Night* et *Gl'Ingannati*," *Études Anglaises*, XIII (1960), 1-9; Jim C. Pogue, "*The Two Gentlemen of Verona* and Henry Wotton's *A Courtlie Controversie of Cupids Cautels*," *Emporia State Research Studies*, X (1962), 17-21. See also Geoffrey Bullough, *Narrative and Dramatic Sources of Shakespeare* (London, 1961), I, 203-66.

11. The strongest advocate of this notion is Oscar J. Campbell, who not only believes that Shakespeare based his play on the lost *Felix and Philiomena*, or some other Italianate play like it, but also argues that certain features of Shakespeare's comedy were inspired by the *commedia dell' arte.* "The Two Gentlemen of Verona* and Italian Comedy," *Studies in Shakespeare, Milton, and Donne* (New York, 1925), pp. 49-63.

12. Arden, p. xxxii.

13. New Cambridge Shakespeare, p. xiv.

14. *Ibid.,* p. xv.

15. Though seeming to accept this explanation at the time, the younger of the two editors has more recently rejected it in his volume on the comedies. J. D. Wilson, *Shakespeare's Happy Comedies,* p. 43.

16. Parrott, *Shakespearean Comedy,* p. 113.

17. Arden, p. xxxvii.

18. Charles Lamb, *Tales from Shakespeare* (Everyman Library, 1961), p. 90.

19. Sargent, "Sir Thomas Elyot and the Integrity of *The Two Gentlemen of Verona,*" p. 1179.

20. Chambers, *Shakespeare: A Survey,* p. 56.

21. For some of these defenses see W. W. Lawrence, "The Meaning of *All's Well That Ends Well,*" *PMLA,* XXXVII (1922), 418-69; Alwin Thaler, "Shakespeare and the Unhappy Happy Ending," *PMLA,* XLII (1927), 736-61; Samuel Asa Small, "The Ending of *The Two Gentlemen of Verona,*" *PMLA,* XLVIII (1933), 767-76; Sargent, "Sir Thomas Elyot and the Integrity of *The Two Gentlemen of Verona,*" pp. 1166-80; *The Two Gentlemen of Verona,* ed. John Munro, *The London Shakespeare* (London, 1957), I, 264-66.

22. J. D. Wilson, *Shakespeare's Happy Comedies,* p. 43.

23. John F. Danby, "Shakespeare Criticism and *The Two Gentlemen of Verona,*" *Critical Quarterly,* II (1960), 320.

24. For a different view of the song see John H. Long, *Shakespeare's Use of Music: A Study of Music and Its Performance in the Original Production of Seven Comedies* (Gainesville, Florida, 1955), pp. 57-58.

25. In addition the song justifies Julia's presence in the scene, and forwards the action by revealing Proteus' betrayal of her. She identifies the song as his, for when the host asks if "the music likes [her] not," she responds: "You mistake: the musician likes me not."

26. This view of Julia's character is in contrast to Professor Charlton's notion that her conception is "under no obligation whatever to the code of romance." *Shakespearian Comedy,* p. 40.

27. *Ibid.,* p. 42.

28. *Ibid.,* p. 41.

29. Some critics consider it a flaw: "Of the thin jesting and quibbling and light bawdry, I say nothing now: that flaw, for flaw it is, can be dealt with later." G. Gordon, *Shakespearian Comedy* (Oxford, 1944), p. 58.

CHAPTER IV

1. *The Plays of William Shakespeare,* ed. Samuel Johnson (London, 1765), II, 224.

2. *Love's Labour's Lost,* ed. Richard David. The New Arden Shakespeare (Cambridge, Mass., 1951), p. xvi. Cf. E. J. West, "The Essential Theatricality of *Love's Labour's Lost,*" *College English,* IX (1948), 427-29.

3. J. D. Wilson, *Shakespeare's Happy Comedies* (London, 1962), pp. 65-75.

4. C. L. Barber, *Shakespeare's Festive Comedy* (Princeton, 1959), p. 88.

5. *Ibid.*

6. J. M. Robertson, *The Genuine in Shakespeare* (London, 1930), p. 11.

7. Harley Granville-Barker, *Prefaces to Shakespeare* (Princeton, 1947), II, 414.

8. J. D. Wilson, *Shakespeare's Happy Comedies,* p. 64.

9. For brief reviews of the different dates assigned to the play see the editions of *Love's Labour's Lost* in *The London Shakespeare,* ed. John Munro (New York, 1957), I, 160-62; and in the New Arden Shakespeare, ed. Richard David (Cambridge, Mass., 1951), pp. xxvi-xxxii.

10. See J. W. Lever, "Three Notes on Shakespeare's Plants," *RES*, n.s., III (1952), 117-29.

11. T. W. Baldwin, *Shakespeare's Five-Act Structure* (Urbana, Illinois, 1947), pp. 579-625.

12. Among the more recent studies of the date of *Love's Labour's Lost* are: H. B. Charlton, "The Date of *Love's Labour's Lost*," *MLR*, XIII (1918), 257-66, 387-400; H. D. Gray, *The Original Version of Love's Labour's Lost* (Palo Alto, 1918); Austin K. Gray, "The Secret of *Love's Labour's Lost*," *PMLA*, XXXIX (1924), 581-611; Rupert Taylor, *The Date of Love's Labour's Lost* (New York, 1932); Fred Sorensen, " 'The Masque of the Muscovites' in *Love's Labour's Lost*," *MLN*, L (1935), 499-501; W. Schrickx, "Shakespeare and the School of Night: An Estimate and Further Interpretation," *Neophilologus*, XXXIV (1950), 35-44, and *Shakespeare's Early Contemporaries: The Background of the Harvey-Nashe Polemic and Love's Labour's Lost* (Antwerp, 1956); Walter Oakeshott, *The Queen and the Poet* (London, 1960), Chapter IV, *passim*; Alfred Harbage, "*Love's Labour's Lost* and the Early Shakespeare," *PQ*, XLI (1962), 18-36.

13. The connection was first pointed out by John Phelps in an essay in *The Baltimore News*, June 24, 1899, and later reprinted in the *Shakespeare Association Bulletin*, XVII (1942), 97-102. See also Abel Lefranc, "Les Éléments Français de *Peines d'Amour Perdues* de Shakespeare," *Revue Historique*, CLXXVIII (1935), 411-32, and his *Sous le Masque de William Shakespeare* (Paris, 1918-19), II, 17-103. Sir Sidney Lee had seen a connection between the Princess's embassy in the play and a later visit of Catherine to Henry of Navarre at Saint Bris in 1586, *Gentleman's Magazine*, October, 1880. This later visit, however, was of a sort which would scarcely suggest the atmosphere and general action of Shakespeare's play. In the 1586 visit, Catherine's daughter Marguerite, Navarre's estranged wife, did not accompany her mother, nor did the "escadron volant"; and the object of this visit was to offer Henry a divorce from Marguerite.

14. The allusions or echoes are listed in great detail by Rupert Taylor in *The Date of Love's Labour's Lost* (New York, 1932), pp. 34-51, 91-112. See also Eugene J. Kettner, "*Love's Labour's Lost* and the Harvey-Nashe-Greene Quarrel," *Emporia State Research Studies*, X (1962), 29-39.

15. See E. K. Chambers, *William Shakespeare: A Study of Facts and Problems* (Oxford, 1931), I, 335-36; also the study of the relationship in Taylor, *The Date of Love's Labour's Lost*, pp. 1-9.

16. *Gesta Grayorum*, ed. W. W. Greg (Oxford, 1914), pp. 54-55.

17. Sorensen, " 'The Masque of the Muscovites' in *Love's Labour's Lost*," pp. 499-501.

18. *Chronicles of England, Scotland, and Ireland* (1587), III, 805.

19. For studies of Raleigh's relationship to the play see especially Frances A. Yates, *A Study of Love's Labour's Lost* (Cambridge, 1936); M. C. Bradbrook, *The School of Night* (1936); Schrickx, "Shakespeare and the School of Night: An Estimate and Further Interpretation," pp. 35-44; Oakeshott, *The Queen and the Poet*.

20. For a rejection of the theory see Ernest A. Strathmann, "The Textual Evidence for 'The School of Night,' " *MLN*, LVI (1941), 176-86; and his *Sir Walter Raleigh: A Study in Elizabethan Skepticism* (New York, 1951), pp. 262-71.

21. It is the date, 1594 or 1595, first proposed by Malone, supported by E. K. Chambers, and now accepted by the most recent editors of the play.

22. See for instance H. B. Charlton, "*Love's Labour's Lost*," *The Library*, VIII (1917), 355-70; H. D. Gray, *The Original Version of Love's Labour's Lost*; John Dover Wilson, ed., *Love's Labour's Lost*, New Cambridge Shakespeare,

1962 (1923), pp. xx-xxii, 98-135; Greta Hjort, "The Good and Bad Quartos of *Romeo and Juliet* and *Love's Labour's Lost*," *MLR*, XXI (1926), 140-46; Chambers, *William Shakespeare: A Study of Facts and Problems*, I, 333-35; Leo Kirschbaum, "Is *The Spanish Tragedy* a Leading Case? Did a Bad Quarto of *Love's Labour's Lost* Ever Exist?" *JEGP*, XXXVII (1938), 501-12; W. W. Greg, *The Editorial Problem in Shakespeare* (Oxford, 1942), pp. 126-28; *Love's Labour's Lost*, New Arden Shakespeare, pp. xvii-xxvi.

23. Marguerite's own account, *Memoires de Marguerite de Valois*, appeared in 1628.

24. See O. J. Campbell, "*Love's Labour's Lost* Re-Studied," *Studies in Shakespeare, Milton, and Donne* (New York, 1926), pp. 3-45.

25. See Daniel G. Boughner, "Don Armado as a Gallant," *Revue Anglo-Americaine*, XIII (1935), 18-28; and "Don Armado and the *Commedia dell' Arte*," *SP*, XXXVII (1940), 201-24. For attempts to fix the source of "The Nine Worthies" see Lefranc's theory that the play is based on Richard Lloyd's *A briefe discourse of the most renouned actes, and right valiant conquests of those puisant Princes, called the Nine Worthies* (London, 1584), in *Sous le Masque de William Shakespeare*, II, 17-41). See its refutation in John Hawley Roberts, "The Nine Worthies," *MP*, XIX (1921-22), 297-305.

26. J. D. Wilson, *Shakespeare's Happy Comedies*, p. 60.

27. *The School of Night*, p. 153.

28. *Ibid.*, p. 161.

29. O. J. Campbell, *Shakespeare's Satire* (London, 1943), p. 25.

30. A. K. Gray, "The Secret of *Love's Labour's Lost*," pp. 581-611.

31. Oakeshott, *The Queen and the Poet*, p. 122.

32. The essay is printed by Yates, who discovered it, in her *Study of Love's Labour's Lost*, pp. 206-11.

33. *Love's Labour's Lost*, New Arden Shakespeare, p. xlviii.

34. Such an extreme position may lead to some far-fetched conclusions, such as the notion that Shakespeare may have "ridiculed Raleigh's academic pretensions by presenting him as the pedant Harvey, himself disguised as Armado." *Love's Labour's Lost*, New Arden Shakespeare, p. 1.

35. Walter Pater, *Appreciations* (London, 1924), p. 169.

36. T. M. Parrott, *Shakespearean Comedy* (New York, 1949), p. 124. This interpretation of Berowne's character would be hard to reconcile with the theory that "his name and some of his characteristics—notably his use of astronomical metaphors, his combination of anti-Petrarchan woman-hating with a lofty philosophy of love—were deliberately meant to recall Bruno to the audience." Yates, *A Study of Love's Labour's Lost*, p. 127.

37. Parrott, *Shakespearean Comedy*, p. 125.

38. Pater, *Appreciations*, pp. 162-63.

39. Barber, *Shakespeare's Festive Comedy*, p. 89.

40. New Arden Shakespeare, p. xv.

41. H. B. Charlton, *Shakespearian Comedy* (London, 1938), p. 270.

42. Charlton, "The Date of *Love's Labour's Lost*," p. 388.

43. Gladys Doidge Willcock, *Shakespeare as Critic of Language* (London, 1934), pp. 8-9.

44. Yates, *A Study of Love's Labour's Lost*, p. 195.

45. Bradbrook, *The School of Night*, p. 161.

46. Oakeshott, *The Queen and the Poet*, p. 109.

47. Campbell, *Shakespeare's Satire*, p. 29.

48. Professor Harbage believes that the "structure of *Love's Labour's Lost* is radically different from that of typical Shakespearean comedy, and the dif-

ference is in the direction of Chapel and Paul's drama of the eighties—in the grouping and balancing of characters, the at-least-perfunctory deference to the 'unities,' the fairly equitable distribution of lines among the characters, the emphasis upon words at the expense of action, the use of scenes as set pieces rather than as links in an integrated plot." *"Love's Labour's Lost* and the Early Shakespeare," p. 29. Though the structure of *Love's Labour's Lost* is admittedly weak, it must be observed that the grouping and balancing of characters is to be found in such later and greater plays as *A Midsummer Night's Dream* and *As You Like It*. Furthermore, the play simply adheres to the unities even as *Othello* and, in part, *The Tempest* do, both of them later and again greater plays. As to an equitable distribution of lines among the characters, all that can be said is that Berowne seems much more articulate than the other lords.

49. J. D. Wilson, *Shakespeare's Happy Comedies*, p. 73.

50. *Ibid.*

51. Though expressed in different terms, the same general interpretation of the "ladies' bizarre commands" at the conclusion is given by Barber in his *Shakespeare's Festive Comedy*, p. 112.

52. M. C. Bradbrook, *Shakespeare and Elizabethan Poetry* (London, 1951), p. 215. Miss Bradbrook sees this aspect of Berowne's character only in his being "both guilty of courtly artifice and critical of it," and in his playing "a double game with language throughout."

53. Later on, after he has vowed to abjure rhetoric, he declares to Rosaline: "My love to thee is sound, sans crack or flaw." On this point see the excellent commentary in Barber, *Shakespeare's Festive Comedy*, pp. 103-13.

54. The episode bristles with references to the lords' wits, and it is interesting to note that the term "wit" appears forty-one times in the play, while only five times in *A Midsummer Night's Dream* and eight in *The Merchant of Venice*. In *Much Ado*, as we should expect, it occurs twenty-seven times.

55. The Princess can censure fantastical language directly as well as obliquely through her own idiom. When Armado enters the stage to consult the King about the play of the "Nine Worthies," he says

> Annointed, I implore so much expense of thy royal sweet
> breath as will utter a brace of words.

Princess. Doth this man serve God?

Berowne. Why ask you?

Princess. 'A speaks not like a man of God's making.

(V, ii, 523-29)

56. On the theme of the play see a stimulating essay by Cyrus Hoy, *"Love's Labour's Lost* and the Nature of Comedy," *SQ*, XIII (1962), 31-40.

57. See H. B. Lathrop, "Shakespeare's Dramatic Use of Songs," *MLN*, XXXIII (1908), 1-5; Louis B. Wright, "Extraneous Song in Elizabethan Drama After the Advent of Shakespeare," *SP*, XXV (1927), 261-74.

58. J. R. Brown, *Shakespeare and His Comedies* (London, 1957), p. 134.

59. B. H. Bronson, "Daisies Pied and Icicles," *MLN*, LXIII (1948), 35-36.

60. R. B. Browne, "The Satiric Use of 'Popular' Music in *Love's Labour's Lost,"* XXIII (1959), 148.

61. Barber, *Shakespeare's Festive Comedy*, p. 118.

62. Richmond Noble, *Shakespeare's Use of Song* (London, 1923), p. 36.

63. *Ibid.*, p. 33.

64. *Ibid.*, p. 35.

65. The ironies of the song are noted by Robert B. Sharpe in *Irony in the Drama* (Chapel Hill, 1959), p. 140.

66. The view proposed by Schrickx that "the reference to Mercury and Apollo can be explained as Shakespeare's saying that his poetry is better than Chapman's" is the sort of extreme to which the search for topical meaning may lead. "Shakespeare and The School of Night: An Estimate and Further Interpretation," p. 38.

CHAPTER V

1. On this see S. B. Hemingway, "The Relation of *A Midsummer Night's Dream* to *Romeo and Juliet*," *MLN*, XXVI (1911), 78-80; Kenneth Muir, "Shakespeare as Parodist," *N&Q*, CXCIX (1954), 467-68; also his *Shakespeare's Sources* (London, 1957), I, 46; and his "Pyramus and Thisbe: A Study in Shakespeare's Method," *SQ*, V (1954), 141; Ernest Schanzer, "*A Midsummer Night's Dream* and *Romeo and Juliet*," *N&Q*, CC (1955), 13-14.

2. For a convenient list of dates proposed by eighteenth- and nineteenth-century scholars see *A New Variorum Edition of Shakespeare*, ed. H. H. Furness (Philadelphia, 1895), p. 267.

3. In his variorum edition Furness cites different kinds of such evidence with the dates derived therefrom. *Ibid.*, pp. 248-64.

4. Among those who have set 1594-96 as the probable date of the play are the following: Henry Cunningham, Arden Shakespeare, 1905, pp. xxxiv-xxxv; E. K. Chambers, *William Shakespeare: A Study of Facts and Problems* (Oxford, 1931), I, 360; Peter Alexander, *Shakespeare's Life and Art* (London, 1939), p. 106; G. Bullough, *Narrative and Dramatic Sources of Shakespeare* (London, 1961), I, 367; Muir, *Shakespeare's Sources*, I, 47. F. H. McCloskey argues that in Bottom's song (III, i, 128-36) Shakespeare is alluding to "A Poem of A Mayde Forsaken," which had appeared, he conjectures, in the 1594 edition of *The Arbour of Amorous Devices* and that therefore the play was written after that date. See "The Date of *A Midsummer Night's Dream*," *MLN*, XLVI (1931), 389-91. On the date of the play see also Burns Martin, "*A Midsummer Night's Dream*," *TLS* (January 24, 1935), p. 48; Sidney Thomas, "The Bad Weather in *A Midsummer Night's Dream*," *MLN*, LXIV (1949), 319-22; W. J. Lawrence, "The Date of *A Midsummer Night's Dream*," *TLS* (December 10, 1920), p. 826; and his "A Plummet for Bottom's Dream," *Fortnightly Review*, CXVII (1922), 833-44; J. D. Wilson, New Cambridge Shakespeare (Cambridge, 1953), p. 94; Edith Rickert, "Political Propaganda and Satire in *A Midsummer Night's Dream*," *MP*, XXI (1923-24), 53-87, 133-54.

5. J. D. Wilson has argued that Shakespeare revised the play not once but twice. See New Cambridge Shakespeare, pp. 77-100. In the first revision, according to this view, Shakespeare added the greater part of the fairy scenes and the clowns and their interlude. In the second revision he modified the fairy scenes, rewrote the opening of Act V, and provided the fairy-masque at the close with which he replaced the duplicate ending of Puck's epilogue which had been written, according to Professor Wilson, for the first performance of the 1592 version in a public theatre. For comment on this theory see E. K. Chambers's review of the New Cambridge edition of the play in *MLR*, XX (1925), 340-45. See also W. W. Greg, *The Editorial Problem in Shakespeare* (Oxford, 1942), pp. 124-26; and Hazelton Spencer, "A Nice Derangement: The Irregular Verse-Lining in *A Midsummer Night's Dream*, Act V, Sc. i, ll. 1-84," *MLR*, XXV (1930), 23-29; also *TLS* (December 18, 1924), pp. 857-58.

6. *Henslowe's Diary*, ed. W. W. Greg (London, 1904), I, 19-20. Greg calls it

"a new play," rather than the old one by Richard Edwards, which had been acted before the Queen at Oxford on September 3, 1566. *Ibid.*, II, 168. See also Dorothy Bethurum, "Shakespeare's Comment on Medieval Romance in *A Midsummer Night's Dream*," *MLN*, LX (1945), 85-94. Miss Bethurum speculates that the lost play led Shakespeare to write *A Midsummer Night's Dream* in order to parody the sort of romantic comedy of the eighties to which *Palamon & Arsett* probably belonged.

7. For Chaucerian echoes in the play see *ibid.* and Neville Coghill, "Shakespeare's Reading in Chaucer," *Elizabethan and Jacobean Studies Presented to Frank Percy Wilson* (Oxford, 1959), pp. 86-99.

8. See T. P. Harrison, Jr., "Shakespeare and Montemayor's *Diana*," *UTSE*, VI (1926), 72-120. From the *Diana*, Shakespeare may have received the hint for the love-juice although he could have found it also in Chaucer's *Merchant's Tale* (l. 2258).

9. Madeleine Doran, "Pyramus and Thisbe Once More," *Essays on Shakespeare and Elizabethan Drama in Honor of Hardin Craig* (Columbia, Missouri, 1962), pp. 149-61.

10. On the literary parody in the Pyramus and Thisbe playlet see G. E. Arkwright, "The Death Songs of Pyramus and Thisbe," *N&Q*, 10th Series, V (1906), 341-43, 401-3; and Doran, "Pyramus and Thisbe Once More," pp. 160-61. A. G. van Kranendonk argues that the playlet reflects the style, diction, and mannerisms of the *Faerie Queene*. "Spenserian Echoes in *A Midsummer Night's Dream*," *English Studies*, XIV (1932), 209-17. In the title and some of the lines in Thisbe's lament Shakespeare may have been glancing at *The Lamentable Tragedy Mixed Full of Pleasant Mirth, Conteining the Life of Cambises King of Persia.*

11. For evidence of Shakespeare's use of these sources see Muir, *Shakespeare's Sources*, I, 31-47. The argument that Shakespeare borrowed from Mouffet's poem, originally advanced by Margaret L. Farrand and supported by A. S. T. Fisher and Kenneth Muir, is rejected by Geoffrey Bullough and Douglas Bush. See Margaret L. Farrand, "An Additional Source for *A Midsummer Night's Dream*," *SP*, XXVII (1930), 233-43; A. S. T. Fisher, "The Sources of Shakespeare's Interlude of Pyramus and Thisbe: A Neglected Poem," *N&Q*, CXCIX (1949), 376-79, 400-2; Douglas Bush, "The Tedious Brief Scene of Pyramus and Thisbe," *MLN*, XLVI (1931), 144-47; Bullough, *Narrative and Dramatic Sources of Shakespeare*, I, 373-76. For a general study of the sources see Frank Sidgwick, *The Sources and Analogues of A Midsummer Night's Dream* (London, 1908).

12. On this see Doran's excellent essay, "Pyramus and Thisbe Once More," pp. 149-61.

13. For sources and analogues of Bottom's "translation" see J. R. Moore, "The Transformation of Bottom," *Indiana University Studies*, XIII, No. 72 (1926), 45-50; Sister M. Generosa, "Apuleius and *A Midsummer Night's Dream*: Analogue or Source, Which?" *SP*, XLII (1945), 198-204.

14. In "To the Gentlemen Students of Both Universities," *The Works of Thomas Nashe*, ed. R. B. McKerrow (Oxford, 1958), III, 324.

15. Mercutio's description of Queen Mab in *Romeo and Juliet*, I, iv, 53-95, attributes to her some of the characteristics and functions of Robin Goodfellow.

16. For Shakespeare's conception of the fairies in *A Midsummer Night's Dream* and the influence of that conception on contemporary poetry, see Minor White Latham, *The Elizabethan Fairies* (New York, 1930); also E. K. Chambers, *Shakespeare: A Survey* (London, 1925), p. 77; Muir, *Shakespeare's Sources*, I, 31-47; Ernest Schanzer, "The Moon and the Fairies in *A Midsummer*

Night's Dream," University of Toronto Quarterly, XXIV (1955), 234-46; Bullough, *Narrative and Dramatic Sources of Shakespeare,* I, 370-6.

17. Sheldon P. Zitner, "The Worlds of *A Midsummer Night's Dream," South Atlantic Quarterly,* LIX (1960), 398-99.

18. T. M. Parrott was surely carried away by his enthusiasm for the structure of the play when he wrote of its "mastery of dramatic technique and its power of characterization. . . ." *Shakespearian Comedy* (New York, 1949), p. 125. Adverse criticism of the play's construction is voiced by Robert A. Law, who holds that its "structure indicates the immature playwright, following a 'preconceived pattern' set by two or more of his predecessors in comedy." "The Pre-Conceived Pattern of *A Midsummer Night's Dream," UTSE,* XXIII (1943), 5-6.

19. H. B. Charlton, *Shakespearian Comedy* (London, 1938), p. 103.

20. *Ibid.,* p. 112.

21. *Ibid.,* p. 104.

22. Richmond Noble, *Shakespeare's Use of Song* (London, 1923), p. 53. The same critic's enthusiasm for the success of the song in the play led him to conclude that Shakespeare could not have written it before 1598! *Ibid.,* p. 52.

23. Weston A. Gui, "Bottom's Dream," *American Imago,* IX (1952), 251-305.

24. Gerald F. Jacobson, "A Note on Shakespeare's *Midsummer Night's Dream," American Imago,* XIX (1962), 22.

25. Bertrand Evans, *Shakespeare's Comedies* (London, 1960), p. 34.

26. Harold Goddard, *The Meaning of Shakespeare* (Chicago, 1951), p. 74.

27. Paul A. Olson, "*A Midsummer Night's Dream* and the Meaning of Court Marriage," *ELH,* XXIV (1957), 111.

28. *Ibid.,* p. 107.

29. *Ibid.*

30. C. L. Barber, *Shakespeare's Festive Comedy* (Princeton, 1959), p. 133.

31. It must be noted that though the movement from city to woods and back to city or court is present in most of the later comedies, it does not appear in all. For instance, as we shall see, the structure of *Much Ado About Nothing* and *Twelfth Night* does not utilize the symbolic movement from city to woods and back.

32. Donald C. Miller, "Titania and the Changeling," *English Studies,* XXII (1940), 66-70.

33. Lord David Cecil, *The Fine Art of Reading* (Indianapolis, 1957), p. 52.

34. E. J. West, "On a Purely Playful Hypothesis Concerning the Composition of *A Midsummer Night's Dream," College English,* IX (1948), 249.

35. See Madeleine Doran, "*A Midsummer Night's Dream:* A Metamorphosis," *Rice Institute Pamphlets,* XLVI (1960), 113-35.

36. Alexander, *Shakespeare's Life and Art,* p. 106.

37. Barber, *Shakespeare's Festive Comedy,* p. 129.

38. Bethurum, "Shakespeare's Comment on Medieval Romance in *A Midsummer Night's Dream,"* p. 86.

39. Charlton, *Shakespearian Comedy,* p. 108.

40. *Ibid.,* p. 117.

41. Barber, *Shakespeare's Festive Comedy,* p. 159.

42. Charlton, *Shakespearian Comedy,* p. 121.

43. On this see some excellent comments by George A. Bonnard in his essay, "Shakespeare's Purpose in *Midsummer Night's Dream," SJ,* XCII (1956), 268-79.

44. Charlton, *Shakespearian Comedy,* p. 122.

45. See a fine passage on this in John R. Brown, *Shakespeare and His Comedies* (London, 1957), p. 90.

CHAPTER VI

1. E. K. Chambers, *William Shakespeare: A Study of Facts and Problems* (Oxford, 1931), I, 373. For the alleged relationship between Gobbo and Robert Cecil which Chambers saw and a comment upon it, see John R. Brown's New Arden (Cambridge, Mass., 1955), p. xii.

2. Stephen Gosson, *The School of Abuse,* ed. Edward Arber (London, 1895), p. 40.

3. *Palladis Tamia,* ed. D. C. Allen (New York, 1938), p. 282.

4. For the Dr. Lopez-lupus-wolf relationship see the New Cambridge Edition, pp. 117-18.

5. An allusion to Dr. Lopez in Nashe's *Lenten Stuff* (1599) is cited by J. R. Brown, New Arden, p. xxiv. He also suggests that the hanging of a wolf may be taken literally and that therefore Gratiano's line need not allude to Dr. Lopez. *Ibid.,* pp. xxiii-xxiv.

6. E. Kuhl, "My Wealthy Andrew," *TLS* (December 27, 1928), p. 1025.

7. For further details see New Arden, 1955, pp. xxv-xxvii.

8. E. A. J. Honigmann rejects the theory in "Shakespeare's 'Lost Sources,'" *MLR,* XLIX (1954), 297-98.

9. The theory proposes that the ultimate source of the play is the prompt-book of *The Jew,* that its version was revised by some dramatist or dramatists, that this later version was recast by Shakespeare in 1594, that Shakespeare added a few lines after the execution of Dr. Lopez in the summer of 1594, that he further revised the play before 1598, that this version was transcribed from players' parts, and that to this transcribed text stage-directions and theatrical interpolations were added. For comment on the theory see E. K. Chambers' review of the New Cambridge Edition in *MLR,* XXII (1927), 220-24; B. A. P. Van Dam, "The Text of *The Merchant of Venice,*" *Neophilologus,* XIII (1927), 33-51; W. W. Greg, *The Editorial Problem in Shakespeare* (Oxford, 1942), pp. 123-24.

10. See H. R. Walley, "Shakespeare's Portrayal of Shylock," *The Parrott Presentation Volume* (Princeton, 1935), pp. 211-42.

11. Quoted by John Dover Wilson, New Cambridge Shakespeare (Cambridge, 1953), p. 115.

12. *Ibid.*

13. H. B. Charlton, *Shakespearian Comedy* (London, 1938), p. 127.

14. See J. L. Cardozo, *The Contemporary Jew in Elizabethan Drama* (Amsterdam, 1925), p. 309.

15. The same is true of Falstaff in the *Henry IV* plays.

16. Both stories are old, appearing independently in different versions. For the history of the flesh-bond, see J. L. Cardozo, "The Background of Shakespeare's *Merchant of Venice,*" *English Studies,* XVI (1932), 177-86, and *The Contemporary Jew;* also Margaret Schlauch, "The Pound of Flesh Story in the North," *JEGP,* XXX (1931), 348-60. For the history of the casket story see Helen Pettigrew, "Bassanio the Elizabethan Lover," *PQ,* XV (1937), 296-306.

17. The word "insculp't" (II, vii, 57), used nowhere else in Shakespeare, occurs in the English version of the *Gesta* first done by Wynkyn de Worde and "bettered" by Richard Robinson in a collection of stories printed in 1577 and also in 1595. In the *Gesta* a woman is tested to see if she is worthy to become the Emperor's wife. In addition to this change Shakespeare altered the motto on the lead casket. See Geoffrey Bullough, *Narrative and Dramatic Sources of Shakespeare* (London, 1961), I, 460. From *The Jew of Malta* may have come the suggestion to add the story of Jessica and Lorenzo, although

it is as likely that Shakespeare may have received the hint from Book III of Anthony Mundy's *Zelauto* (1580), which combines a version of the pound of flesh story with the theft of the usurer's daughter. See Janet Spens, *An Essay on Shakespeare's Relation to Tradition* (Oxford, 1916), pp. 23-24; and Julia Celeste Turner, *Anthony Mundy* (Berkeley, 1928), pp. 32-34. For other versions and analogues see Beatrice D. Brown, "Medieval Prototypes of Lorenzo and Jessica," *MLN*, XLIV (1929), 227-32; also James L. Wilson, "Another Medieval Parallel to the Jessica and Lorenzo Story," *SAB*, XXIII (1948), 20-23. For additional minor sources see New Arden, 1955, p. xxxi.

18. M. R. Ridley, *Shakespeare's Plays, A Commentary* (New York, 1938), p. 91.

19. Sigurd Burckhardt, *"The Merchant of Venice:* The Gentle Bond," *ELH* XXIX (1962), 242.

20. Northrop Frye, *Anatomy of Criticism* (Princeton, 1957), pp. 166-67.

21. For comment on this arrangement see E. J. West, "The Use of Contrast in *The Merchant of Venice,*" *SAB*, XXI (1946), 172-76.

22. See comments by Burckhardt, *"The Merchant of Venice*: The Gentle Bond," p. 243.

23. For comment on the rhythm of Shylock's speech see John W. Draper, "The Tempo of Shylock's Speech," *JEGP*, XLIV (1945), 281-85.

24. Cf. T. M. Parrott, *Shakespearean Comedy* (New York, 1949), p. 139.

25. Like Prince Hal's early association with Falstaff, Bassanio's first interest seems to be with Portia's wealth, and even in his brief description of her beauty he speaks of her "sunny locks" which "Hang on her temples like a golden fleece."

26. Charlton, *Shakespearian Comedy*, p. 127.

27. *Ibid.*, p. 137.

28. From a structural point of view Shylock's role is like Iago's, Edmund's, Iachimo's, and Falstaff's. Though of the greatest importance to their plays, these characters are not the heroes: the plays in which they appear cannot be called "their" plays.

29. E. K. Chambers, *Shakespeare: A Survey* (London, 1925), p. 111.

30. *Ibid.*, p. 110.

31. See Pettigrew, "Bassanio the Elizabethan Lover," p. 305.

32. For the view that the play is about money see Sidney Finkelstein, "Shakespeare's Shylock," *Mainstream*, XV (1962), 26-42.

33. John W. Draper, "Usury in *The Merchant of Venice,*" *MP*, XXXIII (1935), 47.

34. Violet M. Jeffery, "Shakespeare's Venice," *MLR*, XXVII (1932), 28.

35. Shylock admits the reason he hates Antonio:

> I hate him for he is a Christian.
> But more for that in low simplicity
> He lends out money gratis, and brings down
> The rate of usance here with us in Venice.

(I, iii, 37-40)

And Antonio corroborates Shylock's lines in the following:

> He seeks my life; his reason well I know:
> I oft deliver'd from his forfeitures
> Many that have at times made moan to me.

(III, iii, 21-23)

For a different view see John H. Smith, "Shylock: 'Devil Incarnation' or 'Poor Man . . . Wronged'?" *JEGP*, LX (1961), 1-21.

36. See especially Arthur B. Stonex, "The Usurer in Elizabethan Drama," *PMLA*, XXXI (1916), 190-210; C. T. Wright, "Some Conventions Regarding the Usurer in Elizabethan Literature," *SP*, XXX (1934), 176-97; Draper, "Usury in *The Merchant of Venice*," pp. 37-48; E. C. Pettet, "*The Merchant of Venice* and the Problem of Usury," *Essays and Studies by Members of the English Association*, XXXI (1945), 19-33; B. N. Nelson, *The Idea of Usury* (Princeton, 1949); Bernard Grebanier, *The Truth About Shylock* (New York, 1962), pp. 76-96.

37. For relevant references see Draper, "Usury in *The Merchant of Venice*," p. 41; Arthur Stonex, "Money Lending and Money-Lenders in England During the 16th and 17th Centuries," *Schelling Anniversary Papers* (New York, 1923), pp. 263-85.

38. In England opposition to usury was reflected in legislation that went back to the reign of Alfred, with subsequent periodic legislation against the practice down to the reign of Queen Elizabeth. The two exceptions were "An Act Against Usury" of 1545 (37 Hen. VIII, c. 9) and "An Acte agaynst Usurie" of 1571 (13 Eliz. c. 8), both of which have been referred to above. See Stonex, "Money Lending and Money-Lenders," p. 264.

39. See Stonex, "Money Lending and Money-Lenders."

40. It is interesting to note that only a handful of these antedate *The Merchant of Venice*.

41. III, i, 17.

42. *Timon of Athens*, II, ii, 61, 97, 103; IV, iii, 112. *The Winter's Tale*, IV, iv, 266, 271. See also *Much Ado About Nothing*, II, i, 196; *Romeo and Juliet*, III, iii, 123; *Measure for Measure*, III, ii, 7; *King Lear*, III, ii, 89; IV, vi, 167.

43. Stonex, "Money Lending and Money-Lenders," pp. 269-70.

44. III, i, 47.

45. Shakespeare's failure is noted by C. L. Barber, *Shakespeare's Festive Comedy* (Princeton, 1959), p. 190.

46. Portia's unhesitating offer of the gold contrasts sharply with Shylock's deliberation in I, iii, 1-10, which one critic very properly sees as an expression of "the impersonal logic, the mechanism, involved in the control of money." *Ibid.*, p. 172.

47. See pp. 157, 165-67.

48. Grebanier, *The Truth About Shylock*, p. 31.

49. Nevertheless, some have complained that in depicting such characters as Iago, Macbeth, King John, and Richard III, Shakespeare does not associate their evil with their race or religion as he does in the case of Shylock, thereby wronging deeply the Jewish people. E. N. Calisch, *The Jew in English Literature* (Richmond, Va., 1909), pp. 75-76.

50. Charlton, *Shakespearian Comedy*, p. 129.

51. *Ibid.*, p. 130.

52. Draper, "Usury in *The Merchant of Venice*," p. 37.

53. It should be noted also that in Launcelot's soliloquy where he debates whether to stay with Shylock or leave him, it is his conscience that tells him to stay and the fiend that tells him to leave. II, ii, 1-23.

54. John E. Hannigan, "Shylock and Portia," *SAB*, XIV (1939), 172.

55. *Ibid.*, p. 174.

56. Graham Midgley, "*The Merchant of Venice*: A Reconsideration," *Essays in Criticism*, X (1960), 119-33.

57. Charlton, *Shakespearian Comedy*, p. 146.

58. *Ibid.*, p. 151.

59. *Ibid.,* p. 137.

60. *Ibid.,* p. 152.

61. E. E. Stoll, "Shylock," *JEGP,* X (1911), 236-79.

62. John R. Moore, "Pantaloon as Shylock," *Boston Public Library Quarterly,* I (1940), 33-42.

63. Barber, *Shakespeare's Festive Comedy,* p. 183.

64. Shylock is a far less comic character than the faceless Don John, who occupies an analogous position in *Much Ado About Nothing.*

65. Professor John Dover Wilson is right in saying that Shylock is a greater character than Barabas because, unlike Barabas, "he is one of ourselves." *Shakespeare's Happy Comedies* (London, 1962), p. 108.

66. On the Shylock-Antonio relationship see Charles Mitchell, "The Conscience of Venice: Shakespeare's Merchant," *JEGP,* LXIII (1964), 214-25. See also Frank Kermode, "The Mature Comedies," in *Early Shakespeare,* eds. John Russell Brown and Bernard Harris (London, 1961), pp. 211-27.

67. This is what the song is intended to do, not to guide Bassanio's choice, as some critics believe. For the latter interpretation, going back to John Weiss, *Wit, Humour, and Shakespeare* (Boston, 1876), p. 312, see R. Noble, *Shakespeare's Use of Song* (London, 1923), pp. 44-49; Austin K. Gray, "The Song in *The Merchant of Venice*," *MLN,* XLII (1929), 458-59; and J. D. Wilson, New Cambridge Shakespeare, pp. 149-50, and *Shakespeare's Happy Comedies,* pp. 99-100.

68. For comment on the history of the debate of the eye and the heart see W. A. R. Kerr, "Le Cercle d'Amour," *PMLA,* XIX (1904), 48-57; H. R. Lang, "The Eyes as Generators of Love," *MLN,* XXIII (1908), 126-27; James Holly Hanford, "The Debate of Heart and Eye," *MLN,* XXVI (1911), 161-65; Charles R. Baskervill, "Bassanio as an Ideal Lover," *The Manly Anniversary Studies* (Chicago, 1923), pp. 90-103. *A New Variorum Edition of Shakespeare,* ed. H. H. Furness (Philadelphia, 1895), pp. 141-42. The medieval poem "The Eye and the Heart," edited by Eleanor Hamond in *Anglia,* XXXIV (1911), 235-65, appears to be the only English treatment of this old theme.

69. J. D. Wilson, *Shakespeare's Happy Comedies,* p. 114. Though Gratiano is not an altogether attractive character, Professor Wilson goes too far in calling him a "storm-trooper." *Ibid.,* p. 113. He also makes the comment that Shakespeare's friends, "the earls," would have acted towards Shylock as Antonio does in "spurning him like a dog and bespitting him. . . ." *Ibid.*

70. See for instance Barbara K. Lewalski, "Biblical Allusion and Allegory in *The Merchant of Venice,*" *SQ,* XIII (1962), 327-43.

CHAPTER VII

1. E. K. Chambers, *William Shakespeare: A Study of Facts and Problems* (Oxford, 1931), I, 387.

2. Edward Arber, ed., *A Transcript of the Registers of the Company of Stationers of London, 1554-1640* (London, 1875-94), III, 37.

3. New Cambridge Shakespeare (Cambridge, 1953), pp. 102-7.

4. Chambers, *William Shakespeare,* I, 385-88; W. W. Greg, *The Editorial Problem in Shakespeare* (Oxford, 1942), pp. 121-23; Allison Gaw, "Is Shakespeare's *Much Ado* a Revised Earlier Play?" *PMLA,* L (1935), 715-38.

5. The story of Claudio and Hero goes back to fourth-century Greek romance of *The Loves of Chaereas and Callirhoe* by Chariton of Aphrodisias. A long list of analogues followed, including the Spanish romance *Tirante el Blanco* (printed in 1511) of John Martorell; an episode in *Orlando Furioso*

(1516); the twenty-second novella of Matteo Bandello's *Novelle* (1554); and the story of Phedon and Claribell in the fourth canto of Book II of the *Faerie Queene*. From Bandello, perhaps through Belleforest's *Histoires Tragiques* (1582), Shakespeare took the setting, some of the names, and most of the elements of the Claudio-Hero story, and to these he added details from either Ariosto or Spenser. For studies of the sources see Charles T. Prouty, *The Sources of Much Ado About Nothing* (New Haven, 1950); also F. C. Danchin, "Une Source de *Much Ado About Nothing*," *Revue Anglo-Americaine*, XII (1936), 430-31; Mackie Langham Bennett, "Shakespeare's *Much Ado About Nothing* and its Possible Italian Sources, *UTSE*, XVII (1937), 52-74; Alwin Thaler, "Spenser and *Much Ado About Nothing*," *SP*, XXXVII (1940), 225-35; Abbie Findlay Potts, "Spenserian 'Courtesy' and 'Temperance' in *Much Ado About Nothing*," *SAB*, XVII (1942), 103-11, 126-33; D. J. Gordon, "*Much Ado About Nothing*: A Possible Source for the Hero-Claudio Plot," *SP*, XXXIX (1942), 279-90.

6. Prouty, *The Sources of Much Ado*, p. 63.

7. *Ibid.*, p. 35.

8. Professor Thaler points to a difference between the roles of Ariosto's Dalinda and Spenser's Pryene: Dalinda is a willing and conscious agent of the slanderer's efforts to win her mistress while Pryene, like Margaret, is innocent. "Spenser and *Much Ado*," p. 234.

9. For these parallels between the two pairs see Mary Augusta Scott, "*The Book of the Courtyer*: A Possible Source of Benedick and Beatrice," *PMLA*, XVI (1901), 475-502. Geoffrey Bullough, *Narrative and Dramatic Sources of Shakespeare* (London, 1961), I, 78-80, has suggested that Count Ludovico da Canossa's remarks on indirect ways of wooing sound very much like a germ of the Benedick-Beatrice relationship. The following paragraph is a good example: "I have also seene a most fervent love spring in the heart of a woman, towarde one that seemed at the first not to beare him the least affection in the worlde, onely for that they heard say, that the opinion of many was, that they loved together. And the cause of this (I believe) was that so generall a judgment seemed a sufficient witnesse, that he was worthie of her love. And it seemed (in a manner) that report brought the ambassade on the lovers behalfe much more truer and worthier to be believed, than he himselfe could have done with letters or wordes, or any other person for him. . . ."

10. For parallels between characters in *The Faerie Queene* and *Much Ado*, see Potts, "Spenserian 'Courtesy' and 'Temperance' in *Much Ado*."

11. *The Faerie Queene*, VI, viii, 22.

12. In addition to the obvious parallel with Mirabella, Beatrice is said to have connections with Briana, the Blatant Beast, Ate, Sclaunder, Phaedria, and Britomart. See Potts, "Spenserian 'Courtesy' and 'Temperance' in *Much Ado*."

13. E. K. Chambers, *Shakespeare: A Survey* (London, 1925), pp. 127-35.

14. It should be noted in passing that this theme of deception is admirably sustained by a large number of images of bird-snaring and angling, especially in the scenes wherein Benedick and Beatrice are intended to eavesdrop on the conversations about them.

15. Benedick's first words in the play question Hero's legitimacy (I, i, 101).

16. When he learns that a marriage is imminent, Don Pedro asks: "What is he for a fool that betroths himself to unquietness?" (I, iii, 143).

17. Prouty, *The Sources of Much Ado*, p. 40.

18. Richmond Noble calls it the "earliest example of the genuine dramatic song rendered by an adult actor that we have from Shakespeare's hands," but he says nothing about the function of the song. *Shakespeare's Use of Song* (Lon-

don, 1923), p. 64. Louis B. Wright argues that the song "was intended as a bit of entertainment by the talented vocalist in the company. . . . " See his "Extraneous Song in Elizabethan Drama After the Advent of Shakespeare," *SP*, XXIV (1927), 263. Finally, John H. Long is convinced that the song "apparently serves no dramatic function other than to reflect the light and humorous spirit of the scene in which it is placed." *Shakespeare's Use of Music: A Study of Music and its Performance in the Original Production of Seven Comedies* (Gainesville, Florida, 1955), p. 125.

19. This has to do with the proud rejection of love and wedlock, not their "dreary conventions," as some believe. Benedick says clearly that he had railed against marriage, not its conventions.

20. Beatrice's lines are in alternate rhyme whereas the rest of the scene, with the exception of a single couplet (ll. 105-6), is in blank verse.

21. See above, p. 190.

22. See above, p. 181.

23. Prouty, *The Sources of Much Ado*, p. 63.

24. In this analysis of the play's action I am indebted to an excellent essay by T. W. Craik on *"Much Ado About Nothing,"* *Scrutiny*, XIX (1953), 297-316.

25. This view was first proposed by Nadine Page, "The Public Repudiation of Hero," *PMLA*, L (1935), 739-44.

26. Prouty, *The Sources of Much Ado*, p. 63.

27. *Ibid.* For comments on this interpretation see especially Kirby Neill, "More Ado About Claudio: An Acquittal for the Slandered Groom," *SQ*, III (1952), 91-107; and also Craik, *"Much Ado About Nothing."*

CHAPTER VIII

1. "If you were to go to *As You Like It* for the story you would, in Johnson's phrase, 'hang yourself.'" Helen Gardner, *"As You Like It,"* in *More Talking of Shakespeare*, ed. John Garrett (New York, 1959), p. 20.

2. Writing in 1946 and following John Dover Wilson, John Palmer took it for granted that Shakespeare wrote the play in 1593: "Shakespeare, writing his first draft of 'As You Like It' in 1593, could hardly forbear to remember that in Christopher Marlowe England had just lost an author who had made a very notable contribution to the sylvan muse." *Comic Characters of Shakespeare* (London, 1946), p. 28. Palmer adopts 1593 as the date of the play without further comment on the matter.

3. For his arguments see New Cambridge Shakespeare (Cambridge, 1948), pp. 107-8.

4. E. K. Chambers, *The Year's Work in English Studies, 1926* (Oxford, 1928), p. 126.

5. *Ibid.*

6. John Dover Wilson, *Shakespeare's Happy Comedies* (London, 1962), pp. 143-44.

7. See pertinent comments by Edwin Greenlaw in "Shakespeare's Pastorals," *SP*, XIII (1916), 121-54.

8. In his edition of *English Pastorals* (London, 1895), E. K. Chambers, somewhat unguardedly, affirms that "Shakespeare glorified the prevailing fashion in *As You Like It."* p. xxix.

9. In *3 Henry VI*, King Henry alludes to the contrast between the life of a shepherd and that of a king and he dwells upon the passing of time in the country which curiously anticipates the same motif in *As You Like It.*

O God! methinks it were a happy life
To be no better than a homely swain;
To sit upon a hill, as I do now,
To carve out dials quaintly, point by point,
Thereby to see the minutes how they run,
How many makes the hour full complete,
How many hours brings about the day,
How many days will finish up the year,
How many years a mortal man will live.

(II, v, 21-29)

10. This is the chief motive, for instance, in the most influential Italian pastoral plays, Tasso's *Aminta* and Guarini's *Il Pastor Fido*.

11. This, I believe, is what attracted Shakespeare to the novel rather than "Orlando's blindness and the bewildering play of the various planes of reality offered by Rosalind's disguise. . . ." Marco Mincoff, "What Shakespeare Did to *Rosalynde*," *SJ*, XCVI (1960), 82. Mincoff is led to this conclusion by his notion that the play owes its success to the "complete and harmonious fusion of . . . two comic themes, love's foolishness and clash between appearance and reality."

12. Charles Knight argued that Shakespeare used the poem (Geoffrey Bullough, *Narrative and Dramatic Sources of Shakespeare* [London, 1961], II, 148), and W. G. Stone lists a half-dozen parallels between the play and *The Tale of Gamelyn*. "Shakespeare's *As You Like It* and *Rosalynde* Compared," *Transactions of the Shakespeare Society*, II (1880-85), 277-93.

13. Mincoff, "What Shakespeare Did to *Rosalynde*," p. 79.

14. It must be stressed again that in the play the pastoral incidents are far more than what one critic calls "fair and graceful ornament upon [the] structure, bringing with them a smack of the free, rude, countryside, or a faint perfume of the polished Utopia of courtly makers." W. W. Greg, *Pastoral Poetry and Pastoral Drama* (London, 1906), pp. 412-13.

15. Mincoff ("What Shakespeare Did to *Rosalynde*," p. 89) believes that "Under the Greenwood Tree" may have been suggested by Corydon's praise of the shepherd's life in *Rosalynde*, ed. W. W. Greg (London, 1907), p. 49; and that "Sylvius's fugue of love (V, ii, 91 ff.) may have been inspired by Montanus's pleadings to Phoebe." *Rosalynde*, ed. Greg, p. 119.

16. The general correspondence in the action of the novel and the play is treated by Mincoff, "What Shakespeare Did to *Rosalynde*," p. 86. See also Stone, "Shakespeare's *As You Like It* and *Rosalynde* Compared," pp. 277-93; Albert H. Tolman, "Shakespeare's Manipulation of his Sources in *As You Like It*," *MLN*, XXXVII (1922), 65-76; Edna Davis Romig, "*As You Like It*: Shakespeare's Uses of his Source, Lodge's *Rosalynde*," *University of Colorado Studies*, XVI (1929), 300-22; Kenneth Muir, *Shakespeare's Sources* (London, 1957), I, 55-66; Bullough, *Narrative and Dramatic Sources of Shakespeare*, II, 143-57.

17. Rosader considers that Rosalynde would doubtless love him "more willingly" if she heard of his wealth, most of it inherited from Saladyne, should the latter be left a prey to the lion: "for women's eyes are made of Chrysocoll, that is ever unperfect unless tempered with gold. . . ." *Rosalynde*, ed. Greg, p. 95. Such contemplations on Orlando's part are clearly inadmissible in Shakespeare's comedy, for they would violate his conception of both Orlando and Rosalind.

18. Charles Prouty, "Some Observations on Shakespeare's Sources," *SJ*, XCVI (1960), 71.

19. Silvius' wooing is mocked also by Touchstone, and here again the precise

point satirized is his romantic wooing so that Silvius' pastoralism is mocked by an attack upon his romanticism.

20. Bullough, *Narratve and Dramatic Sources of Shakespeare*, II, 231.

21. Cf. R. P. Draper, "Shakespeare's Pastoral Comedy," *Études Anglaises*, XI (1958), 3-8.

22. P. V. Kreider, "Genial Literary Satire in the Forest of Arden," *SAB*, X (1935), 214.

23. Cf. Draper, "Shakespeare's Pastoral Comedy," p. 4.

24. Some (cf. Palmer, *Comic Characters of Shakespeare*, p. 38) have taken Touchstone's mockery of Corin's rusticity at face value, but the jester is nothing if not ironic, both in his exchange with Corin and in his brilliant first meeting with Jaques reported by the latter. Incidentally, Touchstone's irony escapes Jaques too, and in that fact especially lies the jester's superiority. For an analysis of the Corin-Touchstone debate see James Smith, *"As You Like It,"* *Scrutiny*, IX (1940), 9-32.

25. It has been argued that in "comparison with [Touchstone's] nihilistic cleverness Corin's pastoralism has much more solid worth . . . and that [their] debate also reveals that Corin's attitude is a much healthier one than Touchstone's." Draper, "Shakespeare's Pastoral Comedy," p. 7. In a strict biographical sense it may seem so, but Touchstone's comments are to be taken in a philosophic, not a biographical, sense. Thus those comments have a larger meaning and application than Corin's. The latter believes that what is proper at court would be out of place in the country. Touchstone implies that the ways of life, in court or country, are fundamentally the same. Cf. H. Jenkins, *"As You Like It,"* *Shakespeare Survey*, VIII (1955), 48.

26. Although Jaques belongs to the play for the sake of a few speeches, those speeches are relevant to the theme of the play, whether the character appeared in the play's earliest draft or was added later. The view has been expressed that Jaques' "speeches . . . make not the least addition to the main story, for even Mercutio's Queen Mab speech has not so complete an irrelevance to the time and place." John Wilcox, "Putting Jaques in *As You Like It*," *MLR*, XXXVI (1941), 39. It may be said that Touchstone's speeches likewise add no more to the story, but of course what is significant is what he *says* about the pastoral and romantic themes. And this is true also of Jaques' comments including his most famous speech, as well as of Mercutio's Queen Mab passage. In each case the function of those speeches is to record a point of view which is needed for a final synthesis. Mercutio's Queen Mab speech mocks the extreme romanticism of lovers', courtiers', lawyers', soldiers' dreams as opposed to his own self-conscious, matter-of-fact attitude to life. The speech may not add to the story of *Romeo and Juliet*, but that it is most revelant to the theme of the play is difficult to deny.

27. Gardner, *"As You Like It,"* p. 31.

28. Cf. O. J. Campbell, "Jaques," *Huntington Library Bulletin*, VIII (1935), 100.

29. On the relationship of the two characters see some excellent comments in Robert Hillis Goldsmith, *Wise Fools in Shakespeare* (East Lansing, Michigan, 1955), pp. 89-93.

30. C. L. Barber, *Shakespeare's Festive Comedy* (Princeton, 1959), pp. 226-27.

31. This view is somewhat different from that which sees the ultimate meaning of the songs as an invitation to "an ideally leisured existence which gives men and women the opportunity to enjoy life, to come to full stature as human beings. . . ." Draper, "Shakespeare's Pastoral Comedy," p. 12. This of course is what the songs say in part, but they say more and they say all in a

tone which, as we have noted, serves to oppose or control the extreme assertions about both the innocence of Arden and man's inhumanity to man.

32. We can see why Jaques avoids the Duke's society as much as he can. He "is too disputable for my company," says Monsieur Melancholy, and it is clear that he would disagree sharply with a man who finds "good in everything." In any case it should be noted that Arden reflects a variety of sermons, some for Jaques, others for the Duke.

33. Cf. Draper, "Shakespeare's Pastoral Comedy," p. 11.

34. Here we must take note of a feature of the play's structure which can be misunderstood. Although Rosalind's role has to do chiefly with the love theme, we should not therefore conclude that she has no connection with the pastoral theme. C. L. Barber finds that the play "is composed in two movements, of about equal length, the first developing the pastoral theme, the second the romantic." See "The Use of Comedy in *As You Like It*," *PQ*, XXI (1942), 358. It is true that a great deal more is said about the pastoral theme in the first half of the play than in the second. This is inevitable since Shakespeare transfers his chief characters to a pastoral scene that at once demands comment. But it should be noted also that the love theme fills the entire play, beginning with the first meeting of Orlando and Rosalind in the second scene of the first act. Furthermore, the pastoral theme is not laid aside after its early appearance but is carried through the rest of the play. Silvius and Phoebe are lovers, but they are presented as pastoral lovers, who appear together onstage for the first time as late as III, v. Audrey makes her first appearance in III, iii, and William makes his in V, i. The song, "It was a lover and his lass," celebrating the ways of "pretty country folks," is sung in V, iii. There is no division of any sort between the two themes. On the contrary, not only are they most closely related structurally but they also make their point by means of that relationship.

35. For some excellent comments on this point see Barber, "The Use of Comedy in *As You Like It*," pp. 362-63.

36. E. E. Stoll, *Shakespeare's Young Lovers* (London, 1937), p. 73. For the multiple ironies here and elsewhere in Shakespeare, see Robert B. Sharpe, *Irony in the Drama* (Chapel Hill, 1959), Chap. V.

37. Draper, "Shakespeare's Pastoral Comedy," pp. 5-6.

38. *Ibid.*, p. 3.

CHAPTER IX

1. There are other similarities with earlier plays. Viola's disguise recalls that of Portia and Nerissa, of Jessica and Rosalind. Sir Toby and Aguecheek recall Falstaff and Slender, and the trick played on Malvolio looks back to the trick played on Benedick and Beatrice.

2. *A New Variorum Edition of Shakespeare,* ed. H. H. Furness (Philadelphia, 1901), p. xii.

3. New Cambridge Shakespeare (Cambridge, 1939), pp. 100-1.

4. Leslie Hotson, *The First Night of Twelfh Night* (New York, 1954), pp. 229-30.

5. *Ibid., passim.*

6. *Ibid.*, p. 63.

7. *Ibid.*, p. 180.

8. II, iii, 110-21. The song is to be found in Edward H. Fellowes' edition in *The English School of Lutenist Song Writers*, Series II, Vol. IV (London, 1959), 24-25.

9. Geoffrey Bullough, *Narrative and Dramatic Sources of Shakespeare* (London, 1961), II, 270-71. For minor details Shakespeare may be indebted to *Gl'Ingannati*, first performed in 1537, which is the ultimate source of all versions, including *Gl'Inganni* (1562) by Nicolò Secchi and Curzio Gonzaga's *Gl'Inganni* (1592). In the Induction to the play there is a Fabio and also a Malevolti, as well as a reference to *la notte di Beffana*, which some believe may have suggested the title of Shakespeare's play. Although *Gl'Ingannati* is closer to Shakespeare's play, it is nevertheless true that Curzio Gonzaga's *Gl'Inganni* gives Cesare (Cesario) as the name of the disguised heroine. In connection with the names of the chief characters it should be noted also that in Emanuel Forde's *Famous History of Parismus* (1598) there is a Viola who is shipwrecked while following her lover in the disguise of a page. See Bullough, *Narrative and Dramatic Sources*, II, 363-71. It has also been proposed that another play by Nicolò Secchi, *L'Interesse* (c. 1547), may have suggested the duel between Sir Andrew and Viola. See Helen A. Kaufman, "Nicolò Secchi as a Source of *Twelfth Night*," *SQ*, V (1954), 271-80.

10. See Violet A. Wilson, *Society Women of Shakespeare's Time* (New York, 1924), pp. 238-56.

11. See Fitzroy Pyle, "*Twelfth Night, King Lear*, and *Arcadia*," *MLR*, XLIII (1948), 449-55.

12. See Oscar J. Campbell, *Shakespeare's Satire* (New York, 1943), p. 83. See also Paul Mueschke and Jeannette Fleisher, "Jonsonian Elements in the Comic Underplot of *Twelfth Night*," *PMLA*, XLVIII (1933), 722-40.

13. Even Malvolio's "examination" for diabolical possession cannot in any of its details be interpreted as a glance at public process of the law either in a particular case or general practice. See C. J. Sisson, "Tudor Intelligence Tests: Malvolio and Real Life," in *Essays on Shakespeare and Elizabethan Drama in Honor of Hardin Craig* (Columbia, Missouri, 1962), pp. 183-200.

14. On the other hand it is perhaps going too far to say that Shakespeare "invented the story of Malvolio, and used it with rare skill as the foundation of the play." Milton Crane, "*Twelfth Night* and Shakespearean Comedy," *SQ*, VI (1955), 7. Nor is it quite accurate to call Malvolio "the most comical and most ridiculous character in the play." Sen Gupta, *Shakespearian Comedy* (Oxford, 1950), p. 168. In Shakespearean romantic comedy the most comical characters are misguided or disdainful lovers, or the self-dramatizing lover whose language is fraught with hyperbole and his passion with sentimentality, the lover who believes himself a realist yet who all along responds to love in the romantic manner. The most comical characters in such comedy are the king and his lords in *Love's Labour's Lost*, Benedick and Beatrice, Orlando and Rosalind, Orsino and Olivia.

15. It is interesting to note that his cross-gartered yellow stockings may be intended to show him as a lover and more particularly as a jealous one. See M. Channing Linthicum, "Malvolio's Cross-gartered Yellow Stockings," *MP*, XXV (1927), 87-93; also M. P. Tilley, "Malvolio's Yellow Stockings and Cross Garters," *SAB*, XII (1937), 54-55. Yellow is also the color of the narcissus, that is, a symbol of self-love. See Hotson, *The First Night of Twelfth Night*, p. 98.

16. In his rigidity, his lack of self-awareness, and his obsessive concern with certain proprieties, Malvolio approaches the Jonsonian humour character.

17. His *raison d'être* is thus much more significant than might appear on the surface. His role in the play is not, for instance, "so that Shakespeare's lovers may preserve their status free from the nothing-if-not-critical comic scrutiny which would otherwise expose their romantic pretensions to the withering winds of laughter," Melvin Seiden, "Malvolio Reconsidered," *Univer-*

sity of Kansas City Review, XXVII (1961), 106-7. Incidentally, the lovers do not escape comic scrutiny in the play.

18. Cf. Harold Jenkins, "Shakespeare's *Twelfth Night*," *Rice Institute Pamphlet*, XLV (1959), 28-29.

19. Something like this takes place during the initial meeting of Touchstone and Jaques, reported by the latter, in which Touchstone tells him precisely what he wants to hear and in the terms he himself would have used.

20. On this see pertinent comments in Gupta, *Shakespearian Comedy*, p. 165; and L. C. Salingar, "The Design of *Twelfth Night*," *SQ*, IX (1958), 122.

21. Cf. some relevant remarks in John R. Brown, *Shakespeare and His Comedies* (London, 1957), pp. 176-77.

22. Morris P. Tilley, "The Organic Unity of *Twelfth Night*," *PMLA*, XXIX (1914), 550-51.

23. John Hollander, "Musica Mundana and *Twelfth Night*," *Sound and Poetry* (English Institute Essays, 1956), pp. 73-74.

24. John Hollander, "*Twelfth Night* and the Morality of Indulgence," *Sewanee Review*, LXVIII (1959), 234.

25. This overstress on the play's metaphor can be seen in Professor Hollander's suggestion that Orsino's name reflects and defines his nature: "Orsino—the bear, the ravenous and clumsy devourer." *Ibid.*, p. 224.

26. Hollander, "Musica Mundana and *Twelfth Night*," p. 75.

27. Furnivall, quoted in Furness, *Variorum*, p. 385.

28. S. Nagarajan, " 'What You Will': A Suggestion," *SQ*, X (1959), 61.

29. J. W. Draper, *The Twelfth Night of Shakespeare's Audience* (Palo Alto, 1950), p. 249. This and other views of Professor Draper have been answered by N. A. Brittin in "The *Twelfth Night* of Shakespeare and Professor Draper," *SQ*, VII (1956), 211-16.

30. Jenkins, "Shakespeare's *Twelfth Night*," p. 21.

31. It has been suggested that Feste and Viola "represent the golden mean of temperance, in whom reason and emotion are at poise." Tilley, "The Organic Unity of *Twelfth Night*," p. 558.

32. John Dover Wilson, *Shakespeare's Happy Comedies* (London, 1962), p. 172.

33. Whether written by Shakespeare or borrowed, the song illustrates his ability to endow complex function to music and song, both thematic and structural. For in addition to its obvious thematic meaning the song leads to more riotous singing which in turn brings the protesting Malvolio to the stage. And out of this emerges the conspiracy against him. In spite of this, some critics have failed to see the dramatic relevance of the song and its perfect blending with its context. See for instance L. B. Lathrop, "Shakespeare's Dramatic Use of Songs," *MLN*, XXIII (1908), 3; John H. Long, *Shakespeare's Use of Music: A Study of Music and its Performance in the Original Production of Seven Comedies* (Gainesville, Florida, 1955), I, 169. The authenticity of "O Mistress Mine" has been the subject of a long debate, dealing mainly with the relationship of the song in Shakespeare's play to a tune (without words) by the same title in Thomas Morley's *First Booke of Consort Lessons* (1599). Was the song, words and tune, an old one or did Shakespeare compose his own words, and if so did he employ Morley's tune? Did Shakespeare and Morley collaborate? Is there any connection between Shakespeare's song and Morley's tune? See E. Brennecke, Jr., "Shakespeare's Collaboration with Morley," *PMLA*, LIV (1939), 139-49; Sydney Beck, "The Case of 'O Mistress Mine,'" *Renaissance News*, VI (1953), 19-23. Edward H. Fellowes saw no connection between Morley's tune and Shakespeare's song and believed that

the dramatist probably rewrote an old song. See Richmond Noble, *Shakespeare's Use of Song* (London, 1923), p. 82.

34. Capell thought it was either a popular song of the day or it was composed by William Kempe, who, he believed, had played the part of Feste. Furness, *Variorum*, pp. 313-14. H. B. Lathrop considered the song extraneous and not by Shakespeare. "Shakespeare's Dramatic Use of Songs," p. 2. L. B. Wright insisted that the song "has no relation to the play." "Extraneous Song in Elizabethan Drama After the Advent of Shakespeare," *SP*, XXIV (1927), 263. John R. Moore thought it might have been an interpolation. "The Songs of the Public Theaters in the Time of Shakespeare," *JEGP*, XXVIII (1929), 182. And John Dover Wilson is convinced that the song was written by Robert Armin. New Cambridge Shakespeare, p. 170. Finally John H. Long follows L. B. Wright and H. B. Lathrop, saying that "there does not seem to be any reason to doubt their conclusions." *Shakespeare's Use of Music*, I, 180.

35. "Feste the Jester," in *A Book of Homage to Shakespeare*, ed. I. Gollancz (Oxford, 1916), pp. 164-69.

36. Noble, *Shakespeare's Use of Song*, p. 85.

37. John Weiss, *Wit, Humor, and Shakespeare* (Boston, 1876), p. 204.

Index